THE ESSEX SYMPOSIA
literature / politics / theory

Uses of history

Uses of history
Marxism, postmodernism and the Renaissance

EDITED BY
FRANCIS BARKER, PETER HULME
AND MARGARET IVERSEN

MANCHESTER UNIVERSITY PRESS
MANCHESTER AND NEW YORK

Distributed exclusively in the USA and Canada by
ST. MARTIN'S PRESS

Published by Manchester University Press
Oxford Road, Manchester M13 9PL, UK
and Room 400, 175 Fifth Avenue,
New York, NY 10010, USA

Distributed exclusively in the USA and Canada
by St. Martin's Press, Inc.,
175 Fifth Avenue, New York, NY 10010, USA

A catalogue record for this book is available from the British Library

Library of Congress cataloging in publication data
Uses of history : Marxism, postmodernism, and the Renaissance / edited by Francis Barker, Peter Hulme, and Margaret Iversen.
  p. cm. — (Literature, politics, theory)
  Includes bibliographical references and index.
  ISBN 0–7190–3512–0 (hardback)
  1. Historiography. 2. History—Philosophy. I. Barker, Francis, 1952– . II. Hulme, Peter. III. Iversen, Margaret Dana. IV. Series.
D13.U78   1991
907'.2—dc20   91–17278

ISBN 0 7190 3512 0 hardback

Photoset in Linotron Sabon with Syntax
by Northern Phototypesetting Co. Ltd., Bolton
Printed in Great Britain
by Billings of Worcester

Contents

THE ESSEX SYMPOSIA
literature / politics / theory

Preface to the Series

In the 1990s the new critical theory of the 1970s and 1980s is firmly established in university departments and publishing houses alike, but with the constant risk that its original cutting edge will be blunted by its currency. Hence our insistence on the three terms in the title of this series: the engagement of theory with literature needs to grasp the political questions at its centre.

Between 1976 and 1984 the annual Sociology of Literature conference at the University of Essex provided an important forum for those interested in left literary and cultural theory in England. Ten volumes of proceedings were published, and some of the papers were collected under the title we now use for this series. The ethos of those conferences, baldly stated, was an engagement with the theoretical work published, especially in France, during the 1960s and 1970s from a position of commitment to a left politics. The conferences and their proceedings stressed the need to place theory within its political and historical contexts, and to test its potential in the re-reading of literary and cultural texts.

The new sequence of volumes to which this book belongs has a different configuration from that first series, but builds upon its work: in that sense it is a continuation of the project long associated with Essex. The principles behind the intervention remain the same: the process is different. These books present advanced research by people working in this new critical field. Contributors have been invited with a view to achieving a mix of established and younger writers from Britain and abroad, representing a variety of relevant theoretical approaches. In each case participants have been asked to prepare a draft paper in advance of a symposium held at Essex. At the symposium the pre-circulated papers have been discussed, and the direction of the volume assumed a clearer shape. Papers have then been rewritten in the light of the discussions. The resulting volume is intended to have a greater coherence (though not necessarily internal agreement) than the normal collection of essays, and the underlying commitment is to collective and dialogic methods of work and publication.

The Editors

Introduction

The focus of this book is on contemporary literary and theoretical studies in the area of the English Renaissance. It seeks to offer some positive contributions to the interpretation and criticism of an area of historical culture which has yielded in recent years the most challenging debate in literary criticism. But the current vitality of Renaissance studies stems not only from the interest of particular interpretations of specific works and authors, but also from the fact that the field has become an arena for the exploration and discussion of the underlying theoretical methods and assumptions which make interpretation possible. Not least, Renaissance studies has become the testing ground for the very viability of *historical* interpretation as such. In an important respect then, this book also grows out of a sense that today history is in question, in theory and in practice; that 'history' as a signified, as a set of discursive practices, as an objective process, and as the sphere of human agency is in important ways now – for better or worse – a politically and theoretically contested terrain.

Whether at the level of the theoretical critique of history which has been conducted in a number of academic disciplines from a variety of philosophical perspectives, or in the cultural and social sphere, or at the level of practical political perspectives, we seem to live in a time when both radical and, perhaps more surprisingly, conservative thought is articulating itself in a decisive break from the past, as we enter, it is held, the new epoch of postmodernity.

What has come to be called postmodernism presents, of course, some very broad and complex cultural, theoretical and political problems. Issues surrounding the conceptualisation of postmodernity as a distinct new moment or as a critique of the none the less still unfinished modern project have engaged artists, critics and theorists in many different fields recently. Many of these broad problems are addressed in the second volume of this series, *Postmodernism and the re-reading of modernity*. But if there is a wider postmodernism, the principal concern in this book is the questioned status of history in light of what is often called in general 'theoretical postmodernism', when this is taken to be the effects of the ensemble of critical perspectives which has come to be called variously 'contemporary theory', or sometimes simply 'theory'.

Theory in this sense includes the legacy of the Saussurian critique of signification, the structuralist explanation of narrative as synchronic structure and the subsequent poststructuralist critique of system and totalisation, psychoanalytic emphasis on the unconscious and the decentring and fragmentation of the categories of experience and the subject, deconstructive distrust, in the name of *différance*, of what it takes to be the metaphysics of presence, and Lyotard's famous 'definition' of postmodernism as 'incredulity towards metanarratives'. If theory is so understood it is clear that postmodernism entails a decisive loosening or weakening of the erstwhile epistemological certainties, ontological groundings, rhetorical protocols and existential authenticities that once apparently made 'history' if not unproblematical at least inescapable. For it is hard to see how there can be any effectively historical knowledge or any political practice grounded on such knowledge if there can be no certainty that words refer to things, that structures and regularities inhere in the organisation of discourse and society, that people and peoples experience their own lives, and that their narratives and narration make sense. The very possibility of history, as the domain of human action – let alone its ethical or political appropriateness as a site or a mode of understanding – is cast into radical doubt. Today we even get *pronunciamentos* to the effect that history has come to an end.

At the theoretical level there are, of course, a number of problems with lumping these various perspectives and critiques together as if 'postmodernism' were one 'school of thought', or indeed as if the critical thought of the twentieth century were not only an undifferentiated medium, but one that has precipitated out in the post-war period into a unitary, new problematic. Postmodernism is frequently used as a stalking horse in this way, but if so its own commitment to de-totalised knowledges and local strategy is belied. Nor is it the case that it is only 'postmodernism' which has committed itself to the critique of 'historicism'. As evidenced even within the limits of the present volume (see especially the papers by Jean Howard and Lisa Jardine), varieties of feminist thought whether postmodernist or socialist have raised trenchant questions about whether the whole enterprise of history – even radical history – is not deeply implicated in the perpetuation of patriarchy. Some feminists have recommended the rejection of history altogether, asking whether liberation for women could ever be achieved within perspectives based on historical analysis, when 'history' is seen as nothing but the masculinist, triumphalist narrative of what was in fact the oppression and subordination of women. Equally, Marxism itself has often been as committed to the critique of historicism as it has been to historical criticism.

Just as it is a distortion of history to forge out of the critical thought of the twentieth century a unitary postmodernism, so is it similarly unhelpful to assume of those forms of critical practice most keen to retain some sense both of history and of the value of historical thought, that this is, or ever was, simply a matter of clinging to linear narratives positivistically grounded in 'things as they are' or 'as they were'. Of the critical perspectives in play in the contemporary debate over history, (versions of) Marxism might be expected to be most committed to 'history'. But what in detail the historical commitment of any particular 'Marxism' in fact looks like is very complex. It is by no means clear, for example, that the form of history at work in Marxist texts is the simply linear narrative which postmodernists reject. Instead it might assume a diacritical concept of historicity suggesting both the embeddedness and the contingency of historical phenomena, situated in but not bounded by their moment, located rather in complex time. Certainly it would be difficult to ascribe simple linearity to Walter Benjamin's sense of the present shot through with past and future temporalities, or to the complex temporal metaphorics of Marx's historical writing in the *The Eighteenth Brumaire* (see Francis Barker's essay in this volume).

Consideration of other relevant conceptual figurations of historical time, Marxist and otherwise, also suggests a more differentiated picture than postmodernism allows. Gramsci's important sense of hegemonies and counter-hegemonies of the conjuncture, for example, or Althusser's formulation of contradiction and overdetermination as key formations in historical process – a theorisation coupled in Althusser's work, of course, with a systematic critique of an unacceptable historicism in the Marxist tradition itself – are both instances from within that tradition where history is certainly not understood either as simply linear or recognisably narrative. (A complication of the recent debate has been in any case the variant status of 'historicism' as a word, a concept and a 'value'.) Or again, to choose examples from outside Marxism and even critical of it, positions as diverse as Raymond Williams's vocabulary of 'emergent', 'dominant' and 'residual', or Michel Foucault's sense of the 'history of the present', both again suggest the *inherent* complexity with which historical time has been conceptualised by radicals.

Within the practice of academic historiography there have also been challenges to the traditional topics and methods. Even if dominantly history in the academy still largely means the facts as they were, none the less various 'revisionisms' on the right and radical alternative historiographies on the left have contested the validity, relevance or accessibility of those facts: popular history, especially 'history from below'; oral history; the women's history which has been 'hidden from history'; the proliferation of alternative, dissident or contestatory 'historicities' (for example, post-colonial history's rewriting of Eurocentric and other imperialist perspectives from indigenous viewpoints); and new kinds of histories associated with, for example, the *longues durées* of, say, economic, climatological and cultural change; the blurring of boundaries between historiography, sociology, anthropology and cultural studies; the formation or discovery of new historical objects such as the body, sex, the subject, now seen as having histories whereas previously they were thought to be natural givens; and so on. In other words, what history is, as seen from the perspective of recent challenges to the intellectual and political assumptions of received historiography, is an extremely complex and critical set of divergent and often conflicting perspectives and practices, raising concomitant problems of the truth of experience and of record, and the wider problems of the authenticity of access to the past whether oral or textual, witnessed or archival.

In part the logic of these developments suggests that history is too important to be left to historians. Indeed, the questioning of 'history' has informed wider radical political and intellectual agendas for some time. If history is not to be either simply the concern of professional academics, or more generally the story told by the victors of previous social conflicts – a narration which frequently occludes those very conflicts themselves, and which invariably seeks to legitimate, naturalise or otherwise dehistoricise the resulting rule of a particular class or élite – then whose history is 'history' to be, and for what purposes? How is the systematic distortion of the representation of the subordinated and oppressed, and even the systematic erasure of the subaltern groups, classes and genders altogether from what then counts as history, to be overcome? How is the formation of legitimating traditions and 'heritages' which in place of history underwrite the dominant ruling and governmental strategies of the present moment – ideological history – to be resisted? If 'history' were to be de-naturalised thus and made historical again, what role should 'fiction' rather than 'truth' be seen as playing in what is then shown to be something made rather than something providentially or pragmatically given? What efforts can be made, in theory and in practice, to wrest back history for what Benjamin called 'the tradition of the oppressed', to remake the story, and in remaking the story of the past and the present, remake the future? What would a radical history of the future look like? Neither teleological unfolding nor simply 'one damn thing after another', what, in short, would be the proper forms and processes within which to think such a radical sense of history? These, and other questions like these, are asked explicitly or implicitly in the present volume.

In literary and related studies these concerns have been most intensely focused and most suggestively explored recently, in the English-speaking world, in work on the English Renaissance and early modern period. This is perhaps partly owing to the circumstance that Renaissance studies as a discipline and as an academic tradition has always been markedly historical and, in the positivist sense, historicist. It is not simply that it addresses writers who lived and texts which were written a long time ago but that it has secreted within itself particular scholarly techniques, archival procedures, textual rigour (in the bibliographical sense), a definite although usually not overt 'philosophy of history', and a profoundly conservative politics (often in the form of an explicit nostalgia) which all serve to secure a certain tendentious sense of what history is and what historical enquiry consists in. The cultural and political investment in Britain in Shakespeare as the national poet who acts as guarantor of both the language and the literature 'as such', and in the 'age of Shakespeare' as a – frequently re-invented – heroic moment in the national past, has been matched in many ways in the United States and elsewhere in the English-speaking world by the similar use of Shakespeare to underwrite similarly conservative definitions of literature, culture, history, and similarly elite, patriarchal, Western versions of the past.

But if in recent years new forms of critical enquiry have been seen as breaking away both critically and politically from this 'old historicism', and if the heartland of traditional literary study seems at last to have opened up to the new, theoretically-informed perspectives, the conceptual problematic of the contemporary debate is complicated and even somewhat paradoxical. (Aspects of this process are considered in Howard Felperin's paper below.) In the United States this has meant 'returning' to history after the anti-historicist moment of deconstruction in the 1970s, and before that the textually fetishising, context-less New Criticism. But despite its name, the 'New Historicism' is more or less thoroughly committed to the use of interpretative strategies which often leave unexplored the nature of the historical address involved. It has been criticised by some for its political ambivalence; others, as Felperin here, have put in question the extent of its break with older methods of historical scholarship.

If New Historicism is principally an American 'movement', new work in Britain has taken on different forms. On this side of the Atlantic important contributions to the field – including what has come to be called 'cultural materialism' – have been made, partly drawing on and partly distinguishing themselves from an indigenous Marxist historiography and literary criticism, but also in debate with the American critical formations as well as sharing some of the theory and method that informs them. The British work, tending to be more politically explicit than its United States counterpart, has entailed the continuation of the strong engagement with history that has always characterised radical left criticism, but with a newly energised focusing of its concerns in the early modern period.

It would be however an over-simplification of the shape of the contemporary field to suggest that even the new work is neatly divided into two schools of criticism (with what ever points of contact and divergence among them), one British and one American. Setting aside the bulk of unreconstructed christian, monarchist, humanist, and formalist work which continues to be produced annually, it is clear that a much more complicated map needs to be drawn than that suggested above. Much of the important recent work is difficult to categorise, as individual books may eclectically permutate Marxist, feminist, deconstructive, New Historicist, semiotic and psychoanalytic perspectives and methods of interpretation in ways that defy generic labelling (and often flout – deliberately or not – theoretical consistency). And even if other texts may exemplify only one of these 'approaches', the overall ensemble of which the field is constituted is characterised more by overdetermined complexity than by simple grouping; and also of course by some very sharply polemical conflicts.

As with the more general question of history and historicisation, the political dimension of Renaissance literary and cultural studies is the most important concern at present. Recent debate has focused on questions of the political functions of the texts we are addressing when we read Renaissance works. The majority of the new criticism focuses on Shakespeare and the drama (and this is so directly or indirectly of the essays printed here) and there has been considerable debate as to whether Elizabethan and Jacobean theatre underwrote the sovereign power of its historical moment, as some have argued, or whether, by contrast, it consists in a canon of radical texts which prefigure theoretical and political themes of the present moment. This in turn raises questions about the politics of the interpretative strategies themselves. Is not the attraction of the 'subversion and containment' model of the operation of Renaissance power in the work of Stephen Greenblatt, the principal exponent of the New Historicism whose *Renaissance self-fashioning* is usually taken as its founding text, that as a hermeneutic approach it remains ambivalent? The literary or dramatic text may contain moments of subversion, but these moments can then be seen as indeed contained by – and even as charismatically strengthening – the power they apparently contest, permitting such slippery interpretations to appeal to both radical and conservative persuasions simultaneously. In various ways this was the main single issue discussed at the Essex Symposium. In any case, it will be clear from papers in this volume, and from the explicit and implicit relations among them, how politically charged the very matter of historical remembering and forgetting is, even in the academy. It is an important preoccupation here, and in the series this volume inaugurates, that there are important political issues at stake in contemporary criticism and theory, not just in the sense that sometimes apparently theoretical debates are often surrogates for political argument, but that intellectual positions are themselves inevitably political and that much depends – politically – on the way in which 'the question of history' in particular is addressed.

A sense of the centrality and complexity of the problem of 'history' and the particularly intense form this takes in current critical work on Renaissance literature lay behind the convening of the Symposium on which this volume is based. The project of the Symposium was to examine the conceptual vocabulary and the cultural politics of contemporary work in this field. Among the 'founding questions' around which the Symposium was organised, and which were sent out to potential contributors, were the following: why this current historical or anti-historical interest in the Renaissance? is 'the Renaissance' an acceptable category or should it be criticised and abandoned? what is meant by 'history' and why, if at all, is it important? is there anything in 'history' for women, or was it a masculine fiction from the start? are the uses of history at stake here, if not 'history' itself, profoundly Eurocentric in formation? how historical or historicist is the New Historicism in fact? are, on the other hand, post-historical positions tenable? what are the politics of the different strands of new work and of their apparent or implicit contention: do they help to provide, or do they incline to exclude, discourses of gender or class? how do they situate themselves, if at all, in relation to the abiding emphasis on historical understanding of the various formations of Marxism? what does Marxist criticism of the Renaissance have to say of *its* historicity in the light of postmodernism? is it necessary to account for what have been perceived as major differences if not antagonism between British and American work?

A group of prospective contributors emerged from among those who responded positively to the invitation to address these and similar questions, and they were asked to prepare draft papers on topics of their choice within the general framework established by the editors. For contingent reasons, some of this initial group found themselves unable to be present at the meeting. The Symposium was held in Wivenhoe House at the University of Essex, on 19–21 March 1989 and was attended by the editors, the present contributors, and by members of the Essex Early Modern Research Group which then consisted of Maurizio Calbi, Tracey Hill, Paula Hutchings and Steve Speed, as well as Francis Barker and John Joughin. Annabel Patterson of Duke University also presented a paper, ' "The sweat of other men": Milton and the ideology of work', but has not included it here. At the Symposium the draft versions of the essays printed here, which had been circulated in advance, were introduced by their authors and were then either discussed directly or allowed to trigger wider consideration of the problems of the field.

We have not thought it appropriate to try to give here a blow by blow account of the discussions which took place at the Symposium: the papers, which have been revised – in some cases lightly, in some cases very fully – subsequent to the Symposium and in the light of the discussions which took place, must speak for themselves, as must the implicit and explicit relations among them.

It is in the very nature of a project conceived as a dialogic encounter that the Symposium and the volume do not follow a single theoretical or political 'line'. Broadly speaking the positions represented here are situated on the political left, and within the scope of the new work on the Renaissance, but there are none the less many divergences and some clear differences among them. However, the papers also have some things in common, not least their shared response to one of the increasingly prevalent challenges to the validity of historical work in general, and an engagement with the early modern moment in particular, a challenge which can be succinctly expressed as 'why bother?' 'What possible point (one strand of – postmodern? – argument goes) can there be in knowing about the past, even assuming that access to the historically "real" independent of the discourses in which it is investigated or constructed were possible?' Several different answers have been given to this more or less serious question. There is of course the simply positivist (in Renaissance studies, often antiquarian) sense of knowledge being a good in itself and one relatively simply available. None of the contributors to this volume holds that position. But another response – which *is* represented here – is that which dwells on the critical importance of historical difference: if the early modern moment is on the threshold of our own modernity, then the understanding of its contingency can help not only to defamiliarise our own historical epoch by seeing how what appears natural to us was in fact constructed out of the struggles of the earlier moment, but also to glimpse alternatives to our own situation, not in the sense of the possibility of or desire for a nostalgic return to the feudal, but in the sense of grasping in the fullest possible way that historical contingency, that sense that history is something made not given, and therefore remakeable, capable of transformation, in our own moment. And another response again involves the way in which, for a variety of reasons, the study of this period, inflected as it has been in recent years by contemporary theoretical and critical concerns, has become an important site where problems within critical and historical theory itself have been negotiated or where different critical theories (including theories of the nature and value of history) have confronted each other.

In general this debate, as we have tried to stress throughout, is implicitly (and preferably explicitly) political. In all of the essays in this volume there is an underlying sense of historical work as being not simply the recovery of the past, but of the working through of pressingly contemporary questions in relation to the understanding, even the construction, of the past. Emphases vary among the contributors as to the degrees of 'presentness' and 'pastness' at stake, and whether this is at the relatively abstract level of theory or the very practical matter of particular issues such as AIDS and plague, or at another level the concern with issues of pedagogy at stake in Graham Holderness's essay. Engagement with the question of history – whether with a positive or a negative orientation towards the value of 'history' and 'historicism', whether in more theoretical or predominantly 'practical' form – is evidenced in all of the contributions.

The essays printed here – to which we now in detail turn – represent a particular constellation of the current problems and issues as focused by the way in which a number of writers saw fit to address the theme of 'Marxism, postmodernism, and the Renaissance: the uses of history' (the original title of the Symposium which we have re-arranged as the title of this volume). Because of the dialogic character of the project of both the Symposium and the volume, there is potentially a multiplicity of possible cross-connections – whether explicit or implied – among the essays and their assumptions. This has made the problem of ordering the essays acutely difficult. The order chosen makes a certain sense to the editors; but it is only one choice among many others which would have been equally appropriate and plausible. In a sense, even as we now identify what are for us some of the significances of the essays we leave it to the reader to construct others.

Catherine Belsey's paper takes a fresh look at the antithesis between history and fiction in the light of postmodern theory. Within the traditional academy 'history' generally signifies 'what really happened', the facts of the matter, as opposed to various kinds of fiction. Some writers are allowed to have been 'historical' (Scott, for example), but for the most part the more historical then the less literary. Shakespeare's history plays have always been taken as the best example of this case: as Belsey puts it, they have been seen as 'art, not life, imagination and not truth'. In Renaissance studies the respect for 'history', manifest in the inter-war period in the work of Tillyard, was never entirely dislodged by the New Criticism, at least in England. Shakespeare in particular and the Renaissance more widely were part of a national cultural life signified by the notion of an 'English History'. In Belsey's account this growing investment in the idea of a national history – buttressed during the Second World War – was already symptomatic of an anxiety about the present: the crisis of a postmodern (post-Holocaust, post-Hiroshima) world in which the optimism behind Enlightenment values seemed newly empty. (In retrospect, the key document of this 'moment' is Adorno and Horkheimer's *Dialectic of Enlightenment*, published in 1947, though section iii of Belsey's paper allows Tillyard himself to be a more complex figure than often assumed, his reading peculiarly 'postmodern in spite of itself'.) The seeds of epistemological scepticism had also already been sown – Belsey highlights Saussure's lectures from the second decade of the century; although it would only be after 1968 that their product began to have any significant influence in British and North American intellectual life.

Belsey's narrative of modern theory sees a straight and relatively unproblematic line from Saussure to Lyotard. *The postmodern condition* is introduced as the logical culmination of nearly a century's work, dethroning in its slender pages the last of the previously unchallenged metanarrative signifiers, history. The postmodern condition is defined by Lyotard as 'incredulity towards metanarratives'. After Lyotard, the authority of the very idea of a single historical trajectory, which has meant so much to so many attempts to understand and change the world, has been – so the story goes – destroyed.

Of all the participants in the Symposium Belsey was least troubled by the implications of Lyotard's arguments. For almost everybody else, a commitment to some sense of our title words 'History' and 'Marxism' meant that Lyotard's positions should be approached with, for example, the kind of 'unease' (Belsey's word) that Fredric Jameson shows in the introduction to the English translation of *The postmodern condition* on the grounds that to embrace the postmodern seems to leave no space for *any* of the traditional categories of Marxism. Belsey does not feel this unease. The 'grand narrative' of the modes of production would indeed fall (or at least be read as an ingenious myth) but this,

she feels, is no great loss. The important work of Marxist analysis can
go on as before, with *The Eighteenth Brumaire* offered as an exemplar,
in its own way as much one of Lyotard's *petits récits* as Derrida's 'story'
of the history of philosophy.

Within Renaissance studies one version of the postmodern is, for
Belsey, best exemplified by the New Historicism. At its most brilliant,
the self-conscious fragmentation and arbitrariness of New Historicist
work manifests all the qualities that Lyotard identified with one manifestation of postmodernity. If Tillyard was telling of heroic quests and
voyages of discovery, Belsey says, the expeditions described by the New
Historicists are 'voyages of colonisation and ruthless conquest'. In the
course of describing and characterising the New Historicism, Belsey
displays scepticism towards this version of the postmodern. The hard
and brilliant surfaces of New Historicist work seem only to reflect a
narcissistic play of mirrors in which there is no place for political
intervention and transformation. There is here, as elsewhere in the
volume, a drawing-back from the 'elegant pessimism' of New Historicism, and the search for a different space in which to develop a more
clearly political work of reading and analysis. For Belsey (perhaps
unlike the others here) the foundation for this work is still to be found in
Lyotard, but above all in his emphasis on contradiction (*plus marxiste
que les marxistes*), on which can be built a set of 'modest narratives' that
would aim to undo the founding oppositions of contemporary capitalism.

In retrospect Shakespeare's history plays can be seen as grappling
with surprisingly similar issues to those Belsey confronts in the first half
of her paper. In particular the second tetralogy tells a story of change
which begins in nostalgia for a lost golden world and ends in
indeterminacy. The issue of *Henry V* is power, that of *Richard II*
meaning. Belsey reads the plays from an openly postmodern perspective
and sees in them marks of a struggle to fix the dominant meanings of the
age. In other words, in Belsey's reading the history plays are indeed in an
unexpected way about history, posing questions that we can now see as
among the conditions of possibility for the revolutionary struggle that
was to convulse mid-seventeenth-century England. It is here that Belsey
finally takes her distance from the New Historicism. Greenblatt's model
of subversion and containment is seen as inadequate to the complexities
of the plays and ungrounded in what we know of Elizabethan history.
In its place Belsey offers a reading that gives more credence to the

resistances voiced within Shakespearean texts, resistances that are inseparable from the 'poetics of Elizabethan power' of which Greenblatt speaks, but which are not always 'contained' by the reaffirmation of that power.

The paper leaves a strong impression of the connections between Shakespeare and the postmodern world. Not in the vapid sense of 'Shakespeare our contemporary', but through the parallels that exist in the relationships between on the one hand Shakespeare and that 'world of plenitude' which his plays acknowledge lost, and on the other our postmodern world and those 'full' narratives of Enlightenment in which (we are told) we no longer believe. For Belsey the Enlightenment separates us from Shakespeare but also allows us to recognise his stories and problems anew, as in some sense still, again, ours.

In his complex and recursive essay 'Which dead? *Hamlet* and the ends of history', Francis Barker observes that the proclamation of the 'end of history', which plays a central part in much postmodernist discourse, has in fact a long history and should be understood in the historical perspective of earlier crises of representation. Like Belsey, he refers back to Shakespeare's own texts to make his point: 'Shakespearean tragedy dramatises an end of history', not least in as much as it is structured around a contradiction between the need to remember and the impossibility of historical discourse. The dead king's ghost insists 'remember me' and Hamlet, dying, begs Horatio to retell his story. Yet a major trope of the play displaces the political task of memory on to the inadequate substitutes of personal grief or collective commemoration of an individual. Barker writes of 'a pattern of displacement and substitution where historical memory is displaced on to and tendentially replaced by the personal version'. These and other tropes bear witness to the very historical pressures which the play seeks to evade.

Other key moments of crisis and ends of history are evoked in the apparently contrasting positions of Marx and Benjamin. Marx, in *The Eighteenth Brumaire*, calls for a proletarian revolution that would dispense with the costumes of the past worn by both the tragic and farcical versions of the bourgeois revolution: his slogan might be said to be 'forget'. Benjamin, on the other hand, warns that if the enemy is victorious not even the dead will be safe – he enjoins us to remember. But are they really so at odds? Barker suggests that the 'history' in Marx's text that we must forget is something more like the empty continuum of historicism, which Benjamin, too, sought to explode, and to which he counterposed the 'tradition of the oppressed', the active memory of the dispatched and the officially forgotten.

The complex dialectical understanding of these two thinkers on ends and beginnings, forgetting and remembering, is contrasted in a later part of the paper with a certain strand of postmodernist thought, especially Lyotard's, which in the name of anti-totalitarianism throws history as metanarrative into the bin of an outmoded modernism. Implicit in Barker's argument is a critique of the notion of history as a simple, linear metanarrative: he ties this misconception of the historical by postmodernism to its forgetting of the long history of the discourse of forgetting. As Barker says, 'the end of history has always been the theme and condition of any radical, historical (and radically historical), practical, thought'. In contrast to the 'breathless novelty' of post-modernist historicism, for Barker 'the end of history' is profoundly historical, and has been since it was possible to think of the present as modern, that is, since the Renaissance.

Barker examines, in parodic and critical form some of the key motifs of postmodernist thought: the non-representational representation of representation and in particular representational technology and the representation of technology; the 'representation' of the 'other'; and substitution of the figures of space for that of time. Informing his at times bitter ironisation of these figures is the conviction that postmodernism is politically complicit with the same aestheticisation of the postmodern world that Benjamin warned against at the end of high modernity.

Finally, Barker questions the politics of postmodernist theory noting, for example, that the call for conceptual undermining and a liberating play of differences can serve as a displacement of political intervention which, in any case, is rendered redundant by the legitimating role 'difference' plays in contemporary political formations. Within this body of theory the proper rejection of historicism is too often a disabling abandonment of historicity as such.

Howard Felperin's paper differs from the others in the volume in so far as it attempts to stand back from the debates elsewhere vigorously engaged, and instead offers to historicise the New Historicism or, as he puts it in his title, the 'two New Historicisms'. From his position on the sidelines of the current debates, Felperin points out, in ironic style, what he sees as the antinomies and paradoxes of current theoretical standpoints. In particular, the New Historicism emerges as remarkably similar to the old historicism from which it supposedly takes its difference. Although previous accounts have tended to form a single critical position out of quite divergent components, Felperin dismantles this fictional construct with some careful attention to the different cultural determinants behind recent United States and British work: studies which share only a common commitment to what Felperin calls 'conventionalism', a post-structuralism which, he argues, too often provides the fashionable trimmings on a rather more sedate model.

The problem with the United States version of New Historicism, as Felperin sees it, is that it is caught rather unhappily between two paradigms. At heart, he suggests, it is a structuralism, wedded to the possibility of 'representation' in a manner not distinct from epistemological realism, committed to a Geertzian idea of a societal 'deep structure' which will limit the otherwise potentially infinite exchange within Greenblatt's new but superficial vocabulary of 'circulation' and 'social energy'. These latter concepts escape the difficulties inherent in an older historicism only at the cost of not being able to provide any historical interpretation at all. The conventionalist trim on this realist model, if taken seriously, renders the latest 'historicism' open to the charge of 'conservative relativisation and recuperation'.

In a word, United States New Historicism is condemned by Felperin as not new and not historical, and therefore without the capacity to be seriously political in the way it at least sometimes suggests it wants to be. Felperin's own position here, judged by his impatience with Greenblatt's residual attachment to some idea of 'the real', indicates his acceptance of the full force of post-structuralist scepticism towards *any* attempts at historiography other than those which recognise their complete factitiousness.

The British model perhaps lacks the sleekness of its United States counterpart but at least runs in the tracks of a well-established historical materialist tradition, allowing it to display quite openly its commitment to political change. In this sense it has, according to Felperin, 'an enormous head start in becoming a genuinely historical and political criticism'. And Catherine Belsey's work (chosen here with Francis Barker's as examples of British 'cultural materialism') is seen to offer itself quite openly as a 'textual construct', leaving no suspicion of the residual realism that dogged Greenblatt.

But this version of New Historicism (not a concept either author applies to their own work), like its United States counterpart, is not that new after all. It might look impeccably Foucauldian in its periodisation and its general account of the emergence of the modern 'subject' – the theme of the two books under discussion; but these again prove to be but the superficial trimmings of post-structuralism, a veneer overlaying a residual affinity with the work of Leavis. Barker and Belsey are read as valuing the pre-bourgeois world over that which replaced it and as therefore demonstrating a nostalgia for the public discourse of a medieval world, God and torture included, a 'social nostalgia' also embraced by the reactionary project of *Scrutiny*. Such supposed similarities – however much difficulty both Belsey and Barker might have in recognising them in their books – would not be altogether surprising: after all Leavis had close, if not comfortable, relations with British Marxism in the 1930s, and the debt of Raymond Williams, coiner of the phrase 'cultural materialism' (which is also not a label that either Belsey or Barker applies to their work), to Leavis is well-attested.

Jean Howard opens her paper with the claim that, among the terms that structure this Symposium, 'postmodernism' is the one which throws into crisis the others – Marxism, Renaissance, history. She also proposes the addition of a further term, 'feminism', with a view to 'thinking an address to history committed to an emancipatory politics without being committed either to Enlightenment epistemology or discourses on truth'. She observes that feminist historians, for example, have for some time been contesting the legitimacy of 'objective' history, anticipating postmodernist critiques and many of the tenets of New Historicism as well. Howard proposes to utilise these resources in her project 'Towards a postmodern, politically committed, historical practice'. She might, in this context, be construed as negotiating a space somewhere between the positions of Belsey and Barker, accepting the full force of postmodern epistemological critiques while at the same time holding on to the idea of an historically grounded scholarly and political project. In other words, she sees scope for a postmodern Marxism, rather than seeing them as necessarily in contest. Howard is equally critical of those de-historicising and aestheticising tendencies within postmodern theory as she is of totalising master-narratives which marginalise the struggles of women, ethnic groups and so on. One tendency might be used to counter the excesses of the other.

The feminist contribution to Howard's model of 'a politically committed, postmodern historical practice' would be to deepen the New Historicist conviction that historical knowledge cannot be disengaged from the concerns of the present and, further, to insist that the concerns of the present must include an emancipatory telos. Legitimate postmodern scepticism about 'Enlightenment' foundational discourses must not to lead to defeatism with respect to the project of freedom and equality for all. In this conviction Howard is close to Barker's position when he invokes Gramsci's 'pessimism of the intellect, optimism of the will'.

If feminists have been able to learn from New Historicists in the past, the reverse should also be possible. The problem Howard sees with New Historicist critical practice is that it is susceptible to turning back into disinterested academic scholarship. This is so because, although it throughly politicises the past, it is reticent about the politics of its own contemporary scene of writing (on this point see also Graham Holderness's paper). Making use of Donna Haraway's notion of 'situated knowledge', Howard sets out guidelines for an historical practice that would avoid both androcentric objectivism and postmodern relativism. As she put it, 'Postmodernism does not mean the disappearance of the real, but rather of a belief in true, complete, unmediated accounts of that real'. With a political goal in view feminist critics and theorists can afford neither the complacency of positivist notions of truth nor the luxury of relativism. They can abide neither historicism nor notions of the end of history.

Lisa Jardine in her ' "No offence i' th' world": *Hamlet* and unlawful marriage', also addresses problems of the historical interpretation of the past from politically explicit positions in the present. Writing as a feminist critic whose work engages with interpretative strategies from within various adjacent disciplines, she none the less begins by separating the project of her work from that of a 'return to "history" ' of the kind which so often in fact conceals a retention of an earlier positivistic historicism. Instead, she seeks to articulate her project with the 'generally progressive trend' of the 'converging practices of social historians, intellectual and cultural historians, text critics and social anthropologists, as they move towards a more sensitive integration of past and present cultural products'.

But if this resists positivism, neither does it entail – even although our access to the past is only possible via 'textual remains' – 'radical indeterminacy'; this is a position which Jardine rejects not least because it is buttressed by the equally unacceptable view that what the textual remains of the past yield is evidence of 'individual subjectivity'. Referring to Greenblatt's notion of self-fashioning and the – anthropological – model and methodology in which it is embedded, she points out that if subjectivity has been shown by Greenblatt to be an aspiration which is 'endlessly deferred and historically incomplete', then the textual remains, and their interpretation, will inevitably be indeterminate too. But in opposition to the view which is focused in this way on subjectivity, Jardine considers another agenda, one which has in her own recent work centred on group consciousness and on intersubjectivity, one growing, moreover, out of 'a strongly felt need to provide a historical account which restores agency to groups hitherto marginalised or left out of what counts as historical explanation – non-élite men and all women'.

Jardine's project is to 'give meaning' to early modern agency and not just to record – like the social historian – the fact of its existence. She cites Greenblatt's approach again, and, behind it, the methodology of the cultural anthropologist Clifford Geertz, for a conversational rather than a positivistic and descriptive model of engagement with other selves; but one which none the less treats with the 'external manifestations of selfhood' as events within the fabric of social relations. But Jardine asserts that there is a drawback for feminist critics in Greenblatt's New Historicist methodology, particularly when it posits a model of subjectivity which reduces the actual to what the New Historicist critic can recognise in the discourses of the early modern period, or at least to what the two discourses (that of the critic in the present, and that of the text in the past) share. It is not only that New Historicist method *assumes* the subjection of women in its coding of power, Jardine argues, but that it depends upon senses of intertextual identity – a 'fundamental difficulty when we are trying to recover female agency from the cultural traces of the past'.

Jardine then focuses her attention on the notions of excess which have characterised commentary on *Hamlet* since Eliot's famous 1919 essay. Remarking critically the recent tendency of some writers, assuming from within a psychoanalytic or deconstructive perspective that desire is 'a permanent condition of language', to collapse incest from a specifically forbidden sexual union into 'a universal tendency towards non-conforming, problematic forms of desirous social relationships', Jardine points out that there is no incestuous relationship, in the specific sense, between Hamlet and Gertrude corresponding to 'the excessive emotion on his side, and the excessive guilt on hers.' In fact Hamlet's emotions are focused on Gertrude's sexual relations with Claudius, a marriage which taken historically is unlawful both in itself, and in so far as it denies Hamlet his lawful succession. This prompts a discussion of what constituted unlawful marriage in the early modern period. Drawing on archival material from the ecclesiastical courts, Jardine analyses the way in which unlawful marriage is connected in canon law with the idea of 'offence caused'. The Levitical decrees, the tables of consanguinity and affinity, also incorporate this idea, and the notoriety of Henry VIII's marriage to the widow of his dead brother, like Claudius's to that of his, confirms the incestuous character of the marriage in *Hamlet*. 'Act I in its entirety dwells deliberately', in Jardine's estimation, 'on incest as a material offence committed against Hamlet.'

This reading suggests an alternative account to that of the man 'dominated', in Eliot's phrase, 'by an emotion which is inexpressible, because it is in excess of the facts as they appear.' In contrast to the guilt of Claudius, Gertrude's guilt is 'culturally constructed so as to represent her as responsible without allowing her agency'. This reading does not exculpate Gertrude, but it makes a great part of the guilt which attaches to her 'a condition of her oppression'. She has indeed committed 'offences recognised within the early modern community', but this is a very different thing from reading her as the 'emotional focus' of the generalised guilt which 'taints the state of Denmark', and the received readings.

Thus, in respect both of the strategies of reading which are deployed *vis-à-vis Hamlet*, and also of the wider problems of historical interpretation, which Jardine's paper implicitly and explicitly engages, the importance of the 'turn to history' is that it is motivated by the potential consequences of shifting the critical emphasis from 'text and discourse' to 'history and agency'. Critical discourses focused on the former still all too frequently 'objectivate' women as inevitably objects of desire, objects of blame, and permanent victims. But concentration instead on the event, and on agency in history as Jardine's paper defines these, dissipates the inevitability of such accounts, and re-entitles the critical, feminist question, 'Who, after all has been wronged, and by whom?'

It was always going to be the case that those symposiasts who associated themselves most closely with a radical politics would want to speak from and to the here and now: in the event almost all the papers demonstrate such concerns. John Joughin's densely written essay presses the question of the present as persistently as any, allowing the parallelisms between the Renaissance and contemporary worlds to reverberate discomfortingly.

The paper begins with the statutes of the plagued city, the legislation with which London made itself a place apart, disciplined the threatening chaos with a civic calculus of order; and with the official plague histories, bland remembrances through which the survivors imposed the hindsight of statistical 'accuracy', forgetting to remember (or remembering to forget) the hasty dispatch of the uncommemorated dead – whose stinking corpses will reappear as punctual mementoes throughout the rest of the paper, unlettered ghosts haunting the margins of the historical 'accounts', preventing the books of the dead from balancing. Memory, here as elsewhere in the Symposium, surfaces as one of key registers of 'history': Joughin's reference – again as elsewhere – is to Walter Benjamin. From this 'plague writing' Joughin singles out as a case history John Allin's letters, reflections in crisis of the plague's critical history, writings not wholly unaware of the special position they occupy and which Joughin highlights with the constant plays of 'script' and 'crypt', 'corpus', 'corpse', and 'corporation'. The body is here fully politic.

The uneasy writing of a history of disease is located in a present conjuncture where the 'envelope' of discourse is now beginning to encase the experience of AIDS. Except of course that the metaphor of message and envelope, inside and outside, is itself part of the problem, part of that set of metaphors which 'informs' (and 'infects') the scientific discourse on AIDS and determines its reception within the wider social domain. In this second half of his paper Joughin looks squarely at a divergence within the oppositional discourse of AIDS, within the writings of those who have rejected the entrenched narratives of 'plague' used as the major signifier in so-called moral crusades. The starting point is Susan Sontag's important *AIDS and its metaphors*. Recognising the necessity of its exposition of the language of stigma, Joughin nevertheless sees a hostage to fortune in Sontag's programme for figural detoxification which opts for the 'demystified' narratives of modern science, as Galenic in their way as Allin's version of the plague, and leaving Sontag inevitably at the mercy of the overdetermination of those discourses of rationality and enlightenment which validate such demystifications. In contrast, 'in the figural frontline', as Joughin puts it, AIDS activists operate a strategy of active discursive involvement under the slogan 'SILENCE = DEATH' which offers a kind of mirror-image of Sontag's deficiencies.

A strong sense of the urgency of strategical questions marks Joughin's paper. The scepticism towards the truth-claims of conventional historiography is as marked here as elsewhere but, *contra* Lyotard, the master tropes of social and cultural analysis are seen as still fully empowered, worryingly insensible to the theoretical inadequacy which is supposed to have undermined their valency. 'Crisis' is finally read as belonging to a language of power, one of those 'ruling ideas' that serves now, as it always has done, as alibi for 'the necessary measures' that the state will put into place to prevent the threatening chaos – and to shore up its own position. The 'use of history' is clearly seen here as a reminder that the claims of the post-men are not as new as their suits.

Graham Holderness's essay is written from the positions, strongly marked in his text, of one who engaged in left political and critical activities thoughout the 1960s and 1970s and of a teacher of drama. On the basis of his experience he argues against the currently fashionable contention that Marxist theory was then, or is now, unreflexive and totalising. Turning the tables, he suggests that contemporary criticism, particularly deconstruction, could learn from the Marxist commitment to integrate theory and practice. His paper, 'Production, reproduction, performance', advocates a critical practice that would be attentive to theatre as a material institution, instead of focusing solely on the play-text. He presses questions about the the uses to which Shakespeare is put in the educational system and in cultural practices such as television, film and exhibitions. 'Shakespeare' and the 'Renaissance' are continually being reproduced and one cannot study this rich history by attending to the text alone nor to it in conjunction with adjacent contemporaneous texts. Holderness is explicitly critical of the New Historicist desire to speak with the dead, which means that 'dramatic texts are returned to the historical culture from which they emanated'. Like Jean Howard, he objects to the way this practice ignores the present context of the critical utterance itself. And although New Historicists juxtapose literary and 'non-literary' texts, they are seen as more securely tied to the textual than the 'cultural materialist' tradition invoked by Holderness.

Holderness advocates a specifically theatrical methodology as an alternative to subject-centred close reading of a single 'authoritative' text. Criticism should understand Renaissance drama as *theatre*, that is, as texts devised for performance and constituted by a history of performances. As an example of the kind of insights this approach would yield, he sketches the performance history of the story of *The taming of the shrew* bringing to light all its centrifugal diversity of significations which are at the same time responsive to changing historical attitudes and anxieties. Unlike the crystalline authoritative text which has been the object of even radical forms of critique, the performance history discloses 'a deeply unstable, volatile entity, chameleon in its adaptability, vertiginously pluralistic in its continual metamorphoses'.

His history of *The taming of the shrew* begins with an account of the way scholarship has marginalised the variant Renaissance instances of it, creating a univocal, authorial origin. Instead of contributing to this process of canonisation, Holderness proposes what he calls 'peripheral analysis'. This could take the form of a study of written adaptations of the story including, for example, the musical *Kiss me, Kate*. His specific interest, however, lies in the history of theatrical reproductions and textual improvisations. He cites one scholar who acknowledges the way a single textual version has been used to signify quite different meanings on stage in response to contemporary attitudes, particularly attitudes to male dominance. But, as he points out, this 'litmus paper' analogy retains the idea of the text's 'inviolable essence' – a fixed quantity capable of registering change.

This fixity of the text is not challenged by deconstructive criticism either which continues to endorse the canonised text. In this respect, theatrical productions of the play have proved more 'deconstructive'. They have amalgamated what scholars have separated as 'good' and 'bad' versions, creatively interpolating elements of the anonymous *The taming of a shrew*. In his ambitious essay, Holderness is not only commending a study of this experimentation and improvisation, he also sees it as a model for criticism and pedagogy able to 'interrogate and re-open the closures of written fiction'.

To 're-open the closures of written fiction' might well be seen as one among the central tasks of this series. In bringing to a conclusion the introduction to this first volume, however, we would like to acknowledge the help we have received with the production of this book. In addition to those who have put such a lot of hard work into writing and presenting the essays of which this volume is made, we would also like to thank the following: The University of Essex, and the Departments of Art History and Theory and of Literature at Essex, for help with the funding of this project; Ann-Marie Deacon, Sylvia Sparrow and Elizabeth Weall for secretarial assistance; and Tracey Hill for making the index.

Francis Barker, Peter Hulme, Margaret Iversen
University of Essex, January 1991

Making histories then and now: Shakespeare from *Richard II* to *Henry V*

CATHERINE BELSEY

I

Shakespeare's history plays are not commonly taken seriously as history.[1] Everyone knows that they are not accurate. Much of the material is pure invention, so the argument goes, and even when it is not, both story and characterisation are significantly modified in the interests of vital and enduring drama on the one hand and the glorification of the Tudor dynasty on the other. Brilliant fictions, and perhaps equally brilliant propaganda, the history plays are understood to be precisely art, not life, imagination and not truth.

Is it possible that this account reveals as much about the literary institution and the distinctions it takes for granted as it does about Shakespeare's texts? History, it assumes, enables us to measure the accuracy of the plays and find them wanting – as truth. At the same time, and paradoxically, imagination throws into relief the dullness of mere empirical fact: art is dazzling where history is drab. In either case the term 'history play' is something of an oxymoron. History, *real* history, stands outside literature as its binary antithesis, fact as opposed to fiction.

Or it did. Our postmodern condition has called into question that antithesis, and perhaps in the process identified 'history plays' as a more sympathetic category for us now. I want, not purely perversely, to read Shakespeare's second tetralogy as history.

II

A generation ago, because it was understood to be outside literature, history constituted the final court of appeal for readers of Renaissance texts. The truth – which is to say, the authority – of an interpretation could be guaranteed by its historical accuracy in the light of our linguistic, cultural, social and political understanding of the period. Scholarship was the mark and criterion of correct reading, and scholarship was synonymous with a grasp of history. A good knowledge of the history of the language was a prerequisite: you had to know what the words of the text *meant*. And in quest of independent confirmation of the meaning, it was widely held, you also needed to know what the Elizabethans *thought*. That would ensure that you had accurately identified what they must have had in mind. Thereafter, texts were fully intelligible only to those who could pick up the allusions within them to contemporary events, however obscure or allegorical. And the same allusions, duly deciphered, could then be used to date the texts in question.

If a certain circularity is evident in this scholarly way with allusions, that is not surprising. It was, indeed, a common feature of scholarship that it was generally brought to bear on the very material which also generated it. Philology was derived, of course, from the study of the documents in the first place, and it was the scholar's reading of the text that made possible the attribution of meaning to specific words and phrases. The meaning of these words and phrases, recurring elsewhere, then produced more readings of more texts. The possibility of an infinite regress was not raised: no one asked what guaranteed the original readings of the original texts.

When it came to cultural history, political predisposition became more evidently part of the hermeneutic circle. F. R. Leavis scrutinised Renaissance poetry for the continuity of felt life in the expressive rhythms of English speech before the fall into writing – and repudiated counter-examples as outside the tradition. E. M. W. Tillyard, meanwhile, read a number of Renaissance plays to find a commitment to order, and discovered in consequence that most of the other plays of the period were also committed to order. And if Tillyard read Renaissance texts for intimations of hierarchy, C. S. Lewis saw the inaugural moment of the Anglican Church wherever he looked.

As these examples indicate, the mood was frequently nostalgic. And even when Christopher Hill fluttered their right-wing reading practices by producing a scholarly, incisive and surely irresistible Marxist account of the Renaissance, including Renaissance literature, it was still with the effect of rediscovering for the admiration of the left a long-forgotten heroism, that of our revolutionary predecessors, recording their exemplary journeys and the dangers they overcame.

That the work was produced should not surprise us. But what needs accounting for is its dominance within the institution, at least in Britain, from the early 1950s onwards. In Renaissance studies even New Criticism never quite succeeded in dislodging the respect for history.[2] This investment in the past was symptomatic of an anxiety about the present, the crisis of the postmodern, precipitated by the Second World War. In the world of the Holocaust and Hiroshima, what price the optimism of the Enlightenment? What purchase now had the conviction that reason and truth must finally inevitably prevail? Nostalgia was the quest for an authentic reference point in the past, a moment of plenitude from which to fend off an uncertain modernity (Doane and Hodges 1987, p. 8), and history guaranteed the truth of that moment, its reality and its certainty. History, in each of its manifestations, was the single, unified, unproblematic, extra-textual, extra-discursive real that guaranteed our readings of the texts which constituted its cultural *expression*. If it was never fully mastered, never absolutely known, if the matter of history was never settled, that meant only that there was more work to be done.

But meanwhile, the same postmodern anxiety also produced a contrary symptom, a counter-current in the literary institution, which called into theoretical question all realities, all certainties, and with them the certainty of history. The work of Saussure, suddenly given a new prominence in the post-war period, put in doubt the possibility of mapping in language the extra-linguistic real. There was, Saussure's work implied, no sure place beyond language to draw from. History was consequently dethroned: it too was linguistic, precisely a story, a narrative, a reading of the documents, and thus no longer able to constitute a guarantee of our readings of other documents. What, after all, could be invoked to guarantee the truth of history itself?

It was Jean-François Lyotard who finally brought it out, who made explicit in *The postmodern condition* exactly what had changed. History itself, the grand narrative, the one story of the single extra-discursive truth, was no longer authoritative. Lyotard defined the postmodern condition as 'incredulity toward metanarratives' (Lyotard 1984, p. xxiv), and incredulity in consequence towards the knowledges and the competences the grand narratives had traditionally legitimated. The authority of the single historical story, with its heroes and voyages

and goals, is, Lyotard argues, deeply political. The knowledge it trans-
mits 'determines in a single stroke what one must say in order to be
heard, what one must listen to in order to speak, and what role one must
play (on the scene of diegetic reality) to be the object of a narrative'
(Lyotard 1984, p. 21). (Feminism and the Civil Rights Movement
could, of course, have told him as much. The history of man, they were
well aware, was the history of white men, and licensed their continued
dominance.) History as progress, as the grand narrative of emancipation, legitimates the bourgeois state, in which the people have finally
won the right to decide, to prescribe norms. History as the story of
freedom represses the role of the economy; it suppresses difference. In
the liberal narrative 'the name of the [single] hero is the people, the sign
of legitimacy is the people's consensus, and their mode of creating
norms is deliberation' (Lyotard 1984, p. 30).

But if in this respect Lyotard was telling the left what it loved to hear,
his analysis of the postmodern also threatened the authority of utopian
Marxism, with its corresponding grand narrative of emancipation, the
story of successive modes of production culminating in the socialist
revolution. This story, Lyotard implied, was no more than the mirror
image of liberal history, and no more credible as a guarantee of truth or
political validity. Almost at once Fredric Jameson, who had written
the Foreword to the English translation of The postmodern condition
(displaying in the process a certain unease about his role), published his
masterly denunciation of the postmodern in the New left review
(Jameson 1984), and Terry Eagleton followed suit in a fluent and witty
repudiation of the postmodern which was also, and explicitly, a denunciation of Lyotard himself (Eagleton 1985). The source of their anxiety
was the depthlessness of the postmodern, its commitment to surfaces, to
the signifier at the expense of the signified, and its consequent
ahistoricity, its lack of sense of a substantial past. The alternative to a
grand narrative, complete with protagonists representing good and evil,
was, they believed, an unfocused eclecticism, and the implications of
that for our understanding of the political present were to reduce it, in
Jameson's words, to 'sheer heterogeneity, random difference, a
coexistence of a host of distinct forces whose effectivity is undecidable'
(Jameson 1984, p. 57).

Were they right? Is there no alternative to the master-narrative of
inexorable and teleological development, but only a (dis)continuous
and fragmentary present, a world of infinite differences which are

ultimately undifferentiated because they are all confined to the signifying surface of things, Lyotard's notorious degree zero of the postmodern: 'one listens to reggae, watches a western, eats McDonald's food for lunch and local cuisine for dinner, wears Paris perfume in Tokyo and "retro" clothes in Hong Kong' (Lyotard 1984, p. 76)?[3] Is there in practice only a leap of faith, a willed commitment to an increasingly implausible narrative on the one hand, or on the other contemporaneity endlessly deferred, the repeated encounter with absence which must ensue if the fullness of presence is recognised as a chimera?

One of the classic locations of the poststructuralist interrogation of history is Derrida's essay on Michel Foucault's *Madness and civilization*. Foucault's book appeared in Paris in 1961, and Derrida's 'Cogito and the history of madness' was first given as a lecture in 1963. What worries Derrida in Foucault's analysis is the risk of nostalgia which invades not only the record of a fall from a merry and tolerant middle ages but, worse, the assumption of an undifferentiated Greek logos, reason without a contrary. In order to tell the story of the great incarceration of the insane in the seventeenth century, and the division between reason and madness which legitimates it, Foucault seems to posit a lost presence, a world which precedes division. In this sense *Madness and civilization* repeats the pattern of other grand narratives, though in Foucault's project the Christian story of paradise lost supplants the liberal account of progressive emancipation. (Later Foucault's concept of history as genealogy would engage with the dangers of metanarrative and its quest for origins (Foucault 1977b, pp. 139–64).[4]) There was, Derrida insists, no fall, and from the beginnings of Western philosophy no undifferentiated logos, but only 'reason divided against itself since the dawn of its Greek origin' (Derrida 1978, p. 40).

Derrida's account of Western metaphysics might easily be read, therefore, as an affirmation of a single, continuous present, characterised ultimately by absence, twenty-five undifferentiated centuries of beleaguered logocentrism. Derrida too tells a story, however, or perhaps a series of stories, and in this sense history reappears in his account of philosophy. But it returns, predictably, not as master-narrative but only as change, not as extra-discursive explanation and guarantee, but as textual difference. If madness has any continuous meaning, Derrida asserts, 'it simply says the other of each determined form of the logos'. Each determined form is inevitably different, and in these differences it is apparent that philosophy too has a history.[5] By establishing a continuity, Derrida argues, he is not defending a single and eternal condition of philosophy. 'Indeed, it is exactly the contrary that I am proposing. In question is a way of accounting for the very historicity of philosophy' (Derrida 1978, pp. 58–60).[6]

This historicity is altogether more modest, more unassuming than the grand legitimating narratives, something closer, perhaps, to Lyotard's *petits récits*, the little stories which are in his analysis 'the quintessential form of imaginative invention' (Lyotard 1984, p. 60). Lyotard is not opposed to narrative: his own book tells the story of the emergence of the postmodern within modernism. Narration, after all, constructs objects of discourse, 'objects to be known, decided on, evaluated, transformed . . .' (Lyotard 1984, p. 18). How else but by telling new stories are we to challenge the limits of what one must say in order to be heard? But the *petits récits* lay no claim to extra-discursive authority, to mastery or to the abolutism of truth. They acknowledge the process that Derrida calls differance, by which signifying practice itself necessarily differentiates and distances all that is extra-linguistic.[7] They explicitly make meanings, make histories.

From the perspective of the literary institution it might be argued that the New Historicism has replaced the old historicism of Tillyard and C. S. Lewis in something like the way Lyotard's short stories supplant the grand narrative. Offering a generalisation which necessarily suppresses important differences, I want to suggest that at its most brilliant, its most elegant, New Historicism is characteristically postmodern. It records no heroic quests, no voyages of discovery, no dangers triumphantly overcome. On the contrary, the expeditions it describes are more commonly voyages of colonisation and ruthless conquest. It is anything but nostalgic in its account of a world dominated by power, which produces resistance only to justify its own extension.[8] Sophisticated to the point of scepticism, the work of Stephen Greenblatt, Jonathan Goldberg, Steven Mullaney and others is self-consciously fragmentary, arbitrary. But its degree zero is the eclecticism of the anecdote, the single esoteric text, the improbable reading. Its theme is not change, since the history it recounts is rarely diachronic. The sleek surfaces of New Historicist writing propose no programme; they offer the minimum of evaluations and trans-formations, except in so far as they transform into its opposite the grand narrative itself; and in consequence they legitimate no political intervention.

In the analysis of Jameson and Eagleton the postmodern is a single, unitary, undifferentiated, non-contradictory phenomenon, the deadly cultural manifestation of late capitalism. (Marx would perhaps have been surprised by this unwillingness to acknowledge contradictions.) But in Lyotard's account the postmodern is itself divided. If functionalism produces an analysis of society as a single whole, in which culture is non-contradictory, or power always succeeds in pre-empting challenges to its own increased mastery (produces them, indeed, for that purpose), there is another sociology, derived this time from the Marxist account of society as a site of struggle. It follows that there is also another postmodernism, this time of the left, which emphasises dissension,[9] difference as opposition, and a possible consequent historicity which tells of the *resistance* that continues to challenge power from the position of its inevitable, differentiating other.

It is not this emphasis on struggle which is above all important for us in Marxism now? What distinguishes Marxism is not, in other words, its grand narrative, the inexorable succession of the modes of production, but its analysis of contest, the classes confronting each other locked in contradiction and conflict. Marx's grand *history* is intelligible now as breathtakingly inventive, ingenious myth, the story of a struggle for power which repeats itself and differs from one historical moment to the next.[10] Though it offers a brilliant framework, the attempt to work in detail with the Renaissance as the encounter between feudalism and capitalism runs, it seems to me, into endless problems of historical specificity. Marx's account of *the relations of production*, however, so daring in the nineteenth century, and still politically indispensable now, has not been superseded by postmodernism or poststructuralism. Marx saw labour as the other of capital: not its binary opposite, but the condition, at once necessary and menacing, of its existence.[11] And his dangerously radical gesture was to analyse capital from the position of the other.

In this he was not naive. He was, indeed, more sophisticated than the early Foucault of *Madness and civilization*. Foucault set out to write the history of madness from the place of the other, to make the madness which had been silenced by reason the subject, in every sense, of his narrative, to make it speak. Derrida's case against him is that this reversal is impossible. To attempt to give madness a voice is simply to reiterate the distinction between madness and reason, objectifying madness all over again (Derrida 1978, p. 35). Derrida's own practice, by contrast, speaks not of silent madness, but precisely of voluble reason. But deconstruction uncovers the differences *within* rationality, and thus writes of it *otherwise*. Marx also writes otherwise. He does not set out to speak for the working class, but instead he analyses the differences within capitalism, the contradictions which are precisely its undoing.

To attempt to speak on behalf of subversion, to write a history of the working class, or to give women a voice, is in the end to reaffirm the oppositions which currently exist. Our more radical and more modest narratives set out to undo those oppositions themselves, to throw into relief the precariousness of power, of capital, of patriarchy and racism, showing them as beleaguered to the degree that the resistances they produce return to endanger their seamless mastery.[12] This too is a postmodern project, but it is not satisfied with an elegant pessimism. Its mode is to activate the differences and promote political intervention. It tells short stories which are nevertheless stories of change. There are many histories to be made, meanings to be differentiated, dissensions to be emphasised. And if the practice does not promise utopia, it has at least the advantage that it offers the possibility of making a difference.

III

In the light of the postmodern condition, it is no longer strictly true to say that Shakespeare's history plays have not been taken seriously as history. Tillyard took them seriously. Not as historical fact, on the whole, but precisely as grand narrative. According to Tillyard's account, the history plays tell the true story of their own moment, Elizabethan England, in the richness and multiplicity of its culture, its quintessential Englishness, and above all its universal commitment to hierarchic order. 'The picture we get from Shakespeare's Histories is that of disorder' (Tillyard 1969, p. 15), but this is only on the surface of things. *Behind* the recurring rebellions which constitute the plots, in Shakespeare's *mind*, is the great Elizabethan ideal, which the dramatist *must* have shared with his contemporaries, degree cosmically endorsed by the Author of the great chain of being.

Tillyard's nostalgic reading of the plays re-enacts, of course, his relation to his own historical moment. *Shakespeare's history plays* was

published in 1944. All around was disorder. But beyond this there lay as
the solution universal acceptance of the great ideal of hierarchy, not
(and for an intellectual who had experienced the 1930s in Britain it was
necessary to repeat) *not* socialism. Tillyard's book also re-enacts his
own relation to history itself. The Tudors, he insists, look to a grand
narrative of the middle ages which legitimates their own legally precarious but deeply autocratic rule. Tillyard himself looks in turn to
Tudor history for a narrative which legitimates autocracy now. Did it
not, after all, produce the golden age of Elizabeth I and the golden
works of Shakespeare?

Oddly, however, Tillyard repeatedly identifies Tudor history as a
construct, and emphasises its expediency (Tillyard 1969, pp. 36–76).
Obscuring the reality of the uncertain Tudor claim to the throne, he
argues, there lies not truth but history-as-myth. Tillyard goes so far as to
denounce Tudor historians who, worried about the empirical evidence,
fail to reproduce the master-narrative. Only the select few could see the
pattern. These include the brilliantly creative Hall, but not Holinshed,
who displays an unintelligent anxiety about whether the details are
accurate (Tillyard 1969, pp. 65, 55–8).

Is Tillyard here compelled to repeat a certain anxiety about his own
grand narrative, to betray an unconscious acknowledgement that it too
represents history-as-myth, designed to keep disorder at bay? Does his
proclaimed contempt for Holinshed imply (by denying it) a fear that an
ordinary empiricist historian, lacking Tillyard's creative flair, might fail
to see into 'the hearts of most Englishmen' of the period (Tillyard 1969,
p. 73), and might read the history of the sixteenth century, and particularly of the 1590s, rather differently? If so, Tillyard shows his reading to
be postmodern in spite of itself, truly of its own historical moment, and
not least in its inability to sustain the opposition between art and
history, fiction and truth.

It is possible to read Shakespeare's history plays otherwise, in ways
which have explicit resonances for us now. The second tetralogy tells a
story of change which begins in nostalgia for a lost golden world and
ends in indeterminacy. Early in *Richard II* John of Gaunt speaks
wistfully of a time when kings were kings and went on crusades
(II.i.51–6), but by the end of *Henry V* the legitimacy of kingship itself is
in question. The issue is power. Similarly, the beginning of *Richard II*
seems rooted in the simple unity of name and things, but the plays chart
a fall into differance which generates a world of uncertainties. The issue

is meaning. And the texts themselves bear witness to the difference within textuality. Read from a postmodern perspective, they reveal marks of the struggle to fix meaning, and simultaneously of the excess which necessarily renders meaning unstable.

IV

The vanishing world to which the opening of *Richard II* alludes is an imaginary realm of transparency, plenitude and truth, where the essential link between signifier and referent has not yet been broken. Names, their meanings and the condition they name are apparently one:

> *K. Rich.*   What comfort, man? How is't with aged Gaunt?
> *Gaunt.*   O, how that name befits my composition!
> Old Gaunt, indeed; and gaunt in being old.
> Within me grief hath kept a tedious fast;
> And who abstains from meat that is not gaunt?
> For sleeping England long time have I watch'd;
> Watching breeds leanness, leanness is all gaunt.
> The pleasure that some fathers feed upon
> Is my strict fast – I mean my children's looks;
> And therein fasting, hast thou made me gaunt.
> Gaunt am I for the grave, gaunt as a grave,
> Whose hollow womb inherits nought but bones.
>   (*King Richard II*, II.i.72–83)

For Richard this reiteration of Gaunt's name, specifying in a series of figures its meaning and its cause, is no more than an instance of the play of the signifier: 'Can sick men play so nicely with their names?' (II.i.84). But from the point of view of the audience, the sequence has the effect of producing a convergence on a single truth, identifying a unified state of being, gaunt by name and gaunt by nature.

Ironically, this affirmation of plenitude, of the fullness of truth in the signifier, is also an assertion of absence, of leanness, fasting, the hollow womb of the grave. Its occasion is the absence Richard has made in the political and the symbolic order. John of Gaunt is dying of grief for a land which has no heirs, a realm whose lineage is coming to an end as Richard fails to *live* the true and single meaning of sovereignty: 'Landlord of England art thou now, not King' (II.i.113). Richard divorces the name of the king from the condition, leasing out the realm and banishing Bolingbroke.

Gaunt's grief is also for his own heir. The name of Duke of Lancaster has a material existence: it is a title, an entitlement, meaning land, a position, an army, power. By sending his son into exile, Gaunt protests, 'thou dost seek to kill my name in me' (II.i.86), to end the dynasty and expropriate the land.[13] Thus Richard, already identified as the murderer of Gloucester, is now represented as causing the death of Lancaster.

It is not, of course, to be done by fiat. Lancaster is not merely a name but a material presence. Since the title is precisely an entitlement – to property and to power in the realm – the inscription of power in the symbolic order cannot be created or destroyed by an act of individual will, not even the sovereign's. In the opening scene of the play Bolingbroke, Duke of Hereford, nephew of the dead Gloucester, challenges the king in Mowbray. In Act II Bolingbroke, his identity transformed by his father's death, returns to challenge the king again by reclaiming his title, in all its materiality: 'As I was banish'd, I was banished Hereford; / But as I come, I come for Lancaster' (II.iii.113–14); 'I am come to seek that *name* in England' (II.iii.71, my emphasis).

But as in Gaunt's sequence of figures, here too the names of England and Lancaster are linked as elements in a system of differences where meanings are interdependent. All names are authorised by inheritance, as fathers are authors of their children. The inscription of authority in a name is reciprocal and differential, not individual, and it is specified by blood. In consequence Bolingbroke is entitled to argue, 'If that my cousin king be King in England, / It must be granted I am Duke of Lancaster' (II.iii.123–4). It is not granted, of course. In the event, the king's repudiation of the symbolic order, which also guarantees his own succession, impels civil war to manure the ground with English blood – in another but, of course, related sense of the word 'blood'.

There is thus only a brief moment in Act I when the truth of things is perceived to reside in names, when the grand simplicities appear to be in place, or when the (royal) sentence seems absolute. By naming the banishment of Mowbray and Bolingbroke the king is able to bring it about – or to repeal it. Richard sees Gaunt's grief signified in his tears and reduces the term of Bolingbroke's exile. Bolingbroke draws attention to the inscription of power in the signifier:

How long a time lies in one little word!
Four lagging winters and four wanton springs
End in a word: such is the breath of Kings.

(I.iii.213–15)

But within the system of differences which gives meaning to kingship, inscribes the power in royal utterances, kings are only the location of authority, not its origin. In practice Richard cannot give meaning to his sentences or deny meaning to the names of his subjects. His words are absolute only on condition that they remain within the existing system of differences. He, like his subjects, is subject to the symbolic order, which allots meaning to the orders he gives.

Richard transgresses this system of differences when he tries to remake the meaning of kingship in the image of his own desires. His predecessors lived the regality of their name, Gaunt complains. Their sovereignty was thus synonymous with England's, and the realm was a 'sceptr'd isle', an 'earth of *majesty*' (II.i.40–1, my emphasis). But this world of unity and plenitude is already lost. Richard-as-England has consumed England's material wealth in riot, misusing his sovereignty to mortgage the land, devouring in the name of his title his own entitlement. He has thus turned the sceptre against the isle, majesty against the earth itself, and in consequence fragmented the singleness of the realm.[14] The 'teeming womb of royal kings' (II.i.51) is now, according to the logic of Gaunt's rhetoric, empty, and it is this absence of heirs which propels one of its few remaining denizens towards the grave, 'Whose hollow womb inherits nought but bones' (II.i.83). Richard violates the symbolic order, and in consequence his words lose their sovereignty: Bolingbroke returns, repudiating the royal sentence of banishment.

Richard makes a gap between names and things, between kingship and its referent, majesty, and Gaunt cannot live in the new world he makes. But Bolingbroke belongs there already, and thus proleptically identifies himself as Richard's heir even more surely than he is his father's. Gaunt offers consolation for exile in the supremacy of the signifier:

Go, say I sent thee forth to purchase honour,
And not the King exil'd thee; or suppose
Devouring pestilence hangs in our air
And thou art flying to a fresher clime.

Look what thy soul holds dear, imagine it
To lie that way thou goest . . .

(I.iii.282–7)

But his son recognises the power to remake the referent in accordance
with the signifier as precisely imaginary:

O, who can hold a fire in his hand
By thinking on the frosty Caucasus?
Or cloy the hungry edge of appetite
By bare imagination of a feast?
Or wallow naked in December snow
By thinking on fantastic summer's heat?

(I.iii.294–9)

But if Bolingbroke recognises the differance that Richard has made,
or has made evident, the difference and the distance between the
signifier and what it re-presents, Richard himself is tragically unable to
do so. This is the dramatic irony of what follows, as Richard, deserted
by 12,000 Welshmen, clings to the imaginary sovereignty of the
signifier:

Is not the King's name twenty thousand names?
Arm, arm, my name! a puny subject strikes
At thy great glory.

(III.ii.85–7)

In practice, we are to understand, the unity of the king's name and
kingship itself have fallen apart. The realm has deserted him for
Bolingbroke, and Richard is king precisely in name only.

Meanwhile, the new and silent sovereign says nothing, uses few
words, or none (IV.i.290). It is Richard himself who employs the breath
of kings to strip away the signifier of his own monarchy: 'What must the
King do now? . . . Must he lose / The name of king? A God's name, let it
go' (III.iii.143–6). But like Gaunt, he cannot survive in the world of
differance, where if he is not king he has no identity at all: 'I must
nothing be' (IV.i.201). 'What says King Bolingbroke? Will his Majesty /
Give Richard leave to live till Richard die?' (III.iii.173–4). As Marjorie
Garber points out, the king performs an act of erasure, as differance
thus invades his identity, enters into the selfhood of Richard:

I have no name, no title –
No, not that name was given me at the font –
But 'tis usurp'd. Alack the heavy day,
That I have worn so many winters out,

And know not now what name to call myself!
O that I were a mockery king of snow,
Standing before the sun of Bolingbroke
To melt myself away in water drops.

(IV.i.255–62)

He is already a mockery king, other than himself, figured here as insubstantial, a snowman visibly melting away, though it is worth remembering, of course, that his name, his entitlement, will return to haunt the remainder of the second tetralogy (Garber 1987, pp. 20–1).

V

Richard fails to find a means of holding the signified in place, guaranteeing his title. The Bishop of Carlisle proffers the grandest of all grand narratives:

Fear not, my lord; that Power that made you king
Hath power to keep you king in spite of all.

(III.ii.27–8)

And Richard reiterates it (III.ii.54–62). But the play at once subjects the master-narrative of divine protection for divine right to ironic scrutiny, as first Salisbury and then Scroop deliver their *petits récits* of desertions and defeats. If God has the power, he signally fails in a fallen world to exercise it on behalf of his anointed deputy. The only power on earth that supports the materiality of titles is the law of succession, and Richard breaks it by seizing Bolingbroke's title (II.i.195–208).

Bolingbroke's regime becomes in consequence one of bitter uncertainties, of conflicts for meaning which are simultaneously conflicts for power. These constitute the story of the reign of Henry IV, but the uncertainty begins in the deposition scene in *Richard II*, when it becomes apparent that the word is no longer anchored in the referent, no longer names a single, consensual object. The Bishop of Carlisle defends Richard's sovereignty in the name of the transcendental signified: the king is 'the figure of God's majesty' (IV.i.125). In consequence, he argues, 'My Lord of Hereford here, whom you call king, / Is a foul traitor to proud Hereford's king' (IV.i.134–5). As he concludes his argument, Northumberland steps forward on behalf of Hereford (now Lancaster; now England?) and turns the verbal and political tables on Carlisle: 'Well have you argued, sir; and for your pains, / Of capital treason we arrest you here' (IV.i.150–1).

In a world of differance who is the traitor? who is the king? When in
Act I Mowbray and Bolingbroke accuse each other of treason, the truth
is available: in the following scene the exchanges between Gaunt and
the Duchess of Gloucester make clear to the audience that Richard is
responsible for Gloucester's murder. But in the new world of differance,
who can be sure? If Richard is king, Bolingbroke is a traitor. But is he? If
Bolingbroke is king, Carlisle is a traitor. But is he? Richard's breach of
the symbolic order has divorced the name of king from the power,
laying bare a world of political struggle for possession of meaning,
property and sovereignty. In this new world it is not a name but the
allegiance of the Duke of York and of 12,000 Welshmen which proves
decisive. The orders of the mockery King are now subject to confirmation by Bolingbroke:

> For do we must what force will have us do.
> Set on towards London. Cousin, is it so?
> *Bol.*   Yea, my good Lord.
> *K. Rich.*
> Then I must not say no.

> (III.iii.207–9)

Bolingbroke comes back to claim his title in the name of law, but his
victory, the play makes clear, is an effect of force, not legality. Nevertheless, the repressed law of succession returns to disrupt the reign of
Henry IV. It is Mortimer's legal title as Richard's heir which cements the
quarrel between Hotspur and the king (*1 King Henry IV*, I.iii.77 ff.,
145–59), and if Mortimer is not the motive, he is none the less the
legitimating occasion of the rebellion which constitutes the main plot of
the *Henry IV* plays.[15]

Henry V is legally and unequivocally king, and he manages to bring
the law of succession into line with political strategy when his
Archbishop of Canterbury adduces legal authority for the war with
France. Part of Henry V's claim to reunite the name of king and the
power that belongs to it depends on his identity as a man of the people.
He himself declares his ordinariness as he wanders in disguise among
the common soldiers on the eve of Agincourt: 'Though I speak it to you,
I think the King is but a man as I am'. And if the utterance is an
equivocation, exploiting the plurality of the signifier, the speech goes on
to specify more clearly the unexceptional nature of the king: 'all his
senses have but human conditions; his ceremonies laid by, in his
nakedness he appears but a man' (*King Henry V*, IV.i.100, 103). The

scene presents the king as a popular hero and thus helps to legitimate his sovereignty.

In Williams, therefore, who is also a man of the people, Henry encounters a figure who represents both his similitude and his differentiating other. At the moment of victory Williams, a man as he is, will apparently give back to Henry in his own person the king's desired self-image, while still preserving his independence, his defining alterity (IV.viii.45–55). But on the eve of Agincourt, the climactic battle of the play, Williams challenges on behalf of the people the justice of the king's war. The issue is ostensibly what it means to die well. The official position is apparently that if the king's cause is good, and the soldiers' consciences clear, death is no real threat to them. Williams sees it differently. From the point of view of the ordinary soldier, death is not simply a question of conscience, an affair of the soul, but a matter of 'legs and arms and heads, chopp'd off in a battle', of mutilated bodies on the battlefield, 'some swearing, some crying for a surgeon, some upon their wives left poor behind them, some upon the debts they owe, some upon their children rawly left. I am afeard', Williams continues thoughtfully, 'there are few that die well that die in a battle; for how can they charitably dispose of anything when blood is their argument?' (IV.i.133–43).

If Williams's role in the play identifies his as the voice of the people, his final sentence specifies the nature of the challenge he delivers: 'Now, if these men do not die well, it will be a black matter for the king that led them to it; *who to disobey were against all proportion of subjection*' (IV.i.143–5, my emphasis). Williams does not propose disobedience to the king: he accepts his subjection. But what he says locates the initiative for the war and the consequent responsibility for the legs and arms and heads, the widows and orphans, solely with the monarch.

Uniquely in the history plays, the people are here presented without irony – without comedy and without the differentiating, distancing effect of an inadequate purchase on the language. We might think of other, contrasting figures in the second tetralogy, whose marginality is inscribed precisely in their precarious command of English. This includes most of the women: Mistress Quickly, a sort of Mrs Malaprop *avant la lettre*, Princess Katherine, whose foreignness is so engagingly comic in one of the most patriarchal wooing scenes in all of Shakespeare, and Lady Mortimer, a Welsh speaker confined to communicating in looks and kisses. It also includes the Gloucestershire rustics, as well as Fluellen, Jamy and Macmorris, the three captains representing Wales, Scotland and Ireland; and it includes poor Francis the drawer, who is not allowed to string two words together – for the greater glory of Prince Hal and Poins. Williams, on the other hand, speaks standard English, fluently and persuasively, on behalf of the people. And the people put a strong case that the king has no moral entitlement to risk *their* bodies, *their* lives and the security of *their* families in *his* war. Henry's answer evades the issue, although he has the last word and to this extent Williams seems to concede his case. The whole question is apparently dissipated in the victory celebrations, as the king fills Williams's glove with (ironically?) crowns (IV.vii.56). But it is not necessarily forgotten, and the audience is left to consider the problem implicitly raised in the debate. Has the sovereign the right to demand obedience to the point of death? What are the rights of the people? What are the limits of sovereignty? Who is entitled to define them, to impose them? *What is the meaning of the king's title?*

The encounter with Williams prompts Henry himself to ponder the last of these questions. What differentiates the king who is a man of the people from the people themselves? The answer he gives is no more than idle/idol signifying 'ceremony', but this only prompts further questions. Is ceremony material, substantial: 'What are thy rents? What are they comings-in?' (IV.i.239). Does ceremony entail power, or is it no more than an empty signifier, a form, an illusion:

> O, be sick, great greatness,
> And bid thy ceremony give thee cure!
> Thinks thou the fiery fever will go out
> With titles blown from adulation?
> Will it give place to flexure and low bending?
> Canst thou, when thou command'st the beggar's knee,
> Command the health of it? No, thou proud dream.
>
> (IV.i.247–

What, then, does it mean to say, as Henry does, 'I am a king . . .' (IV.i.255)?

This question runs all the way through the presentation of Henry V and his prodigal antecedent, Prince Hal, in the curious displacement and differentiation of his identity which recurs in all three plays. It is not duplicity of character which is in question: the plain style of his rhetoric marks Hal–Henry as precisely authoritative to the degree that he is seen to be straightforward. It is rather that the text consistently affirms what he is not: not a party to the crime of Gadshill, not governed by Falstaff, not given to displays of hysterical heroics like Hotspur. He is not a lover (*King Henry V*, V.ii.120ff.), not a private man (IV.i.233). And when he takes the audience into his confidence, it is to tell them that he is not what he seems, as he promises to 'falsify men's hopes' (*1 King Henry IV*, I.ii.204). Even his eloquence itself has the effect of dispersing his identity. In the Archbishop's account,

> Hear him but reason in divinity . . .
> You would desire the King were made a prelate;
> Hear him debate of commonwealth affairs,
> You would say it hath been all in all his study.
>
> (*King Henry V*, I.i.38–42)

As Jonathan Goldberg puts it, 'the very mastery of discourse that he displays leaves obscure who he is, where he is in his discourse' (Goldberg 1985, p. 132). In the critical encounter with Williams Henry's equivocation simultaneously conceals and seeks a truth: 'I think the King is but a man as I am'. Even the opening Chorus of *Henry V*, which has no motive for equivocation, cannot locate him: 'Then should the warlike Harry, like himself / Assume the port of Mars . . .' (5–6). Always defined by analogy, like war, like himself, able to be portrayed (re-presented) like Mars, he is, he tells the Princess Katherine, only a plain soldier. He is one who so much exceeds his own self-definition, however, that he is also in the same scene a plain king (*King Henry V*, V.ii.142, 124, 165). It is as if the text cannot find a way to specify the thing itself, to make present the character of kingship.[16]

Since the play cannot settle on an answer to the problem of what it means to be a king, it throws into question the nature of both sovereignty and meaning. In a world of differance presence is necessarily an illusion, to the extent that absolute meaning, whether as material substance or pure intelligibility, is always deferred, relegated, supplanted by the signifier itself. But if meaning is not fully present, it is not an absence either, not a space to be vacated at will. Henry V's 'ceremony' is not in that sense illusory: it is precisely an instance of the materiality of the signifier, 'place, degree, and form / Creating awe and fear in other men' (IV.i.242–3). It elicits obedience, though it cannot ensure it, and in that sense it represents power, but a power which, without metaphysical guarantees, is always unstable.

Ultimately, outside the fictional world of the history plays, the people were to repudiate, in the name of law, the law of succession, the power of ceremony, and the monarchy with them. In the 1590s the revolutionary struggle was half a century away. Are the questions posed by Shakespeare's history plays among the conditions, nevertheless, of the possibility of that struggle? If so, we are entitled to read the plays not only as interrogating the absolutist claims of the Tudor present, but as raising a broader issue for the immediate future. This is the question that Brecht was to reformulate in another political crisis: 'who does the world belong to?' Who is *entitled* to property and power?

Williams demonstrates that the royal meanings do not go uncontested. In the *Henry IV* plays it is Falstaff who consistently represents the refusal of monarchic order. His emblematic significance reaches its climax when he performs in play the role of king to Hal's prince – and recommends the company of Falstaff (*1 King Henry IV*, II.iv.408–16). But resistance is evident throughout in Falstaff's repudiation of all orthodox values: heroism, military discipline, law, truth, honour, and inevitably, authorised meaning:

> Marry, then, sweet wag, when thou art king, let not us that are squires of the night's body be called thieves of the day's beauty; let us be Diana's foresters, gentlemen of the shade, minions of the moon; and let men say we be men of good government, being governed, as the sea is, by our noble and chaste mistress the moon, under whose countenance we steal.
>
> (*1 King Henry IV*, I.ii.22–8)

These squires of the night's/knight's body/bawdy/booty are revellers, lechers and cutpurses, as both plays make clear; and the proposition that Hal as king should redefine them by royal fiat as 'men of good government' is comic partly to the extent that it parodies the early scenes of *Richard II*. Such, Falstaff absurdly implies, is the breath of kings: it has the power to invert the system of differences which allots meaning. The concluding pun ('steal') specifies the real nature of the anarchy Eastcheap represents: crime is a refusal of control, of legality, of the sovereign's authority, just as the pun itself, an instance of the dispersal of meaning, insists on the refusal of the signifier in its wayward plurality to be confined to any single, authorised signified.

Henry IV, we are invited to understand, deserves Falstaff. Eastcheap represents the inevitable return within his regime of the lawlessness by which he became king. Henry cannot exercise control – over the rebels or over Eastcheap – because he is not morally or legally entitled to the throne he holds. But Henry V changes all that. He does penance for his father's crime, rejects Falstaff, brings treason remorselessly to justice,

and displays at Agincourt that he has secured the popular obedience
that he thus so richly deserves. Act V of *Henry V* duly celebrates the
victory of the ideal Christian king.

But at the end of the play, in a speech possibly written for Falstaff to
perform, though attributed to Pistol in a version of the text from which
Falstaff has been excised, it appears that resistance to the monarchic
and symbolic order is about to begin all over again, and in exactly the
same punning terms as before:

> Old do I wax; and from my weary limbs
> Honour is cudgell'd. Well, bawd I'll turn,
> And something lean to cutpurse of quick hand.
> To England will I steal, and there I'll steal.
> (*King Henry V*, V.i.78–81)

VI

It is worth remembering, whatever Tillyard may have argued about the
unthinkable nature of rebellion in the sixteenth century, that it was the
anarchic Falstaff whose reappearance Elizabethan audiences clam-
oured for. And for this reason too, when Stephen Greenblatt assures us
that the audience of *2 Henry IV* does not leave the theatre in a rebellious
mood, or that the doubts raised about Henry V merely serve to heighten
his charisma, I am compelled to wonder what can be the *grounds* of
Greenblatt's certainty (Greenblatt 1985, pp. 41, 43). Not, I suspect, the
text.[17] And not what we know of Elizabethan history.[18] What then? A
politics which faces the present in the conviction that domination,
however regrettable, is inevitable, fact of life? I hope not.

Shakespeare's own practice of history-making is more complex and,
ironically, more contemporary. When Greenblatt urges in the same
essay that we need 'a poetics of Elizabethan power', and goes on to
argue that this 'will prove inseparable, in crucial respects, from a poetics
of the theatre', I find myself in wholehearted agreement with him
(Greenblatt 1985, p. 44). But a poetics of power would take account of
the possibility of resistance, not simply as power's legitimation, its
justification or glorification, as the New Historicists seem so often to
argue, but as its defining, differentiating other, the condition of its
existence precisely as power. And it would recognise the corresponding
possibility that resistance is not tamed in the end. Meanwhile, a poetics
of the theatre would take account of the ubiquity of resistance to power

as a requirement of plot, and of the corresponding possibility that resistance is not always 'contained' by the reaffirmation of power. And finally, to do justice to the complexity both of power and of Shakespeare's theatre, we need in addition a theory of textuality which understands meaning as differed and deferred, differentiated by and distanced from the signifier, so that it cannot be fixed by any reading, however supple, which treats texts as ultimately undifferentiated, homogeneous and univocal.

Nostalgia for lost plenitude, for the unity of words and things, is a longing for the imaginary, a desire for the simplicity and certainty of a world which precedes the symbolic difference. This is a world without visible power, since power is a relation of difference. But because certainty implies metaphysical guarantees of the singularity of meaning and the truth of things, it is also a world which is in practice deeply authoritarian. The condition of differance, meanwhile, ensures only that nothing is certain. Presence is deferred, meanings no more than differential. Differance precipitates doubt. The questions about power that differance prompts are not answered by reference to metaphysics. On the contrary, they concern a political relation, and one which, since it is an effect of difference, always inclines towards struggle.

Shakespeare's history plays know this. The world of plenitude was always already lost. It has no place outside the memory of an old man whose name is his condition and signifies an absence. Differance invades the opening scene of *Richard II*, and the plays go on to depict a succession of struggles which pose questions concerning the proper location of power in the present and in the future. The second tetralogy charts a descent from absolutism to the moment when the people confront the King, who cannot give them an adequate answer. It ends at this point. Unable to foresee the Revolution of the 1640s, the history plays leave kingship in question. But do they not also indicate in the process that the world belongs to those who are prepared to take it?

Shakespeare's histories refuse to constitute a grand narrative. They do not recount Tillyard's story of legitimate monarchy betrayed by monstrous rebellion, of hierarchy divinely endorsed. (But then in practice Tillyard was never sure they did.) Instead, these pre-Enlightenment texts propel their audience towards the as-yet unpresentable, the possibility of histories made by the people. Rejecting the transparency of names, they tell of political struggle and of the difference within the signifier. Of course, Shakespeare made free with his sources in a way that no serious historian could now countenance. But ironically, does he not in other ways, in spite of the historical difference, display some of the concerns which impel our own postmodern and radical *petits récits*?

Extraordinarily enough, the second tetralogy, read from the present, might perfectly well adopt as an epigraph Lyotard's call to arms at the end of his essay, 'What is Postmodernism?':

> Let us wage a war on totality; let us be witnesses to the unpresentable; let us activate the differences and save the honor of the name. (Lyotard 1984, p. 82)

The difference between our histories and Shakespeare's is decisive, an effect in part of the intervening Enlightenment. At the same time, however, the Enlightenment is no longer the condition that our postmodern culture aspires to. And to that extent it constitutes a space across which we are able to perceive Shakespeare's questing, questioning stories otherwise, and perhaps also to accord them a new kind of recognition.

Notes

All Shakespeare quotations are from *The Complete Works*, ed. Peter Alexander (Shakespeare 1951).

1 One possible exception is Tillyard's glowing account of the depiction of the middle ages in *Richard II* (Tillyard 1969, pp. 258–65).

2 The situation must have been rather different in the United States. Jean Howard claims that what New Historicism supplanted was formalism, not old historicism (Howard 1986, pp. 14–15), and David Simpson contrasts the 'return to history' and 'deconstruction' (Simpson 1987–8). Paul de Man, whose scepticism about history features prominently in Simpson's analysis, had relatively little influence in Britain in the 1970s, whereas Althusser, Macherey and Foucault were probably more influential in Britain at that time than they were in America. See also Wayne 1987, pp. 53–4.

3 Eagleton, who seems to miss the venom in this French irony at the expense of American culture, solemnly reminds us that there are millions of people who never jet-set at all, but go to work every day and educate their children (Eagleton 1985, p. 72).

4 'Nietzsche, genealogy, history' was first published in 1971.

5 Derrida finds an analogy – but only an analogy, he insists – between Descartes and St Anselm; and the Cartesian Cogito is repeated – but only 'up to a certain point' – by the Husserlian Cogito.

6 For a detailed and sophisticated discussion of this essay see Wordsworth 1987.

7 For an account of differance see Derrida 1987, pp. 8–9 and 1982.

8 Stephen Greenblatt points out that this reading of the New Historicist account of resistance is based only on his essay 'Invisible bullets', but he cites no counter-

examples (Greenslatt 1990, p. 75).

9 See Lyotard 1984, p. 61; Derrida 1978, p. 39.

10 I refer here to the story of successive modes of production. Specific analyses, like *The Eighteenth Brumaire*, for example, are in quite a different category, and in many ways a model for us now.

11 Ironically it is the non-Marxist Lyotard who draws attention to Marx's insistence on the spuriousness of the unity of capital. Writing of the postmodern fission of the pretension to a single purpose, he adds, 'since Marx, we have learned that what presents itself as unity . . . is the imposter-subject and blindly calculating rationality called Capital' (Lyotard 1987, p. 180). Compare the Marxist Jameson: 'anyone who believes that the profit motive and the logic of capital accumulation are not the fundamental laws of this world . . . is living in an alternative universe' (Jameson 1988, p. 354). Like Jameson's explicitly utopian Marxism itself, the reductiveness of this totalising proposition calls into question the value of his plea for totalisation.

12 For a feminist instance see Jardine 1985. The plea here is that we should take the opportunity to write woman differently.

13 Cf. Mowbray who, because he is accused of treason, stands to lose his name to Richard (I.i.167–9), and is therefore defending the rights of his 'succeeding issue' (I.iii.20). The titles and thus the estates of traitors were forfeit to the Crown.

14 This was pointed out to me by Gareth Edwards.

15 And, of course, of the Wars of the Roses in *Henry VI*.

16 I owe this point, or something like it, to Richard Burt.

17 For a discussion of the ambiguity of the play see Rabkin 1981, pp. 33–62.

18 Several of the speeches which, as Greenblatt acknowledges, generate the greatest scepticism concerning the legitimacy of the King's authority, did not appear in the quartos of 1600 and 1602. These include the Archbishop's dubious motives for justifying the war (I.i), most of the speech before Harfleur (III.iii. 11–41) and the whole of Henry's meditation on kingship (IV.i.226–84). (See Greenblatt 1985, pp. 42–3.) Annabel Patterson argues persuasively that the reason for the exclusions from the quartos was political: these speeches, like the epilogue, could be seen at the time as undermining the authority of the Queen's magnificent predecessor and prototype. But there is no reason to suppose that they were not included in the performance (Patterson 1989).

Which dead?
Hamlet and the ends of history[1]

FRANCIS BARKER

I

Despite pretensions to contrariety, and for all its refusal of epistemology, the theory of postmodernism, especially when it treats knowledge, continues to tend itself to take either the rationalist form of a discourse of the knowing subject or the empiricist one of a discourse about the existing object. Failing thus to escape a founding Cartesianism, it is either 'theoretical' in the sense of being a more or less rigorous discourse about discourse; or it purports to describe – or even to participate in the existence of – a 'condition'.[2] It either proposes that because the erstwhile guarantees which it takes once to have secured knowledge are now without foundation we cannot know what we know (and never could) but only and merely 'know' it (in the sense that knowledges simply take their epistemologically indifferent places among all other, equally non-privileged discourses). Or on the other hand, the 'problem of knowledge' notwithstanding (and not, apparently, applying to the theory of postmodernism itself), it can confidently adduce not just the loss of the privilege of knowledge, but a whole new state of affairs (which includes, but is not exhausted by, new forms of non-guaranteed knowledge), a state of affairs which it purports to describe well, even truthfully, while other discourses rest on illusion because they have failed to notice the changes and have not understood that where once they were secure they cannot now, under a changed 'condition', remain so. But if, in each case, postmodernism involves 'incredulity towards metanarratives', all this begins to become serious when one of the simultaneous localisations and globalisations of its account of knowledge in particular, and of the present moment more generally, occurs when the post-industrial theme of the end of ideology has grown over into senses of the end of history.[3] And where again these two forms insist. Either, it has become near orthodox to hold, we must abandon, epistemo-theoretically, historical discourse as now understood to be overweeningly objectivist or, worse, totalising; or history in an objective sense has come to an end, supplanted by the famous new condition which is not, in its own self-estimation or in any received sense, historical.

In both cases surely, some grave problems would be entailed for those who study historical literature, let alone for those who still use historical discourse for the wider purposes of the explanation of the present and the formation of strategies for the future?

But if these 'ends' (and the word may disclose more than it knows) are radical, are they not also signs of crisis and able to be read as such? If they do indeed present *grave* problems – the death of history, the end of the possibility of the intelligibility of its writing – are they new problems? It seems unlikely when so many other contexts, and earlier conjunctures, with – by definition – less novelty, have also developed languages not just of the end of history but of incredulity and death.[4] Of tragedy and farce; of melancholy anti-historicism.

II

Ghost.   Adieu, adieu, adieu. Remember me.

(I.v.91)[5]

Shakespearean tragedy dramatises an end of history. This is inherent in its formation and explicitly figured. To say even that, however, will mean for a moment being incredulous about incredulity, and to begin by looking instead at something 'fundamental': memory.[6]

Signs of crisis are in any case very much to the fore. Indeed, near the beginning, the ghost of a father who was also a king says insistently 'remember me'. At the end the son, now also dying, begs his friend Horatio to survive in order to tell the story. It is the most important thing. A culture is losing its memory. And between this beginning in an injunction to remember and an ending in injunction to narrate, there is a persistent thematic strand of discussion – argument (in the classical dramatic sense as well as in the today more familiar conversational and indeed logical senses) – of memory, pre-eminently in the special forms of mourning and commemoration, as a cultural practice which is coded

– in somewhat abstract and ideal ways – as essential, but which in the event is either absent or crucially damaged. The crisis in memory and narration will turn out to be a crisis in the governing sovereignty of the play and its discursive regime, although possibly not a crisis disclosed 'as such', because as a text and a drama it will resort to displacement and compromise in order to live (or to die) with the radical historical difficulty of the present.[7]

Of the figures of lost plenitude which the tragedies characteristically engender as horizons from which the depiction of the actual deployments of their internal political history depart, the ghost of the elder Hamlet is even more weakly realised than usual.[8] On one hand the voice of the king is coded as the absolute medium of the master discourse of a sovereign power (and this is true even of Claudius despite the fact that that representation may be one of the specious factitiousness of the discourse of a usurper's self-legitimation). But on the other, it is the ghostly trace of a power that has already disappeared into the past. The voice that reminds speaks in pain from beyond the grave, it struggles to be heard across the line between life and death, and in that struggle it at once inaugurates a need and a difficulty which together afflict the play's representations throughout. The story of the killing of the indubitably legitimate king must be told, heard, remembered, and acted on. But in practice it can only be told in pain and only heard with an analogous difficulty; it is hard to remember, and near impossible to accept as the prompt of action.

This double of need and loss, always implicitly articulated against the background of an historicity which cannot in the event quite be present in the dramatisation, then works itself throughout the drama: in some important ways it is the drama. In a variety of figures and situations the need of memory and narration is signalled powerfully, but denied in, and as, practice.

Displacement is a major figure of this doubling. Elsewhere *Hamlet* has been read as incipiently modern.[9] If separations are opening up in the alleged, tendentiously represented, plenitude of the old sovereign order, and if that between the public and the private is a major dimension of them, so too here is the separation between historical and personal memory. Among the transactions of remembering, there is a critical disjunction between history and mourning in a play which, if it initiates a kind of modernity, also hesitates on that threshold. On one hand it is more than 'mere' death which is at stake in the play's task of memory: the king is not an individual, and memory is not personal grief but the record of historical sequence (or in this case, rather, a break in sequence, for arguably discontinuity is the more historical form).[10] But on the one hand Hamlet must remember his father: this is recognisable from within more or less modern liberal humanist perspectives where the emphasis on the authenticity of the personal and the familial both masks and counters the social. It may be the *project* of the text to remember the king, that major sign, still, in the play's world, of historical power. But the mourning of fathers – and the elder Hamlet is not the only one – becomes its dominant articulation.

But this is not simply an 'even' tension in the text between historical and personal memory, as if each were equally present to retrospective analysis of the play as figures of historically separable discursive and political regimes between which the drama is transitional, or as if these were, in a balanced way, present 'existentially' at every moment to the unfolding discourse of the drama as the ambivalence of options between which hesitation and delay is merely inevitable. There is something in each of these formulations, but the structure is not symmetrical. The task of memory (if the present is to be understood and changed) is figured as the memory of the dead, whether as a burden, a duty or a mark of an authentic humanity. But in the event, in the dramatic formation of the matter, rather than memory being understood historically (as the play defines history, of course), it is *displaced* on to mourning. Historical memory *becomes*, or becomes legible *as*, mourning for the 'individual' rather than for the horizon of the historicity previously established. These forms of memory, of the representation of memory – history and mourning – are engaged together in a pattern of displacement and substitution where historical memory is displaced on to and tendentially replaced by the personal version, and considerable analytic and dramatic effort is and would be then needed to unpick and demystify this dehistoricising substitution.[11]

The structure of this displacement is, however, still further complex. It doesn't simply substitute one form for another, but offers instead, at the level of the substitute, of that which is substituted, a dilemma. Mourning takes at least two forms. Within the displacement of history on to mourning, grief is the truly personal version, whereas commemoration is the 'public' form. Both become signs, within the displacement and substitution, of bad remembering; both tend to fail, although in different ways, as a mark of the cultural crisis, and an unwitting exposure of the limitations of the original displacement. If, centrally, and much remarked, Hamlet's grief cannot be the prompt of action, still less of what might be called 'historical action', commemorations – at least in the form of funerals – are also flawed and truncated as in the case of Ophelia's, or are otherwise perceived as inadequate, secret rather than public as is that of Polonius, and in any case quickly forgotten or 'superseded' as is that of Hamlet's father.[12] If the representation of individual death has obscured historical continuity – or discontinuity – in the discourse of the text, commemoration of the individual death then also breaks down as 'collective' acts of commemoration fail, and powerless personal grief alone remains, already hard to narrate, and now redoubled in both its poignancy and its impotence.[13]

The displacement in this way covers its own traces by trailing a false option between grief and commemoration. It offers (this is how the displacement works), a faulty solution to the problem, tempting – even a radical – critique through the necessary criticism of desocialised 'private' grief on to the lure of collective memorialisation as the answer to the problem of the access to, and practice of, history. But if grief is remembering *by* the individual, 'collective' memory, as it is represented here – commemorations as remembering together – are still the remembering *of* the individual: individualism usually trails a lure of the spuriously 'collective'. But that 'solution', the choice of commemoration over grief, without here a closer definition of memory, leaves intact the 'original substitution' which effaced the historical in the first place.

But even so, the very displacement is a mark that the text cannot forget memory.

> *Fort.* I have some rights of memory in this kingdom,
> Which now to claim my vantage doth invite me.
> *Hor.* Of that I shall have also cause to speak,
> And from his mouth whose voice will draw no more.
>
> (V.ii.394-7)

Displacement is here a symptomisation of the crisis of memory; compromise, however, is a *symptom* of the same crisis. The distinction needs to be clarified. It is a cumbersome word, but 'symptomisation' is the right one because it signals more than an 'innocent' symptom. It is a 'second order' symptom, the production of a false sign of the false signs of the sickness of the State, inviting itself to be read as a simple symptom but if decoded as such producing misinterpretation. Of course, in a sense symptomisation is itself symptomatic – for complex reasons, some symptoms 'innocently' take the form of misleadingly interpretable symptomisations (in the sense at work here) – but in any case, compromise, the other major figure of the Shakespearean end of history, is properly a symptom at the first, naive, level. It merely obscures (in the form, of course, of a transparency, a textually *produced* solution), rather than obscures obscurity.

To be more concrete. Fortinbras, himself a ghost of Hamlet,[14] functions to compromise the contradiction between the project and the deployment. A way of putting it would be to say that the play, given that it evidently – and always-already – cannot sustain the representation of what it takes to be sovereign, has, then, in-principle options, each of which is, however, from 'its' point of view, ideologically and culturally impossible, or worse; and that the result of the unacceptability of each is the compromise of and between both. Another way of putting it is to say that in order to solve – or rather, resolve – its ideological-aesthetic problems, the play imposes military rule on itself.[15] Fortinbras is the name of a middle way (a deracination of both options of course) between reinvestment of the centre in presence – the sovereign – and the dramatisation of the transformative destruction of the extant, if residual, discourse of sovereignty (with all of *its* investment not just in the central, legitimate amd legitimated, rule of one, but in the symbology which secures not just a form of government in the narrow sense but the entire practice and imagination of the social hierarchy over which it supervenes and whose economic, social, sexual and authority relations – all complexly but not indifferently interarticulated – it seeks culturally to guarantee as unalterable).[16] If the text can neither reinstate – re-member, in practice – the master-signifiers of the discourse it accepts as sovereign, nor opt for their revolutionary transformation, then Fortinbras is the result: a refiguration of central rule which in narrative terms is more or less arbitrarily produced, even if the play may have made some preparations for his assumption – for compromise isn't merely weak ending from the point of view of aesthetic judgement or judgementalism, but is, rather than anecdotal to its conclusion, structural to the *combinatoire* of the discourses which constitute, which – in the literary sense – *are*, the text. It is a degradation of the symbolic-ideological efficacy of the representation of sovereign rule from which the play both sets out and departs. And it gives the game away. The diminution in affect and charge, as the place of the sovereign gives way to the rule of the military, wins the battle for monarchical nostalgia, for defining history as the question of the lost body of the king or the heir, but loses the war for the continuity of that discourse and that power. If it gets its continuity by force in arms, it has signalled a greater – or rather a bathetically lesser – discontinuity than the one originally protested against.[17] Because the answer is smaller than the question, the reply of the end to the beginning might *almost* be understood as critique.

Like everything else, Fortinbras needs to be read at least twice. From one point of view he, if not Horatio, is Hamlet's son, if we can imagine, in the same historical-critical circumstances and on the precedent of at least one dimension of the play we have, a sequel text which would have to begin, as in a sense the actual play ends, with the ghost of the younger Hamlet enjoining the task of memory and narration and seeking *his* lineal successor. The repetition scarcely even extends imaginatively the text's own strategies in this respect. But Hamlet has no son. If generation is a characteristic but mystified Shakespearean metaphor for historical sequence, here it is unavailable, and an 'end' of history is figured (although even if it is most clearly figured here at the end, this isn't just a closing 'event': 'end of history' is again structural to the discourse of the play, not episodic to its conclusion). But history cannot be allowed to end, and so, from another point of view, Fortinbras must be read again as the figure through which memory gets back on to the tragic scene of the state and even re-establishes something of what was erased in the displacement of history on to grief. The sign of memory Fortinbras invokes as he assumes power, and perhaps even more importantly the injunction to narrative which contains within it the 'legitimating' insistence of Hamlet's dying voice going to Fortinbras – an insistence compared with the urgency of the expression of which the rest is silence – is here re-articulated with something like historicity. The doubling here is that of the need of memory as history, rather than that of history as memory. Mourning and commemoration, among the text's multiple representations of memory and amnesia (in, in each case, both sovereign and critical versions), organising decisive structural and thematic dimensions of the play, have carried, displaced, the historicity without which the crisis of history is, always, unthinkable. The displaced forms survive in one sense (the play ends with a kind of

funeral procession now for Hamlet himself), but are themselves ultimately displaced in another. In as much as the compromise is between
the impossibility of monarchical rule and its continuity, so is it one
between the displacement of memory on to the 'personal' and the claim
of memory – underpinned, to be sure, in this representation of history,
by armed force – as the metaphysical ground of rule. Turning the
question in this way foregrounds the 'real' content of the silence which
succession in this – historical – register must supplant. It is not simply
'individual', existential silence, nor even a generational punctuation,
but rather untelling, unnarration, forgetting, understood as the void
figured by the prospective fear (the futuring equivalent of nostalgia) of a
vacuum in political power and historical meaning.

But indeed it is subject, none the less, to the downbeat – secular and
demystified – which can only assert the continuity of the historical by
displacement, substitution and compromise.[18] While inevitably
engaging, in the only way it can, the dimension of historicity, the
master-discourse, the project, must of course define the historical,
equally inevitably, in terms of the discourse of sovereignty which it
takes to be dominant even although it is residual in terms of dramatic
deployment. The compromise inheres as the very result of this double
coding of that sovereignty as *both* absolute *and* residual, rehearsing at
the end the 'original' ghostly 'presence' of the beginning. That the play
can only code *historicity* as royal *history* (and is therefore historicist),
but that it cannot sustain that code, we might read as – again – critique.
Or at least the bringing to history of the limits of its own formation. And
that reading can be entertained without even having to resort to other
(as it were, extraneous) preferences of our own among the variety of
critical historiographical discourses – or political practices – retro-
spectively thinkable as having been available at the time.

In brief, nothing should prevent *a priori* the thinking of 'ends of history'
as being fully historical. In the very effort, under the form and pressure
of its crisis, to displace, substitute and compromise, *Hamlet* signals the
historicity it both is and at the same time structurally and thematically
denies. And which informs and determines both the impossibility and
insistent return of what it counts as history. In fact, for all its
manoeuvres, and failed symbologies, the only thing it doesn't escape is
historicity. The more it seeks to evade *that*, the more it signals the need
against the grain of which it is formed.

III

Hegel remarks somewhere that all facts and personages of great importance in world history occur, as it were, twice. He forgot to add: the first time as tragedy, the second as farce.[19]

Remembering and forgetting. Unsurprisingly really, Shakespearean tragedy, and postmodern ends of history, are not the only contexts for imbrications of the representation of history and the figure of death. Other texts, other historical conjunctures, have figured the past as 'the dead'.

The burden of the dead is there, certainly, but it is not easy to make precise – and certainly not precisely historicist – interpretations of the first few pages of Marx's text. In the famous invocation and supplementation of Hegel, *The Eighteenth Brumaire of Louis Bonaparte*, it commits itself to figures of repetition, and the repetition of – theatrical – representation. But the metaphors then slide over each other in ways which ask to be interpreted according to received senses of the historical but then resist any clear account of quite which phases or modes of the French revolutionary process are to be thought of as tragedy and which as farce, or exactly how to locate the representational, structural and analytic relations among the repetitions of past models and present guises, either within the decades of the process or between that historical process, or particular phases of it, and earlier historical conjunctures and previous revolutions.

But one thing does seem to be 'clear'. The demystified, proletarian revolution, 'like the revolution of the nineteenth century', abandons the play of disguise. It is defined in opposition to either the tragedy or the farce of the bourgeois revolution; it does without the costumes of previous epochs, and leaves the dead behind. Its slogan, it could be said, is 'forget'.[20]

Walter Benjamin struggled with the memory of Marx's text, and on the face of it there is a contradiction or even a constructable antagonism between them.[21] Marx will consign – with a certain decisiveness – the dead to the grave. If the bourgeois revolution dresses itself in the costume of previous epochs, and if – it isn't clear – the tradition of the dead generations weighs in that sense like a nightmare on the brains of the living, the new revolutionary task will have to figure itself as radically distinct from that figuration of the past. And leave the dead to bury the dead. But Benjamin will say the opposite. His slogan might be said to be 'remember'. Rather than leaving the dead to their burying, he will say that if the enemy wins not even the dead will be safe. Even if the dead merely (and it is more than this) figure a point of – *unnegotiable* – value in the form of providing a measure of how great the threat of the enemy is, they are not, in Benjamin's theses, and must not be, so easily forgotten. He even ventures, against the progressivist logic of post-Enlightenment liberalism the valorisation of enslaved ancestors over liberated grandchildren.[22]

Political contextualisation might provide an explanation of the apparent antagonism between these positions and their oppositions. Marx, it could be argued, writes in a heroically futuristic moment, prospective of the proletarian revolution (not unaffected by the heroic progressivism of his own characterisations of the bourgeoisie) while Benjamin writes in the dark night of Nazism.[23] For Marx, in this reading, the dead can be safely dead (even if they mock – or make a mock of – the present, by providing the guises and the disguises of the past in which the revolutionaries costume themselves). For Benjamin the dead are the only ones who are *not* 'safely' dead, both in the sense that they are not beyond the reach of the enemy, but also, more importantly in the sense that they do continue to haunt the present (although not in Marx's kind of way). But a conceptual rather than a chronological, or even, here, historical, account of the proximity and divergence of the Marxist and Benjaminian vocabularies might prompt rather an interrogation of Marx's sense of 'tradition' (or rather realise that his use of the word is already critical and interrogative) and ask whether that interrogation isn't further conducted – and 'completed' – by Benjamin's even more explicitly diacritical sense of history. Marx urges the revolution of the nineteenth century to abandon the dead in favour of the poetry of the future. For Benjamin the angel of history has its back to the future even as the wind from Paradise compels it forward. If the present generation is endowed with a weak messianic power – whatever that is – it is also the power of the present as a radical discontinuity and not a traditional succession. 'History is the subject of a structure whose site is not homogenous, empty time' and the *jetztzeit* is 'time charged with the presence of the now'. But it is also shot through with the 'past blasted out of the continuum of history', that 'memory ' which 'flashes up at the moment of danger'. If abandoning tradition is what Marx is arguing for, then Benjamin agreed. Tradition, when not articulated historically, is the time of historicism, and continually threatens to become the tool of the ruling classes unless wrested away from conformism by historians – or, presumably, revolutionaries – who have 'the gift of fanning the spark of hope in the past'.

The essential questions are, which dead; which forgetting and which remembering; what relation of the past to the present and the future? There is no contradiction between 'forgetting' the costumes of previous epochs and 'remembering' the tradition of the oppressed.

None of this is designed to serve merely as the citation of the inviolable texts of either a modern or a modernist Marxism, but rather to ask the diacritical question of the postmodern end of history which, in knowing more than it knows, knows thus a lot less. Its erasure of the history of its own vocabulary of forgetting, or ends of history, has, in turn, a history. The end of history is historical, whether we are discussing postmodernism as theory or condition (and its own theoretical bad faith needs to be put to it in this way). *That* end of history is not a new thing but a farcical rediscovery of (an) 'earlier' tragedy. Farcical in its breathless novelty because it doesn't remember – or systematically forgets – that the end of history has always been the theme and condition of any radical, historical (and radically historical), practical, thought. The radical break with the past, in these other contexts which postmodernism knowingly (unknowingly) elides, is not the end of history, but history. Marx again: If the slogan of the revolution of the nineteenth century and, or it may be or, the proletarian revolution, is 'forget the dead', then elsewhere Marx will figure the break with the past as the *beginning* of history; if 'we communists are dead men on leave', no less is the proletarian revolution thought, as the end of pre-history, and communism as the start of human history. History is the move into the radically unknowable future (although not in indeterminate circumstances).[24] For Marx history and tradition are not the same thing. And again, Benjamin agreed. One makes possible the future; it remembers. The other weighs like a nightmare; it forgets.[25]

IV

Human anatomy contains a key to the anatomy of the ape. The intimations of higher development ... however, can be understood only after the higher development is already known.[26]

A *history* of 'postmodernism' (rather than the description of a *condition*) would be hard to write. It would have to be done in at least one of at least two ways: as the recurrence of certain themes, or as the articulation of a dimension of successive, essentially identical, historical conjunctures, successive presents. In the first sense it would stretch, paradoxically, not from about 1960 but from, say, Shakespeare, or – especially if the model of the subject and the object persists in it – from Descartes.[27] It would extend from the Descartes who, at the beginnings of capitalism as a potential world system, left the West the, in one sense, radically demystified, artificial man which amounts of liberal humanism have subsequently strained to animate and recuperate, to, say, *Blade runner*, where the artificial men and women (figured by the film as intimately and intrinsically products of corporation capitalism) search, in a postmodern Los Angeles, for an identity and a past.[28] And there would be at least a certain symmetry (although this is hardly a postmodern form) in a history that would have (the theme of) time, if not 'History', begin in the 'Renaissance' (it would cite Cartesianism or even *Hamlet* as the evidence); and have it end 'now' in the postmodern moment itself. Or in the second sense, it would have to be argued that since it has been possible to think a notion of the present as 'modern' at all (i.e. since the Renaissance), successive conjunctures have had their modern, if not modernist, and postmodern, if not postmodernist, moments.[29] This would come a little closer, in my view, to a more acceptable history of several 'crises of representation', exemplified for present purposes by these brief readings of *Hamlet*, Marx, Benjamin, and by the famous simulacra of postmodernism 'itself'.[30]

But not just crises of *representation*. If the moments of the early modern, of full blown modernity, and of postmodernity, are thought as crises historically, and structurally *as crisis*, then we come to the present not as condition but as crisis, to history as crisis, the crisis of the present, and to the present as history. And if that seems itself like a perpetual 'condition', it is rather more like Benjamin's sense in which the 'tradition of the oppressed teaches us that the "state of emergency" in which we live is not the exception but the rule'.[31]

And that is very far from a 'merely' aesthetic, or representational sense of crisis, especially if we remember the revolutionary character of the conjunctures in question.

But of course there cannot be a history of postmodernism, at least not from within the terms of its own characteristic discourse, whether we think of its high theory or the enigmatic minimalism of its fiction. Despite its avowal of change, if not unknowability, postmodernism in practice figures the stasis of change. The present is figured not as crisis but as, indeed, condition. And if we think of the celebratory dimensions of – cultural – 'postmodernism' in particular, even 'condition' becomes too 'situated' a word for its taste. Easy to recognise, but hard to define, postmodernism is the gloss of consumerism relativised, hardened, and turned into something like a rootless aesthetic of the momentary (*that* then claiming the pseudo-historical authority of the description of a condition). Descriptively, phenomenally, this catches something, to be sure. But postmodernism purchases its own theoretical indeterminacy, or rather imprecision, by the evocation of an ethos, an atmosphere, a style, while abandoning as meta-discursive any account of the determinate production of this condition or aesthetic, or of its historical situation or situatedness.[32]

So, if the capitalism of this postmodernity is a condition instead of a history, postmodernism cannot but be certain figurations of the aesthetic. At least, although not exhaustively these four: (*a*) non-representational representation of representations, and often connected with, in particular, *b*) 'representation' of 'the' 'other'; *c*) representational technology and the representation of technology; and *d*) the space rather than the time of technology in particular and of the condition and the aesthetic in general:

——— Postmodernism has its capital cities. New York, or 'New York', is often cited. Or the Los Angeles of *Blade runner*. Simulacral cities, of course, where the signs are on the streets, and where substance generally has been replaced by sign, in a double sense: it's not just that, in the case of a film, we are looking at a representation of a real city, but that the 'reality' represented is itself representational in its fabric. And not just because *Blade runner* is a film, representational in the ordinary sense, and its Los Angeles a fiction: the 'real' experience of being in New York is often read in this way.

——— And, when not Disneyland, 'pure' simulacra, the *topoi* of postmodernism are, in geopolitical representational terms, hybrid. The postmodern is produced out of the mixing of the metropolitan modern with what has been called 'the modernism of under-development'.[33] The 'charm' of this insists in the glossing of signs of immiseration, usually in significantly 'Third World' forms. If New York can be credibly spoken of as a Third World city (it has been), equally the Los Angeles of *Blade runner* gets its quasi-exotic postmodernity from signs of the 'other' among the ruins of the ideal modern city. The other is not 'there' but 'here'; modernity is and has been now everywhere; the postmodern is the synthetic-aesthetic overdetermination of the numinous presence of the absence of both, or the presence in one of the absence of the other and vice versa. The aesthetic of the postmodern is thus produced as a representational complex of 'over-development' and 'underdevelopment'. At an academic meeting recently, only too aware that it was taking place in a British colony, I asked the speaker about the political geography of postmodernism: I was invited to walk out of the conference building into the streets of Hong Kong if I wanted to 'see' the 'postmodern' ...[34] Multinational capital, presumably, and the signs of 'China'. Banks and ghosts.[35]

It would be tempting to dialecticise, recuperate, and detect in this geopolitically narcissistic complex a progressive moment in its apparent undermining of the substance of the metropolitan. But it would be an uneven dialectic, dominated by the reactionary moment of the complacence of the erasure of the relations which secure this aesthetic by abstraction from, and immunise it against political analysis of, the processes of its production as simulacrum and style.

—— Because it *is* an aesthetic, and the aestheticisation of politics, as Benjamin remembered, has its vicissitudes.[36] In, for example, the consumerisation of a certain politically depoliticised representation, of, say, the 'Sudan' or 'Ethiopia', where in part the 'reality' of the aesthetic of the postmodern is constructed. Those finally comforting television images of 'the starving' – representationally fetishised, however compassionately – wearing wrist watches and trainers. 'The other' as the end of history before it has begun: the double bind of history as Western history, in form *and* substance. There are glosses and glosses. Relatively painless forms of the 'condition'. The complex re-exported, videoed, beamed back again.

—— But if 'we' do indeed live in a world of 'staccato signals of constant information', is it not also one of 'lasers in the jungle somewhere'?[37] If the 'magical is optical' then isn't it so also on a seemingly 'automatic earth' in which military technology – ranged against a mass democratic movement – is the cutting edge of the postmodern: although *that* doesn't figure so prominently in the celebrations of the joyful challenges of post-historical indeterminacy? The celebration of machine intelligence and machine aesthetics might be subjected – at least momentarily – to the criticism of machine use. Even to that of the imagination of a world run, roughly, by 'a loose affiliation of millionaires and billionaires'? Why not? Why should such a 'total-isation' be *a priori* fantastic? After all, 'These are the days of miracle and wonder, this is the long distance call'.

—— Space rather than time. Why not the space of (military) 'tech-nology'? In the new cartographies of the 'postmodern' another *locus* is Michael Herr's *Dispatches*.[38] In his 'Vietnam' of high speed air mobility, Herr writes, attending the multiple ironies of his title, the postmodern war, interpretable, it is said, as space – 'as we moved about the war' – rather than time (or history). There is 'the war' and there is 'back in the world'. Spatialisation.[39] Beyond the modernist theme of the futility of war (not that distant in fact from wider cultural pessimisms of modernism), the postmodern form: the war is post-futile futility: the 'loss of affect'.[40] Not wholly innocent for that. Though Herr went to Vietnam for himself; listened to the language; stuck with the hermeneutic of rock and roll; and didn't presume to speak for anyone else, evading that other sense of representation as not an analytic problem but an imperial weapon.[41] The representa-tional discourses which produce the other as the dead, the ghosts.[42] In which not even the criticism of a technology of major applied death, 'forgetting' on a massive scale, licenses participation. Dis-patches . . .

> Under the general demand for slackening and for appeasement, we can hear the mutterings of the desire for a return of terror, for the realization of the fantasy to seize reality. The answer is: Let us wage a war on totality; let us be witnesses to the unpresentable; let us activate the differences and save the honor of the name.[43]

The difference, or differance, assiduously promoted by some forms of theory today, is pallid when compared either descriptively or agonistically with the difference that a Marx, or a Benjamin – or a Gramsci – were trying to make.[44] It pales into distracting insignificance when taken as an historical diagnosis rather than a critical tool, and when it is brought thereby into what amounts to a symbiotic contact with these relentless, postmodernist, underwritings of the aestheticisation of the current effects of multinational capitalism which it is so frequently used, wittingly or not, to celebrate. It seems to me a shame; because something fundamental *is* disclosed in this elaboration of the way in which we have to think today the continual departure of meaning from itself. Shameful, and sad, that it could have been lent to a relentless sameness in the aestheticised celebrations of an increasing, and increasingly global (and thus undifferentiated), violence. As 'insubstantial' as, but less efficacious than, the staccato bursts of constant information and the lasers in the jungle somewhere which otherwise define the frontline 'experience' of today. When 'poverty' becomes televisual, and otherness provides the style of the lure of consumption, difference – or differance – ought, surely, to have come up against the test of the nightmare of its own neo-liberalism, or worse. Difference, and conceptual undermining, are not, of course, the same as radical political initiatives, and even where there is contiguity or even mutual strategy, not always identical with a radical politics of the left. In the hectic *fashion* for intellectual and cultural postmodernism, far too little thought has been given to ascertaining these distinctions and thinking through their strategic implications. Or rather, it is not so much a matter of deficient or insufficient thought, but of the determined, even intended, politics of these positions and representations. And after all, only the crassest – and today, perhaps, few and decreasingly viable – tyrannies prevent differance. Oppressive societies thrive on difference, even when they are officially democratic, even radically so: unacceptable regimes of left and right actually secure entrenched if dynamic difference(s) – between, for example, the rich and the poor, the fed and the hungry, between those who have power of various kinds and those who have none – and these 'differences' are real and social as well as formal and aesthetic. Whatever their official ideology, most such political formations rather 'prefer', in this practical sense, a certain legitimating 'play'. And are at least untouched by the intellectuals, of the otherwise apparently ubiquitous West, granting themselves that coy privilege.[45]

It is clear that difference in and of itself will not do. Which differences, which criteria of evaluation of differences, which projects for the construction of difference in the future? The questions have to be asked. And answered. If there is a 'postmodern *condition*', for whom it is a condition? Who is conditioned by it, whose existence and practice – if 'humans' are still in the information stream – is conditional upon it, whose existence and practice is *it* conditional upon? *These* questions are no doubt cast in a mode which would appear to postmodernists as all too philosophically realist, and, prefaced as they are by a personal pronoun (albeit relative and interrogative) decidedly humanist in derivation. That will be, or at least appear, as it may.[46] But the line of questioning remains: isn't there too easily available in such discussion a willingness to '*merely*' abandon the 'nineteenth-century' questions of history and totality in favour of the fragmentary, delirious or even ecstatic *jouissance* of the postmodern conceived as an emblem of what is culturally avant-garde without paying any attention to the real power of the political manipulation (and the politics of the means of the manipulation) of representation? The risk in that perspective is that the move beyond authority will be fine with multinational late-capital provided that that rejection is of this metaphysics alone.

But nor should to oppose undifferentiated difference be to allow the accusation of having accepted a position of support for sameness, for totalisation read quickly as totalitarianism. Nothing in the cultural diagnosis at work here hinges on the alleged failure, or consignment to the nineteenth century, or impossibility amid the operations of power today, of the project of social transformation. There *are*, naturally, implications for the forms and methods of political struggle, and in particular for the critique of various kinds of totalisation, whether the perennial debility of a social democracy that still seeks for electoral respectability a metaphysic of 'consensus' or common sense and hands over the radical project of changing 'sense' to the political right, or the 'revolutionary' centralisations of the Leninism which will encode authoritarian teleology in the very organisational forms of the struggle or the revolution. It is, of course, hard to think rationally the dispersal of struggle and, at the the same time, the notion of generalised transformation. But only so *of course* because of the legacy of thinking revolution from within a totalistic conceptual framework which always was idealist and hubristic in respect of the complexity of social reality (which includes, naturally, that metaphysic itself). But another practice altogether is offered in the historical relinquishment of historicism in the name of the new. In postmodernism the proper abandoning of historicism usually masks, as has been argued, the jettisoning of historicity or history as such. But any such neglect of historicism will be futile as long as it is conceived of as merely intellectual and merely negative. The negative project of the lifting of repression or the removal of constraint remains trapped within the problematic of the modern: what has to be thought through is the positive and productive task of constructing strategies of freedom.

Postmodern cancellations of the historical frequently take the form of reinstating the subject – in the substitution of ethics for politics.[47] The *Hamlet* syndrome. I have some sympathy with the idea of a renewed ethical discourse, especially if more epistemology is the alternative. But it might be worth offsetting against that substitution a *political* ethics. The 'sense', like Benjamin's and Gramsci's, that the forces of the enemy are currently formidable and strong should be read as current, historical – and by no means minor, it should not be underestimated – difficulty. But this melancholy historicisation is decisively not an historicism. Instead it recognises the struggle for what it is, a struggle not a teleology, a destiny or a mission (each currently buzz-words in various contexts). There is no God-given or 'natural', or even historical, right to win. Neither history nor historicity can be appealed to in this way. But because of this, that stance is optimistic. And in many respects. But one sense of this is particularly relevant: it entails the refusal, in the face of apparent defeat, to comply with the enemy by giving up the 'original project' (conceived under that historicity which is marked by the diacritic of struggle) and accepting historicism.[48]

Gramsci's 'pessimism of the intellect, optimism of the will' is sometimes invoked. There are of course difficulties with the concept of 'the will', a term which may belong more to the political vocabulary of what Gramsci opposed than what he sought to see overcome: perhaps Gramsci's acute sense of the problematic, historically embedded quality, and the political centrality of the question of language would put the silent inverted commas of irony around the word? Certainly, if the dark night of difficult language is there for Benjamin, no less was it so for Gramsci: localised only too palpably in his case by Fascism's prisons. However, the real 'pessimism', it seems to me, is not the metaphysical reflex of looking into the face of defeat, which each resisted, but that of theorising the post-historical, or even (as fashionable postmodern 'theoretical' formulations have it), the post-political.[49]

Fashionable surrender.

V

It would be strange of me to produce, in writing, a celebration of the Shakespearean text. But I can't stop myself from thinking that if the end of history is to be figured, I prefer the complex transactions of *Hamlet* to the knowing velleities of postmodern ends of history. At least a richer symptomatology. It is a text that signals continuity – the tradition of the memory of the past; the dead as the King – and practises its impossibility. It displaces that conservative historical substance into different forms of mourning, and they then fail as signs of the absence of the historical for which they were substituted. Not content with that negativity the displaced signs of memory are shifted back on to the promise of historical succession (rather than either personal memory or collective memorialisation), but in a form whose secular declination – caught in a network of failing voices, useless audiences, impossible hearing and necessary but inefficient narration – undercuts both the form and the substance of the nostalgic continuity it cannot either dramatise or be. History is at once signalled and 'ends'. But it is a peculiar 'end', of course, which takes the form of the impossibility of history. Because the end in question is not that of history as such but of a certain sovereign discourse still powerful enough dominantly to code what might count as the historical, but already residual enough to need to offer to drag into its end the end of everything, or dominant *and* residual enough to figure 'survival' only in the diminished compromise. But it persists hardly content with that. Isn't the announcement of the end of history intrinsically bound up with the question of history?

In other words, then, it's the sign, despite itself, at a moment of crisis, of – indeed – historicity.

I am certain that the same hermeneutic can be applied to more recent and more contemporary – that is, to other contemporary – 'ends of history'.[50] In the Shakespearean tragic text, and in this 'postmodern condition' there are analogous systems of denial. Summarily, the erasure may be described thus: the denial of historicity is the effacing of domination. They are the same. For me at least, history, in the critical sense, is *difference from domination* – at the descriptive level, the underside of what we have been told, whether the official lies or the naturalised facticity of 'things as they are'; and at the political level the possibility of the practice of the overcoming of these. In this sense even the Nietzschean 'forget' is a call for historicity in that it rejects the way in which the burden of the past is made to substitute for history, and thus encodes the latter not as the sign of change but one, as I have argued, of stasis.

A fundamental critical question always to be asked of the emergence of new discourses is, of course, what and whom does the emergence, and emergency, serve? *Hamlet* signals history when it dramatises the breakdown of the controllingly historicist discourses of its epoch; postmodernism signals historicity not by 'innocent' failure but knowing rejection. Both offer ultimately an impossible and coercive 'choice' between tragedy figured merely as nostalgia and a historicity so flattened figurally, epistemologically and politically as to cancel the question of tragedy, and much besides. But I no more read *Hamlet* and mourn the passing of either feudal or absolutist forms of presence and domination, than I read Lyotard – or Fukuyama – and lament the project of a full sociality and a full liberation, which the one resists weakly because decrepit and the other resists strongly because it fancies that the time of its own banal historicism has come.

To be sure, in one sense the end of history *is* a banally familiar theme. But it is important to risk the difference between an 'end of history' which produces the stasis of change, on the one hand, and on the other, those figured ends of history which have both past and future versions, turnings and orientations, imbricated in an historical diacritic of the historicity of the present. For in another sense end-of-history has still yet to be brought into historically actual contact with the ways in which a Marx or a Benjamin could think the end of a certain history as the beginning of another. Or perhaps, better, the ending of some history as the beginning of others.[51] The agonistic – in both available senses – of the hollowing of any present, may be hard to think, but perhaps not so difficult to feel. But in any case, against either *any* historicism, or confident announcements of the advent of the postmodern (they are often apocalyptic, but not in Benjamin's way that messianic, and in any case historicist), I would counterpose – as 'history', and, more importantly, historicity – the necessary inhabitation of more than one time, with complex memory, in as full as possible a *recognition* of the violence that is 'thus' entailed.

If we must, then, in a special sense, remember (and forget) history, the question of which – or even what – history, remains at this stage open. Simply that which makes a society a society and not merely a machine for domination? Or a life a life, and not just a subjection? Or perhaps the history promised in those whose lives have largely been written out? Rather than the fetishised memorialisation of a dead past, it will certainly have to be a history of the present, shot through with the knowledge and the poetry of that critical part of the present which is the dangerous past. In other words the memory of the future, the history which remains always to be made. And, notwithstanding the criticisms of those who, committed to the charm of the bad new days, confuse memory with nostalgia, a historical practice deploying – in practice – the sense, which is not anecdotal but 'structural' – to both history and the possibility of 'thought' – that things have not always been like this nor need remain so.[52] Where 'this' and 'so' are not so much particles of grammar as historical signs. The sense that if historicity is lost, so too is the capacity to formulate (not just to desire and embrace, but also to know and shape) change.

Notes

1 I would like to thank the other members of the Essex Early Modern Research Group, Maurizio Calbi, Al Constantine, Tracey Hill, Paula Hutchings, John Joughin, and Stephen Speed, for their help and support in the production of this essay. Comment on the paper itself was valuable, and Paula Hutchings in particular was kind enough to give me detailed written criticisms. But it grew out of a climate of discussion forged in a remarkable year of collaborative work.

I would also like to acknowledge my colleague and friend Herbie Butterfield for his assistance, both practical and moral, during the closing stages of the revision of this essay.

And above all Marijn and Alex.

2 I am taking Lyotard's work as the instance which is by now classical; partly because of its substance, and partly because of the widespread influence of the name of his text, not least in as much as it claims to name a 'condition'. See Lyotard 1984.

3 For Lyotard's famous 'definition' of the postmodern as 'incredulity towards metanarratives' – among which 'history' is prominent – see Lyotard 1984, p. xxiv. But the ground has been in preparation for some time: the cognate 'end of ideology' is properly associated with the name of Daniel Bell whose *The end of ideology* (1960) and more recent *The coming of post-industrial society* (1973) and *The cultural contradictions of capitalism* (1976) are notorious landmarks.

And the company kept . . . If Lyotard will have us be incredulous before certain kinds of discourse, others will more bluntly announce the ending of historical process itself, with the politics of this gesture very close to the surface. Published in the US conservative journal *The national interest* in the summer of 1989, Francis Fukuyama's essay 'The end of history' was first influential in Washington and then widely disseminated in many countries, even to the extent of being deemed sufficiently topical for the British newspapers to reprint it. The *best* that can be said for Fukuyama's celebration of the global triumph of capitalism, and the 'end' of any alternative to economic and political liberalism, is that it is tinged with regret: 'The end of history will be a sad time . . . In the post-historical period there will be neither art nor philosophy, just the perpetual caretaking of the museum of human history. I can feel in myself – and see in others around me – a powerful nostalgia for the time when history existed. Such nostalgia, in fact, will continue to fuel competition and conflict, even in the post-historical world, for some time to come' (Fukuyama, 1989). (The second part of the article appeared here clearly enough under the title 'Marxism's failure'.) The 'post-political' is part of this powerful fantasy; cf. note 49 below.

4 Some of what follows is *sotto voce* a critical engagement with the so-called New Historicism in Renaissance studies, and with its wider implications for the political analysis of culture. For the moment, in a preliminary way, however, it may suffice to evoke that by reference to the trajectory of Stephen Greenblatt's work from the now well-known incident on the plane between Baltimore and Boston (which is recounted in the Epilogue to what is in effect the founding text of the New Historicism) to the opening sentence of his most recent full length study: 'I began with the desire to speak with the dead'. This trip from death to death, this figuration of the past as the dead, death-history, requires at least some clarification. See Greenblatt 1980 and 1988. Cf. note 13 and note 42 below.

5 Quotations are from the Arden edition of *Hamlet* ed. Harold Jenkins (London and New York, 1982, rpt. 1986).

6 Fundamental? One of the characteristics of characteristically 'postmodernist' analysis is, of course, to deny, in its own theory and methodology, and in the objects of analysis, any hierarchisation of significance: this is paradoxical in discourses which claim to attend to representation. But even if we agreed to remain at the level of mere 'representation', surely the history of human societies is littered with – and even, arguably, constituted by – the claims of their discursive regimes to locate and to valorise in various patterns of dominance, subordination and dependency: value ranking, logical derivation, material or ideal causality, formations of phenomena and epi-phenomena, and so on? These structures cannot be wished out of existence by remarking that it's all representation; nor understood without seeing that it is power which assembles them, and that it's not merely a case of earlier forms of thought which can now be triumphantly pronounced as being, or having been, in error. Postmodernist theory (which I am taking to be different from postmodern theory) routinely makes these idealist assumptions, which are, in the circumstances, rather touchingly traditional.

7 By definition of the function of 'ruling class' or 'dominant culture' texts, crisis, then as now, will be 'managed' rather than disclosed or acknowledged as such (at least to extent that the ruling culture, in the circumstances of its historical crisis and in view of the current strength of the forces which dissent from or oppose it, is still capable of so doing). Or the pronunciation 'crisis' and its subsequent manipulation themselves form and legitimate strategies of 'management' or control. Elsewhere in this volume John Joughin asks a trenchant question in the very title of his 'Whose crisis?'

8 In *Macbeth* Duncan is short-lived, but a sovereign presence *is* dramatised, if only to maximise the violence of the 'absentiation' which ensues. In *Lear* the map of the realm, and the pastoral language in which the sovereign land is represented, form, *inter alia*, less palpably, this constructed – rather than given – horizon. But in each case the dramatic *and ideological* formation is one of departure from an imagined erstwhile fullness. The present reading of *Hamlet* is parallel to fuller readings of all three texts currently in preparation: see Francis Barker, *Signs of invasion* (forthcoming). Here, then, along the lines of this sense of the *formation* of

Shakespearean tragedy, it will be argued that the cultural forms of mourning and commemoration are themselves uneasily offset against what should properly be called historical memory, but which is given in the signifiers of continuity with the sovereign past, represented by the ghost of the king and the desire for continued narration of his son, but hardly more viable or susceptible of dramatic representation.

9 See Barker 1984.

10 The discussion of discontinuity has probably been most helpfully focused recently by some of Michel Foucault's methodological writing, although the Marxist tradition is not of course unfamiliar with the the conceptualisation of historical breaks at various levels. See in particular Foucault 1978 and 1972.

11 This is the point both of the text's displaced protection of what it cannot protect (see the discussion of 'compromise' below, p. 52), and of the subsequently traditional readings which intrinsically and structurally prefer the personal to the political, and embrace this strange distinction. Not, of course that those readings are therefore unpolitical. On the contrary, if the political in the historical sense is *a priori* beyond their pale, they are none the less only too happy with a nostalgia for Absolutism disguised as the end of politics. The text, by way of the displacements being described here, uncannily conspires, before the event of its having been read in this way, with the terms of this subsequent reading: it is on the threshold of their epoch.

12 In this troubled backgrounding of rites and acts of commemoration – funeral ceremonies in particular – the play tends none the less and thereby to foreground these as by default the sole signs of displaced and substituted memory. It would be wrong to play critically into the hands of that structuration, tempting – and interpretatively rich – as a cultural anthropology of this patterning might be. They are not the only forms, and the contrastive, critical, instances of, say, some of Ophelia's emphases on memory – 'Tis in my memory lock'd, / And you yourself shall keep the key of it' (I.iii.85–6), or 'There's rosemary, that's for remembrance – pray you, love, remember' (IV.v.173–4) – or of the Players represented as 'the abstract and brief chronicles of the time. After your death you were better have a bad epitaph than their ill report while you live' (II.ii.520–2), might prove, in a fuller reading, instructive: not least in as much as they offer, against the odds of the displaced fetishisation of memory, to historicise the present.

13 The failure of both forms doubtless evinces a declination in 'cultural authority'. But it is a cultural authority which in the 'real' historical sequence was already tested and contested by both reformist and revolutionary opposition, and which cannot therefore act as an implicit interpretative norm, as much commentary today assumes. For such commentary – and the 'postmodernist' dimensions of New Historicism, especially its refusal of methodological hierarchisation (cf. n. 6 above), are particularly relevant here – have instated culture in the place of some more 'contradictory' sense of the 'totality', and then read culture in terms of various patterns of reciprocity.

The authorial subject on the plane (see n. 4 above) was reading Clifford Geertz, or trying to. And this is appropriate; Geertz is cited in the introduction to *Renaissance self-fashioning* and there is a notable formal consonance between his anthropological method – which has, of course, much to recommend it – and many of the strategies of New Historicism: interpretative and semiotic rather than positively scientific, performative rather than ideational, particular and essayistic rather than generalisably systematic, descriptive rather than causally explanatory, inflected by 'theory' rather than methodologically regularised, and so on. The ensuing analyses are often strangely in despite of New Historicism having otherwise foregrounded – at least the concept of – power. In what has become known as the 'subversion and containment model', even as it – often brilliantly – tracks the subversive element(s) in the text or the culture, New Historicism none the less seems to snatch defeat from the jaws of victory and to confirm the effectivity of power *figured as* the containment of that very subversion. In any case, if 'subversion' is a key word for such studies, and one which has its uses, to be sure, the conceptual language of New Historicism risks a familiarity with discourses on the right that seek to empower and legitimate domination by a deviant rather than oppositional naming of those who resist its effects. Even on the left, subversion may be a poor name or a poor thing where in reality revolutionary perspectives are either meant or needed. At the very least it should be possible to measure what real distance there is (and there is some) between the demonisation of subversion in order to justify and maintain domination, and the ultimate lack – inherent in the incorporation of subversion into power – of a thoroughgoing critique of domination. The latter tends to offer the political effect of leaving everything as it is, when it doesn't actually debilitate the very idea of opposition in the name of all subversion being a necessary condition of the functioning of power as such. The result is often, in the name of studying the poetics of power, a practical denial of the fact and poignancy of domination, substituting notions of circulation for those of oppression, anxiety for terror.

If the sense of cultural 'reciprocity' – subversion and containment – at work here *is* – however residually – hierarchised, it is none the less without foundation or grounding: as in the famous story, a version of which Geertz quotes, it's 'turtles all the way down'. And in any case eroded as the work develops. Subsequently, instead, power – or 'social energy' – is figured not just as exchange – which is of course an originary concept of (cultural) anthropology – but also as circulation and negotiation which are then the organising metaphors of recent New Historicism, and arguably are not formally that far, in fact, from Lyotard's fully postmodernist language games, and are drained, in any case, of all political force.

Compare Lyotard 1984, *passim* with Greenblatt 1988, pp. 1–20. For Clifford Geertz's methodology see Geertz 1973, esp. pp. 3–30. Cf. also note 42 below. For a positive discussion of the subversion and containment model see Dollimore 1985. See also Howard 1986, Montrose 1986.

14 The constitutive difficulty of the text's production of Hamlet as the prototypical individual of emergent modernity is at once disclosed and betrayed by, amongst other things, the proliferation of 'interference repetitions' of the prince (simulacra which I might be *tempted* now to see as postmodern ghosts). See Barker 1984, p. 39.

15 Terence Hawkes makes a similar point in Hawkes 1986, pp. 92–3, although his sense of the repetition that undermines the ideological effectivity of military power – and which governs the reading more widely – is somewhat formal.

16 This may be a downbeat way of thinking about tragedy, certainly less grand (although perhaps more historically poignant) than other 'theories' of tragedy. But so be it. Not figuring universal and absolute (the word is instructive) loss of value, but – transitional – inability to render value into either dramatic or political practice, at least it doesn't function, compared with some other accounts of the idea of tragedy, as an alibi for its own depoliticisation.

17 The mildly critical value of this bathos may be greater today than when previously it
    would have to have been counterposed to a tradition of reading dominated by
    gentility, academic or otherwise. Since history is now being turned into Heritage, and
    the realm of England thematised in the Disney sense, this failure of enthusiasm in one
    of the key high cultural texts will probably make it even harder to read from a national
    perspective.

18 'Demystified' in this context means 'not claiming the authority of the sacred'. Rather
    than the classically Marxist usage which refers a cultural form structurally to its
    decoded grounding elsewhere in the social formation, the sense here is that quasi-
    'anthropological' (but better historical) idiom which probably began with
    Machiavelli – and which Marx, to be sure, understood and adopted – that, practically
    rather than diagnostically, abandons the transcendentally charged – while continuing
    to manipulate it as a mode of coercion – in favour of force and rationality. See also
    Franco Morretti's account of this dramatic, ideological and historical trajectory
    (Moretti 1988).

19 Marx (1970), p. 96.

20 In this it seems to approximate to the fashionably pleasing, if reductive, reading of
    that other relevant text, Friedrich Nietzsche's 'The uses and abuses of history for life',
    whose drift is also commonly taken to entail not historical forgetting but the
    forgetting of history. Even Fredric Jameson, in his Foreword to *The postmodern
    condition*, speaks of 'the great and still influential essay of Nietzsche on the debili-
    tating influence of historiography and of the fidelity to the past and the dead that an
    obsession with history seems to encourage'. See Lyotard 1984, p. xii. This has a
    certain currency, to be sure, but it remains a misreading and one whose simple
    consonance with Marx's text, as well as being politically implausible, is only con-
    structable on the basis of the latter also being reduced to an essential proposal of
    amnesia. Cf. Nietzsche 1983, p. 63: 'This, precisely, is the proposition the reader is
    invited to meditate upon: *the unhistorical and the historical are necessary in equal
    measure for the health of an individual, of a people and of a culture* (emphasis
    original).

21 See Benjamin 1968 from which the quotations here are taken.

22 It is especially understandable today, without countenancing postmodern critiques of
    the legacy of the Enlightenment, why this reversal of the expectations of progressivist
    ethico-genealogical chronology made sense to Benjamin and should make now a
    similar sense to the *critique* of postmodernist *doxa*: the complexity of Benjamin's
    sense of historical time, and the time of history, resists the conventional postmodern
    flattening.

23 For an apposite reading of the positivity of the Marxist text in respect of nineteenth-
    century capitalism, see Berman 1983, esp. pp. 87–129.

24 Postmodernism routinely conflates unknowability with indeterminacy, and either or
    both with 'undecideability' . . .

25 Despite the apparently radical discontinuity of Benjamin's 'flashes of memory' it is
    important to distinguish none the less between his sense of the tradition of the ruling
    class, the procession of the victors and their cultural spoils, and the altogether
    different 'tradition of the oppressed' which has to be wrested from 'history' and from
    historicism, and which inspires – or indeed, *is* – that historical action. See Benjamin
    1968, pp. 258–9 and *passim*. (I am grateful to Paula Hutchings for this clarification in

particular.)
26 Karl Marx 1973, p. 105.
27 Lyotard's periodisation is precise: the second substantive sentence of his text has the transition to the postmodern age 'under way since at least the end of the 1950s' (Lyotard 1984, p. 1). This very precision, in respect especially of history conceived as chronological sequence, should be an embarrassment in as much as it discloses, against its alternative novelty, the continued attachment of the discourse to the (Cartesian) epistemology inaugurated at the beginning of the modern period.
28 It's frequently cited as exemplary of postmodernism. It plays in Los Angeles in November, 2019. It rains continuously. Coca Cola and TDK adverts move overhead pronouncing incomprehensible, disembodied messages. Gothic-metallic technology and glamorised immiseration; decay. Genetic engineering is available in *sushi* bars. There are blue light effects. And there is Deckard's hardboiled cop voice-over with the usual sentimental half-tones, and Gaff's menacing and ultimately sardonically forgiving *origami*. But the most poignant of the narrative and generic strands of the movie is the quest of the replicants for their own past. As artificial beings they have no authentic history; their search is dominated by the fact that all replicants have built-in termination dates. Their – human, all too human – question is: how long have I got? The search for the past is the memory of the future.
   Blade runner produced by Michael Deeley and directed by Ridley Scott, MCMLXXXII. Cf. Francis Barker, 'The dream of the artificial man', Center for Studies in Contemporary Culture conference on 'The hermeneutics of desire', University of Massachusetts at Amherst, USA, September 1986.
29 Although see also Habermas 1985, pp. 3–4 and *passim*, for a discussion of the historical possibility of the conception of the modern and therefore also of the postmodern.
30 For the 'crisis of representation', connected to a discussion of postmodernity as also a crisis of legitimation, see again, in an appropriate context, Jameson in his Foreword to Lyotard 1984, p. viii and *passim*.
31 Benjamin 1968, p. 259.
32 Situatedness? It's an ugly word which I began to use because it seemed to help with articulating what cannot be articulated: a sense at once of contingency and determination, of the density of an event without resorting to the banality of regarding the context merely as 'background'. It was subsequently elaborated as a – dialectical – concept by the Early Modern Research Group.
33 For Marshall Berman's discussion of the modernism of underdevelopment see Berman 1983, pp. 173–286.
34 The invitation was issued by an American – that is, US – academic who is committed to postmodern*ism*. Doubtless, it would be wrong to overinterpret, but perhaps the current 'theoretical' audibility of the anecdote will license the following speculation. My question was about empire, and about whether the espoused postmodernism wasn't part of at least a representational complex which includes senses of the provincial as the *identical* other side of globalisation – I had in mind, contrastively, the Roman figure of the empire compared with which the US imperium apparently lacks both a capital, a Rome, and, relatively speaking, territorial possession in the empirical sense. The answer didn't convince me that in one major respect postmodernism is not simply 'America' – whether Baudrillard's simulacra or Fukuyama's sad paradise. An

undertow in the discussion is inescapably the way in which some American representations of the present as the end of history (and some European representations – Lyotard?, Baudrillard? – which are essentially American, or, rather, 'American') may participate, knowingly or not, in a (politically *ex post facto*, to be sure) repetition of an originary sense of US historicism, founded as it was on two kinds of break from history; revolutionary severance from Europe, and the erasure of an indigenous history up to and including genocide. The signs of invasion are often of other histories, but recently of history 'itself'.

35 Capitalism is presumably mitigated. Until recently a hazard for motorists in Hong Kong was the fine timing with which elderly Chinese would cross the road. A speeding vehicle, even one driven by a foreign ghost apparently, was an effective way of dispersing the bad spirits which follow at the heels. On the island of Cheung Chau each year pyramids of bread are made for the ghosts of a band of robbers, and other Departed Spirits, who live there. At the culmination of the festival a priest, who alone can see them, observes the ghosts through a jade monocle. When they have eaten their fill he gives a sign and anyone else may take the bread; even the tourists.

It is a peculiar but telling assumption that the postmodern can be *seen* (i.e. that it belongs *in this form* to the sphere of the aesthetic). In this respect, even though properly speaking signs cannot be sensuous-empirical, the signs of 'China' are particularly numinous. But they have a history, in the aestheticised *chinoiserie* of Western artists and collectors, of course, but perhaps as well in the trade and warfare which also stretches back at least to the *European* seventeenth century?

36 See Walter Benjamin, 'The work of art in the age of mechanical reproduction' in Benjamin 1968; esp. p. 244.

37 Paul Simon's song 'The boy in the bubble' on the arguably postmodern *Graceland* album (Warner Brothers, 1986). I am grateful to Thele Moema for clarifying just how politically ambiguous Paul Simon's 'hybrid' encounter with South African music was. But for its following hard on 'Music for peace', and its lack of negotiation with the African National Congress and the mass democratic movement of the cultural boycott of South Africa, it might have been otherwise. The 'Graceland' concert in Zimbabwe with, among others, Miriam Makeba and Hugh Masekela, belatedly mitigated the ambiguity somewhat.

38 Herr 1978.

39 A major theme of Fredric Jameson's seminal article, 'Postmodernism, or the cultural logic of late capitalism' (Jameson 1984) is that of postmodern emphases on space: 'the conception of space that has been developed here suggests that a model of political culture appropriate to our own situation will necessarily have to raise spatial issues *as its fundamental organizing concern*' (p. 89, emphasis added). He too is struck by Herr's writing of the Vietnam War, and associates that representation, along with its imbrication in military technology, with postmodern spatialisation, figured, often, over against time. It is easy to see why: 'Airmobility, dig it, you weren't going anywhere. It made you feel safe, it made you feel Omni, but it was only a stunt, technology. Mobility was just mobility, it saved lives or took them all the time . . .' (Herr 1978, p. 19). But Jameson's reading of postmodernity may concede too much to postmodernism and its 'ends of history', both in general, and in his use of *Dispatches* in particular: key terms for Herr, after all, are *time* and information; see note 41 below.

40 See Jameson 1984, pp. 61ff., for the 'waning of affect' which he, among others, sees as
    another of the principal features of postmodernity.

41 'Talk about impersonating an identity, about locking into a role, about irony: I went
    to cover the war and the war covered me; an old story, unless of course you've never
    heard it. I went there behind the crude but serious belief that you had to be able to look
    at anything, serious because I acted on it and went, crude because I didn't know, it
    took the war to teach it, that you were as responsible for everything you saw as you
    were for everything you did. The problem was that you didn't always know what you
    were seeing until later, maybe years later, that a lot of it never made it in at all, it just
    stayed stored there in your eyes. Time and information, rock and roll, life itself, the
    information isn't frozen, you are.' Herr 1978, p. 22.

42 If Clifford Geertz's cultural anthropology has been adapted to set at least in part the
    methodological agenda of the New Historicism (see note 13 above), and if a key
    article of Geertz's genial method is to figure anthropology as 'conversation', and as,
    for example, 'another country heard from' (Geertz 1973, p. 24 and p. 23), then the
    New Historicism might be invited to clarify this dimension of its politics too. Does not
    'the desire to speak with the dead' inescapably allocate the 'Other' the place of the
    dead . . .? See Greenblatt 1988, p. 1. (Cf. Francis Barker, 'Thick description: the
    theoretical politics of the New Historicism, or, "Turtles all the way down" ', Sixth
    International Conference on Literary Theory 'American Visions, Visions of America:
    New Directions in Culture and Literature', Department of English Studies and
    Comparative Literature, University of Hong Kong, December 1988.)

43 Lyotard 1984, p. 82.

44 Perhaps it would assist some critics if it were pointed out that (although cognate, of
    course) Derridean differance and currently easily fashionable *difference* are not the
    same thing. To take the now famous *dictum* as a case in point, in one sense of course
    there *is* 'nothing outside the text'. But this may be a platitude. To be sure, there is no
    uncultural nature which can act as the guarantee of the truth of the analysis of history.
    But on the other hand, if – to take one limit case – history is 'second nature', the
    problem remains. Weak (in the analytico-philosophical sense) versions of 'the text'
    implicitly address not the textual (cultural and historical) character of Nature, but
    retain the traditional (and, more importantly, traditionalist) understanding of text as
    – empirically – books, writing, etc, and the traditional distinction between words and
    things. Substituting one for the other, the world is made susceptible of *literary*
    criticism . . . Short of some more articulate refutation of this idealism, one might as
    well suppose that this was not what Derrida 'had in mind'. But then to equate these
    'philosophical' problems in the theory of *écriture* with a positive ethics or aesthetics –
    it's hardly a 'politics' – of *unqualified* difference, is, as will be argued below, danger-
    ously if not disingenously mistaken.

45 If disorientation seems to organise the postmodern, might not this loss of the east be a
    complicity with the globalisation of the West? So much for difference.

46 Is it still necessary, even today, to explain *theoretical* anti-humanism?

47 Whether or not it is quite accurate to group him with the postmodernists, a version of
    this move by the Michel Foucault of the later volumes of *The history of sexuality* (if
    indeed they are volumes of the project which was begun under that name) has taken
    up an influential place among the figurations of postmodernity.
        But ethics may not be *necessarily* subjective in the sense of subject-based, although

postmodernism – paradoxically, given its other positions on the fragmented self – does not always free itself from the positivity of this assumption. Or, given that postmodern experience is actually the opposite of experience in that it tends to disorientate the subject born into the modern humanist assumptions and practices which are still the cultural and ideological dominant of the West, and to undermine in concept any notion of the stability or unity of a subject able to have experience in the first place, postmodernism tends to resist the ethical as having no foundation. This too misses at least half of the point.

48 Postmodernism, by contrast, *is* an historicism.

49 At the same meeting in Hong Kong – the context remains significant – Ihab Hassan, who is credited with using the term postmodernism as early as any (although Olsen, with doubtless a quite different valancy, also has a claim), announced the onset of the post-political period . . . He is not alone; cf. note 3 above.

50 i.e. either to those 'ends of history' figured in the more restricted Renaissance studies debate with which this volume is engaged, or those seeking to shape the wider diagnosis of the times in which we allegedly live.

51 'Renaissance studies' today lacks much sense of what in this way might actually be, and be *actually*, at stake. Its significance must surely be its anti-historicism: it is important to get the historicisation right. It is the critical value of alterity on the – revolutionary but then amnesiac – threshold of 'our own' determining history which alone can legitimate the critical value of the study, and its implications for practice. And not just alterity of empirical substance, but also of an interpretative strategy which might have its beginnings – not origins – in a counter-reading of the founding moment of modernity: 'I believe that it is not to the great model of signs and language [*la langue*] that reference should be made, but to war and battle. The history which bears and determines us is war-like, not language-like. Relations of power, not relations of sense. History has no "sense", which is not to say that it is absurd or incoherent. On the contrary, it is intelligible and should be able to be analysed down to the slightest detail: but according to the intelligibility of struggles, of strategies and tactics' (Foucault 1979, p. 33).

52 There is today a strong complicity between the form of the anecdote – a characteristically New Historicist trope, although by no means one confined to that discourse – and the theme of nostalgia. Together they militate against historical criticism. The anecdote mimes a rhetorical legitimation of what then passes for analysis, but at the same time it conspires with the charge that any more 'structured' sense of the interpretatively historical is inevitably nostalgic if it bothers to think cogently 'the past'. Under these circumstances it would be open to much misinterpretation to suggest a parallel with Shakespearean tragedy, itself on the threshold of the modern, and on the threshold of originally modern, if not 'postmodern', ends of history. But – given the necessary caveats above concerning the possibility of unacknowledged containment in the very notion of crisis – is this not a practice of critical thought? Where the delerium or disorientation of the new is represented in Shakespeare as loss and disruption, isn't it possible now to see in such a way of representing the present, not signs of 'the world we have lost', but a lost opportunity for historical strategy?

'Cultural poetics' versus 'cultural materialism': the two New Historicisms in Renaissance studies

HOWARD FELPERIN

Historicism gives the 'eternal' image of the past; historical materialism supplies a unique experience with the past. (Walter Benjamin, 'Theses on the philosophy of history' (Benjamin 1968))

The textualisation of history

Of the diverse schools of criticism to emerge from the theoretical ferment of the 1970s, arguably the most influential in the 1980s – particularly in the field of Renaissance studies – has been the so-called 'New Historicism'. Yet its high institutional profile has made it of late a target of critical and polemical attack from several quarters; so much so that one might be excused for wondering how much longer it will remain alive as a critical movement, let alone influential. So swiftly do our paradigms now seem to shift that the New Historicism could conceivably pass from youthful vigour into obsolescence and decline without ever having attained intellectual and institutional maturity. Such a destiny would be regrettable, because its strengths would remain partly unrealized and its weaknesses imperfectly understood. It would have been denied, in sum, the full exposure, the moment in the sun – for better and worse – enjoyed by the schools it seeks to supplant: the old historicism on the one hand, and new and practical criticism on the other.

It is to some of those weaknesses that I now turn, albeit at the risk of hastening the demise of a critical movement from which I have learned a great deal and for which I have a corresponding respect. In mitigation, I can say only that unlike most recent attacks, the following strictures are *not* directed primarily at the politics of the New Historicism, at a radical will which has occasioned the criticism that 'new historicists do not like "literature"' (Pechter 1987). Nor are my remarks aimed at its style of radical will, which has led some to conclude that it is a 'male historicism and just not feminist enough' (Erickson 1987; Boose 1987; Neely 1988; and Newton 1988). The following critique is directed not at the ideological soundness or unsoundness of the New Historicism, which is of course far from ideologically monolithic, but at certain methodological and epistemological problems raised but not resolved by its practices. These problems arise, I shall argue, out of the difficulty or impossibility of producing a 'textualist' or 'post-structuralist' history, and are themselves contradictions of the New Historicism's moment of emergence, indications of its underlying continuity with older habits of thought to which it is overtly opposed.[1]

To historicise the New Historicism in this fashion, that is, to remind it of its own history, it will be necessary to ask at the outset whether the label 'the New Historicism' is not something of a misnomer: are we really dealing with a single school of criticism? In saying this, I do not intend the sort of qualification that can, indeed should, apply when discussing any 'ism'. Since all 'isms' are umbrella-terms reared high above the diverse movements grouped under them, they are to that extent abstractions much less homogeneous or coherent than they tend to appear in discussion. But that is not the point I want to make. 'The New Historicism' is disunified within itself in a way that goes deeper than the disunified character of all 'isms'. It is disunified in ways that its opponents, preoccupied by its radical politics, have disregarded or discounted, and that it has itself been reluctant, given the institutional advantages of a united front, to acknowledge. The New Historicism, even at the level of abstraction at which 'isms' operate, is at least two distinct historicisms.

To put the matter oversimply for purposes of exposition, there is an American and a British New Historicism, and while they have much in common, they are in certain crucial respects not only 'different', as is now beginning to be perceived, but actually *opposed* (see Cohen 1987, p. 33; Wayne 1987, p. 51). What they have in common is a post-structuralist understanding of literature and history as *constructed textuality* or, to the extent that traditional opposition between the 'literary' and the 'historical' have been shown by this school to be deconstructible, as *constructed intertextuality*. This way of proceeding is sometimes termed 'contextualism'; but more usefully for our purposes, it is also 'conventionalism'. This notion enables us to distinguish both 'New' Historicisms from the 'old'; for their 'conventionalist' understanding of culture as an intertextual construction supersedes an older 'empiricist' or 'realist' identification of the meaning of an historical text with the biographical author's intention or his contemporary audience's understanding of it, as if such things were once monolithically present or linguistically transparent – even for the historical culture concerned – and retain an integrity untouched by the terms and methods of our enquiry into them.[2]

Hence the centrality for both American and British New Historicism of power and politics; for the interpretation of the text of history cannot be 'disinterested' or 'apolitical'. Just as there can be no 'motiveless creation', as Stephen Greenblatt puts it in the closest thing yet to a New-Historicist 'manifesto' (See Greenblatt 1988), so too there can be no motiveless interpretation. Both New Historicisms are thus doubly political, not only in the sense that they are interested in the political motives of the texts they take up, but also in that the texts they produce are themselves politically interested and, generally speaking, make no secret of it – again in contradistinction to the older historicism. They seek, that is, to make a difference in the text of history by actively *rewriting* the Renaissance rather than passively reflecting on it.

Yet even before addressing the larger problems such a project entails, there are crucial differences between the American and British versions of 'the Renaissance'. Such differences reflect the particular political charge and commitment carried by each, and follow from the disparate positions occupied by 'English' within their respective cultures. Consider, for example, their common focus on Renaissance, particularly seventeenth-century, literature. As the moment of transition between medieval and modern England, the seventeenth century is the meeting-ground between historical alterity and contemporary identity, between cultural difference and presence, and as such holds special interest for any self-conscious historicism. Hence the oxymoronic term favoured by many New Historicists: the 'early modern' period. The seventeenth century also holds, as the period of Shakespeare, Donne, and Milton, the strategic high ground in a continuing institutional struggle for control of literary study on both sides of the Atlantic. For British New Historicists in particular, 'English' is not just another subject, and involves more than the skills associated with 'literacy'. For them, 'English' is a matter of national identity, and the seventeenth century a revolutionary moment, a moment of social and constitutional crisis in the past with crucial implications for the political, indeed revolutionary, aspirations of the present. So the political valencies of these related critical movements, given their different institutional positions within the cultures that produced them, are not quite the same.[3]

And neither are their respective theoretical alignments, nor the practical problems that arise in consequence in their dealings with Renaissance texts. For American and British New Historicists have drawn on different intellectual traditions and pursued quite different methods in their respective critical practices. Let us consider the American position first. *Renaissance self-fashioning: from More to Shakespeare*; *James I and the politics of literature: Jonson, Shakespeare, Donne and their contemporaries*; *The illusion of power: political theater in the English Renaissance* – such titles, selected almost at random from the burgeoning shelf, have a lot in common. They announce their topic, and straightaway limit their scholarly focus to a specific set of authors, a king's reign, a historical period. Indeed, the form and style of these titles are distinctly academic; the conventions of the doctoral dissertation in which their authors were well trained are not far away, with watchful supervisors urging economical confinement within accepted historical divisions, and rigorous examiners ready to pounce on any extravagance unsupported by specialist expertise within the delimited field.[4]

More specifically, the academic convention at work in these titles is still that of an older historical empiricism. Its rationale necessitated the establishment of a clear demarcation of the historical subject-matter under study and a carefully measured distance between that subject-matter and its investigator. What such titles still signify, among other things, is 'research' with all its pseudo-scientific, empiricist connotations. 'Research' presupposes a cool, disinterested (indeed, invisible) interpreter bracketed off in the here and now, and an objective body of 'data' sharply visible in the there and then, each standing in a self-contained space and separated from the other by enough distance to enable independence and objectivity in the scrutiny. The historical data, in this case the authors and texts under study, are declared to be 'political' – that seems to be the working hypothesis at its most general – but the politics of the historical scholar – to judge from the titles of these studies – are still implicit or occluded.

Now you cannot judge a book by its cover, or by its title, and neither

Stephen Greenblatt's *Renaissance self-fashioning: from More to Shakespeare* nor any of the other New-Historicist studies cited above is quite the sort of book its title might lead you to expect. After all, these are not works of 'old' but of 'New' Historicism, and that means they know better than to proceed upon the same 'empiricist' assumptions as the older historicism, or to pretend to the same 'objectivity'. Having delimited and distanced the field of enquiry along older empirical lines, New Historicists do not characteristically maintain the pretence of empirical objectivity towards its contents, least of all that of a 'naive' empiricism. Quite the contrary: *nothing is now simply what it appears or as it presents itself to observation* but something else, as anything and everything in the dramatic text reproduces, 'rehearses', and even 'reverses' the power relations of the cultural context (see Greenblatt 1988, pp. 7–9). Tamburlaine's extravagant career, for example, becomes 'an extraordinary meditation' on the destruction of a West African village by English merchant-sailors in 1586, while the rough magic with which Prospero controls his island is analogous to the martial law periodically imposed by the authorities upon the Virginia colony (Greenblatt 1988, pp. 193–4; 1980, pp. 148–63).

This sudden, often surprising, interpenetration of text and context, theatre and culture – indeed, the dissolution of traditional boundaries between them – is of course characteristic of New-Historicist practice. Partly because it began in the 1970s very much as a practice concerned to 'get on with' its work of politicisation, and took theory on board only after the 'fact' and under pressure, the principles on which its subversive or transgressive readings proceed are not always explicit. One critic, not unsympathetic, goes so far as to describe its working assumption as one of 'arbitrary connectedness' between text and context (Cohen 1987, p. 34). This, as we shall see, it not quite the case. But if its persistent reading of Renaissance texts as dark conceits of official authority or ideological 'containment' is more than 'arbitrary', American New Historicism is less than fully or clearly principled in its hermeneutic practices.

What is clear is that its political readings, such as those cited above, do not proceed under the straightforward regime of political allegorisation familiar enough in empirical historicism, within which topical references encoded by the author are read off by contemporary audiences and historical critics 'in the know'. While this procedure was often at work in the early attention to the coterie – and conventionally allegorical – forms of masque and pastoral with which New Historicism began (Orgel 1975; Montrose 1980), later work rarely conforms to this residually empiricist model. Nor does American New Historicism openly embrace – though it does flirt with – a more traditionally Marxist ideological critique, by which the interestedness of the text in promoting or legitimising the political structure of its context of production is unmasked (Greenblatt 1980, pp. 192–222; 1987, p. 258).

The most explicit attempt to date to address such questions has been the 'retrospect' with which Greenblatt introduces his recent collection of essays on Shakespeare (Greenblatt 1988, pp. 1–20). There, he recalls his increasing uneasiness 'with the monolithic entities that my work has posited', the 'sublime confrontation between a total artist and a totalizing society'. That Greenblatt should grow dissatisfied with his residually romantic and idealist conception of Shakespeare as a 'total artist' comes as no surprise. Less predictable, however, is his uneasiness with his other totalisation, an Elizabethan society 'that posits an occult network linking all human, natural, and cosmic powers and that claims on behalf of its ruling elite a privileged place in this network'. He goes on to account for his growing discontent in terms of a heightened awareness, through the work of others, of the ways in which the 'discourse of power' in the period was itself contradictory and contested at virtually every point.

Far be it from me to dispute Greenblatt's account of his disillusionment with an historical hermeneutic that seems as questionable to me as it has come to seem to him. But I want to translate the terms of his disillusionment into those of my own argument, which attempts to identify a deeper source of unease than that which he acknowledges. For his 'totalizing society' whose power structure reinforces itself by appeal to a natural order conceived as rigidly and ubiquitously hierarchical, was not essentially different from that 'posited' by E. M. W. Tillyard and other older historicists forty years earlier.[5] Tillyard documented a society and a Shakespeare for whom hierarchical order was nothing less than a 'world-picture' – and a good thing too. Of course the early Greenblatt, unlike Tillyard, repeatedly registers his astonishment and often his antipathy towards the 'totalizing' Tudor and Stuart culture that he chronicles first in *Sir Walter Ralegh* and more fully in *Renaissance self-fashioning*, in particular towards the absolutism with which its anxious and obsessive authoritarianism is

enforced upon the wayward souls under its sway. One man's order was
certainly another's 'totalitarianism'.

My point, however, is that in moving from Tillyard to Greenblatt
only the political valorisation of such a society had been completed
inverted; the terms of its cognition and construction deployed by
Tillyard, the early Greenblatt, and many others were not essentially
different. Those terms remain basically 'empiricist' or 'realist'. That is,
they all 'posit' Elizabethan society as a historical reality not simply
present – often oppressively so – and univocal to itself, but one whose
historicity exists in its own right – and in a sense for all time – and
remains independent of our efforts to reconstruct it – despite its survival
only in the form of traces. 'Monolithic' indeed. And 'reconstruction' –
as opposed to 'construction' – of the past is distinctly the objective
within the logic of this historical 'realism': if no longer the fully positivist, documentary reconstruction pursued by the older historical
scholarship of a Tillyard, then at least a plausible narrative representation. 'Representations', after all, names not only the journal
Greenblatt has edited, with others, for nearly a decade but the opening
narrative gambit of virtually everything he has written.

The very term 'representation' at once recuperates and sublates this
older historicist and naively realist objective of 'making present again' a
past culture conceived not only as chronologically but *ontologically*
prior to any construction of it. In so doing, it partly rehabilitates a
residually referential aspiration, if not to 'commune', at least to
correspond with the past. This is not the place to elaborate upon the
problems raised (or, more often, repressed) by such a cognitive model.
Against what, for example, could the claim to correspondence be tested,
without independent access to historical 'reality'? How else could the
accuracy, completeness, or vividness of that correspondence be judged?
For such problems have already been confronted and effectively
transcended by the post-structuralist move by which the 'traces' of
history and the constructs of culture have been re-framed on the linguistic model of 'texts' and 'discourses' requiring an ever fresh and
renewable 'construction' rather than the pseudo-empiricist model of
'documents' and 'facts' to be 'read off' in the effort of definitive reconstruction.

That major shift, in which Greenblatt's work has certainly participated, makes possible a rather different account of his change of
attitude from the one he offers. For the transition he describes is a

matter not merely of heightened awareness of complexity and conflict within the same conceptualisation of the field but of a basic change in that conceptualisation. In the course of the theoretical retrenchments of the 1970s and early 1980s, Greenblatt trades in his earlier 'realist' model of history, culture and literature for a sleeker 'textualist' and inevitably 'conventionalist' model. Or perhaps more accurately, he retains his older 'realist' model, but upgrades it by taking on board quite a lot of the new textualist technology arriving from several theoretical directions. The realist narrative structure that dominates his *Sir Walter Ralegh: the Renaissance man and his roles* is by no means relinquished. His essays still characteristically open with an historical 'event' narrated in quasi-documentary detail. But this tactic is now deployed with a new awareness of its status as *narrative*, as something more than a textual and rhetorical construct but less than a documentary 'given'.

The older 'realism' – marked in his latest work by such faintly pejorative terms as 'posit' and 'monolithic' – is now delicately and uneasily qualified by the newer 'textualism'. Thus his revised project is 'to enquire into the objective conditions of the enchantment [of the text], to discover how the traces of social circulation are effaced' (Greenblatt 1988, p. 5). With concepts like 'circulation' – let alone the 'traces' thereof – now in play, Greenblatt has repudiated (having always questioned) the historical empiricism of the likes of Tillyard, and its own traces in his earlier work. But to exchange the totalising reifications of an older historical 'realism' for the differential relations of a newer textualist 'conventionalism', while it might resolve some problems, is to encounter new ones. For the move from history as determinate 'fact' or 'event' to history as constructible 'text' renders this latest historicism open from within to the charge of 'relativism' as no previous historicism ever was, to being dismissed as merely one of many possible and no less plausible constructions of the historical text, and thus to conservative relativisation and recuperation.

Cultural poetics

At the same time, the anthropological emphasis and materialist inflection of the new history on which it depends paradoxically expose it to a reductive 'universalism' and a new 'essentialism'. For beneath the specific Elizabethan historicity it seeks to identify is the concept of a 'deep structure' with which it cannot dispense, and towards which the surface structures of that culture consistently point. Does Greenblatt's latest terminology of 'circulation', 'negotiation', 'social energy' and 'exchange' – basically mercantile, even strangely monetarist, as it is – not effectively render Elizabethan England in terms of a generative grammar of economic exchange common to all societies? On this account, we might be excused for wondering whether we have blundered into a kind of universal bazaar teeming with rug dealers. What with so much exchange taking place in a culture that is, like all others, implicitly based on it, it is hardly surprising to find textual and contextual elements changing places handy-dandy with barely a trace, or the theatre 'rehearsing' or even 'reversing' some feature of the culture that might superficially appear remote and unconnected.

For these newly essentialist categories of 'energy', 'negotiation', and 'exchange' are so inclusive as to apply to virtually every activity conceivable within every historical culture under the sun. Hence the necessity, which Greenblatt himself recognises, of further focusing the principles on which his 'poetics of culture' is to proceed if it is to identify and explore 'the objective conditions' of textual enchantment with any specificity, let alone the intertextual effacements on which it depends. Otherwise, a 'poetics' of culture with some claim to explanatory power would remain beyond reach, and the most we could expect would be another *ad hoc*, proliferating and ultimately arbitrary hermeneutics. Have we not been here before? In Greenblatt's expressed interest in the 'objective conditions' of textual enchantment, is there not a certain sense of *déjà vu*? Having exchanged an 'empiricist' for a 'textualist' model of history and culture, we should not be surprised to discover that a residual – if apparently antithetical – interest in identifying 'objective conditions' is still necessary for the construction of anything like a 'poetics'.

The typology Greenblatt goes on to outline in order to limit, specify and systematise 'the whole spectrum of representational exchanges' (1988, p. 8) certainly creates a familiar illusion of objectivity. Its primary category of 'symbolic acquisition', for example, through which social 'energy' and 'practice' are translated on to the stage, is subdivided into 'metaphoric' and 'metonymic' or 'synecdochic' acquisition. If this sounds familiar, surely it is because Greenblatt's attempt to limit and objectify the potentially infinite variety of dynamic exchange is so openly modelled on the old, reliable opposition of metaphor to metonymy basic to structuralist analysis. For structuralist poetics and anthropology, despite their adoption of the conventionalist model of language, did not cease to think of themselves as 'realisms'. That was why 'deep structures' and 'underlying laws' were required and retained in the first place: to protect against 'relativism'.

The 'knowledge' promised by structuralism, be it of the operations of poetic language or of the cultural function of myth, was meant to be a 'knowledge' *of* something – of something socially and conventionally constructed to be sure, and requiring theoretical work to be understood – but something that was not finally the projection of its own theories and methods. Be it the analysis of a sonnet, a myth, or a culture, structuralist method consisted in taking its object apart and reconstituting it in such a way as to reveal the laws of its functioning. There were a 'method', an 'object', and 'laws' relating the various bits and pieces of the object under analysis were supposed to be independent of the method. After all, the decoding at issue – as anyone recalling Lévi-Strauss's analysis of the Oedipus myth, or Jakobson's of poems by Baudelaire and Shakespeare, will attest – turned on the rigorous teasing-out of the *langue* of their *paroles*, the codes, rules, and grammars that regulated relations among the bits and pieces of the text at hand, the system of differences that made it congenial to analysis on the model of language in the first place. Structuralism was supposed to be a 'realism', whose object was language and its manifold textual and cultural instantiations.

It took a while for us to realise, however, that the system the text was thus forced to yield up was not as 'objective', or susceptible to objectification, as structuralist theory would have it. The text – whether sonnet, myth, or culture – was not structured *as* a language but *like* a language. And not even really like 'a language', but like language as structural linguistics constructs it. Shakespeare's sonnets beautifully illustrate the categories that structural linguistics (and its literary arm, structuralist poetics) consider to be constitutive – and are so, but *constitutive of structural linguistics and structuralist poetics*. Similarly, the Oedipus myth responded obediently to the apparatus of structural anthropology; but how could it do otherwise, when it was reconstituted as a projection of it? A discipline that had conceived of itself as a 'realism' turned out to be a 'conventionalism' after all. One critic aptly invokes James Thurber's classic story of his fumbling efforts to master the use of the microscope, only to discover that the 'variegated constellation of flecks, specks, and dots' he kept seeing through it was

the reflection in the lens of his own eye! (Jameson 1972, pp. 206–7).
Unfortunately, the analogy between 'cultural poetics' and structuralist
poetics and anthropology goes deeper than its exponents might have
wished.

For the New-Historicist act of delimiting its subject matter along
older empirical lines effectively cuts its 'Renaissance' out of the flow of
history and turns it into a slice or cross-section of history. This can then
be studied, like a slide, under the microscope, where it takes on the
aspect of a synchronic system that is certainly culture-specific and
conventional – and displays no shortage of 'energy' and 'circulation' –
but one that has been sealed off from any continuing historical process.
For such questions as what 'writes' the cultural system under study, and
to which culture – Renaissance or contemporary? – it belongs, remain
unexplored and largely unasked. The microscope in use was not
designed to investigate these matters. To be sure, it is no longer 'literature' or 'literary history' that is being isolated as a thing apart –
Greenblatt is quite explicit and consistent on this point – but the
cultural system within which 'literature' is inscribed.

The microscope in use, the method at work, however, is no longer
that of historicism – 'empiricist', 'realist', or any other – but of
structuralism. And this puts into question the historical status of the
enterprise, in so far as it is based on the principle that cultural, like
linguistic, texts are to be analysed as synchronic systems operating in
isolation from all prior and subsequent systems. Structuralist poetics
and anthropology were never meant to be historical and can never be
made historical. Unless Elizabethan literature and society are viewed,
not simply as a textual *system* operating on its own terms – arbitrary,
autonomous, as it were autochthonic – but as a cultural *moment*, laden
with the traces of earlier and the latencies of subsequent moments, there
can be any number of anthropological descriptions, 'thick' and 'thin',
but no historical interpretation.

My point is not simply that American New Historicism is not all that
'new'. I am arguing as well what may be both less clear and more
important: that is not genuinely *historical* or seriously political either,
at least not from the highly politicised viewpoint of certain historical
schools, including that emerging in Britain. In approaching Elizabethan
culture as if it were a self-contained system of circulating energies cut off
from his own cultural system, Greenblatt's cultural poetics relinquishes
its potential for an historical understanding that might exert political

influence upon the present. For such an understanding to arise, the past would have to be constructed not as a remote object – as in empiricism and structuralism alike – but as a vital issue; in terms not of discrete self-containment but of persisting relation. To qualify as a political – as distinct from an antiquarian, archaeological, or anthropological – discourse, the study of past cultures must have present import and consequence. There must be something in it for us beyond curiosity value. In sum, a genuinely *political* historicism inscribes the present as well as the past; it is not only diachronic, but at the very least *dialogic*, if not actually dialectical.

A striking illustration of the limitations of Greenblatt's cultural poetics occurs towards the end of his best-known study (1980, pp. 256ff.). There he discloses his considerable surprise when the 'self-fashioning' from More to Shakespeare he had set out to explore turned out not to be so fully or firmly 'there' as his modern assumptions had led him to expect. It attests to his honesty as a reader that he so openly acknowledges how the texts he reads – and which read him – have forced him to question his own falsely great, if never quite 'Californian', expectations concerning the scope for self-fashioning authorised or even thinkable within Renaissance culture. In these texts, the self-construction he expects keeps collapsing into the social construction he finds; Greenblatt can smell difference when he encounters it. But his surprise in the encounter also attests to an historical understanding insufficiently self-reflective to anticipate the encounter with alterity by inscribing in advance its own position relative to it. Greenblatt experiences history as a kind of 'shock of the old', for which his self-confident title has set him up. Without a philosophy of history that at once relates and differentiates past and present, the historical critic's encounter with the 'other' is bound to come as a shock.[6]

Cultural materialism

These problems in the textual dealings of American 'cultural poetics' are largely absent from those of British 'cultural materialism'. This critical movement traces a path determined by different theoretical alignments and ideological allegiances, and carries in train a rather different set of problems. These are not simply a function of the less fully professionalised institutional structure and the more class-divided society within which the latter operates – more on this shortly – but of distinct intellectual traditions as well, the most obvious and important of these being, of course, Marxism. Whereas cultural poetics inhabits a discursive field in which Marxism has never really been present, its British counterpart inhabits one from which Marxism has never really been absent. This difference has, as we shall see, important consequences, one of which is to confer upon cultural materialism an enormous head start in becoming a genuinely historical and political criticism. Its practitioners seem to have been born into this continuing discourse of history in something of the way the rest of us were born into our native language.

Once again, the titles of its recent productions, as distinct from those of its American counterpart, speak volumes. The auspicious title of *Re-reading English*, the collection to which some of the critics with whom we are concerned contributed essays, foreshadowed an historical criticism oriented as much towards the present as the past, and one in which any safe distance between the two has effectively collapsed. Indeed, 'remaking England' – to maintain their preferred present-participial mode – would have designated no less accurately its quite unhidden agenda. For these critics read and write to change the world, or at least the structure of British society, through the State ideological apparatus of higher education. And unacademic as it may seen to American scholars, they wear their political commitments on their dust-jackets: *Radical tragedy, Political Shakespeare, Alternative Shakespeares, Re-reading Shakespeare*, to cite just a few representative studies.[7]

Ostensibly re-readings of the canonical texts of Elizabethan drama, these studies are hardly less obviously 'interventions' in a political drama closer to home. Such political explicitness contrasts sharply with the ambiguous, gestural, and mainly institutional leftwardness of American 'cultural poetics'. This contrast is not simply a function of differing institutional conventions, though it is that too, but of different philosophies – and experiences – of history. The work of Francis Barker (1984) and Catherine Belsey (1985), for example, engages much the same historical problematic as that explored by Greenblatt of the emergence of a modern selfhood. But they begin not with a determinate subject-matter 'objectively' demarcated in the historical distance, but with the present subject-positions from which they construct and contemplate it. When Francis Barker subtitles his meditation on the fitful appearance of a tremulous, private, modern 'subject' in the literature of the seventeenth century, 'Essays on subjection', he means it in every sense. The historical 'authority' of his work owes more to the self-reflective witness of his modern, liberal-bourgeois 'subjection' *malgré lui* than it does to professionalised, pseudo-objective scholarship.

In fact, Catherine Belsey's *The subject of tragedy* might be mistaken by its title for a politically innocent genre-study of an older kind, tragedy being the noblest 'subject' of them all within traditional, 'humanist' poetics and the form in which subjective 'self-fashioning' has been accorded the highest priority, at least since A. C. Bradley's reading of Shakespeare. (Is this a cunning ploy on the part of Methuen, now Routledge, to sell books to the unsuspecting?) But her subtitle, 'Identity and difference in Renaissance drama', begins to re-frame the subject in question as not eternally given but of relatively recent cultural production and still more recent theoretical concern. In fact, our full-blown, modern preoccupation with 'character' in the plays of the period, however anachronistic and to that extent misplaced, is revealed to be a later stage of the same historical development. In both Barker's and Belsey's work, the inescapability of the historical interpreter's 'presentness' in appropriating the past is capitalised from the outset, in contrast to Greenblatt's attempts to minimise its importance and ignore its consequences.

In the very ease of acceptance and openness of admission of their own 'presentness', however, these cultural materialists exemplify a problem no less vitiating than the denial and back-projection of it by the cultural poeticians. It may actually be the other side of the same problem:

> History is always in practice a reading of the past. We make a narrative out of the available 'documents', the written texts (and maps and buildings and suits of armour) we interpret in order to produce a knowledge of a world which is no longer present. And yet it is always from the present that we produce this knowledge: from the present in the sense that it is only from what is still extant, still available that we make it; and from the present in the sense that we make it out of an understanding formed by the present. We bring what we know now to bear on what remains from the past to produce an intelligible history. (Belsey 1985, p. 1)

Here, in the opening paragraph of *The subject of tragedy*, 'history' is freely acknowledged to be a kind of story-telling towards the present, that is, a textual construct at once itself an interpretation and itself open to interpretation. Even the residual quest for 'objective conditions' seems to have been abandoned.

Perhaps the overt 'conventionalism' of this history of social construction, the self-confessed 'subjectivity' of its 'story of the subject', are only fitting. But before returning to the epistemological status of such a 'history', let me risk crudifying it by attempting to sum it up. For the terms, the discourse, in which this story is told are more than usually inseparable from its subject-matter, story and discourse being in this case one and the same. The story, in outline, begins in what Barker has termed the 'radical alterity' of the Middle Ages, when subjectivity as we know it did not exist as such. The plot thickens only in the latter sixteenth and seventeenth centuries when something like an 'early modern' subject begins to precipitate out of the consolidation of Protestant nonconformism, private enterprise and property, parliamentary democracy, and scientific empiricism. Only then does what Belsey terms the 'discursive knowledge' of the late Middle Ages give way to the 'empirical knowledge' of the modern world.

With it comes a wholly different understanding of the subject, the self, and of course dramatic character. The individual subject, source and site of consciousness and arbiter of the phenomenal world, becomes sovereign, or gathers to itself the illusion of sovereignty. The self, formerly the playground of good and evil, God and the devil, that is, of discursively produced and maintained forces external to it, now becomes an autonomous agency in its own right, no longer constituted as a position in and product of a larger discourse, but constituting its own meaning and truth through observation and ratiocination. The power of defining the human subject hitherto vested in the mutually reinforcing structures of church and monarchy, a power visible, embodied, and enforced in signifying practices of perfect and universal intelligibility, increasingly devolved on to the 'free' individual, a newly autonomous agent capable of self-determination through the exercise of ethical and political choice. Power that was monolithically manifest is now everywhere yet nowhere, inalienable yet invisible in its new inwardness.

In respect of dramatic representation, the sovereign subject's new powers of self-determination have tremendous consequences. They make possible and support the rise of illusionism in the theatre, and the separation of actors and audience by the transparent fourth wall of the proscenium arch. The spectator takes on new interpretive and evaluative prestige as the point of origin of his own 'realistic' perspective, and the actor, no longer the emblematic embodiment of moral roles and social types within a universal discursive system, becomes the imitator of newly individual and psychological beings for whom character is destiny – a notion utterly unthinkable within the culture that produced the *theatrum mundi* of the moralities, but one that would come to be taken for granted in theatrical production and interpretation of the nineteenth and early twentieth centuries.

The story is fresh enough, yet deeply familiar. Where have we heard its like before? Certainly in Michel Foucault's archaeologies of discourse, influential upon all New Historicism, cited early in Belsey's book and crucial to Barker's study of progressive 'disembodiment'. After all, the shift at issue here may be viewed as a local variation on the much larger transition described by Foucault between the medieval and classical epistemes. Foucault's terminology is certainly echoed in these studies, as are the larger conceptual structure and specific institutional focus that go with it. But the nostalgic tone of these British cultural materialists is not really Foucauldian in decisive respects we shall soon examine. Moreover, the concentration on native dramatic texts at the crux of their thesis seems to me to have a more local, though much less obvious and – to the critics in question – less welcome, precedent, and I am not referring to the formative influence of Raymond Williams in particular or of British Marxism in general.[8]

In fact, the thesis that the Elizabethan drama is at best discontinuously 'realistic', that it is an unhomogeneous patchwork of medieval and modern representational modes, and that attempts from the late eighteenth century onwards to discuss it as if it were consistently psychological are a distinctly modern distortion of it, is not of course new. In revealing the discursive discontinuities and instabilities of these plays, as Barker does in his striking discussion of 'presence' versus 'interiority' in *Hamlet*, and as Belsey does in her analyses of conflicting female subject-positions in a number of plays, we are not all that far from the work of Bernard Spivack, Anne Righter, and other 'older' literary historians, who argued the transitional status of Elizabethan dramatic technique against earlier, anachronistic presumptions of a thoroughgoing, if imperfect, naturalism (see, for example, Spivack 1958 and Righter 1961). The focus has shifted, to be sure, from theatrical form as an end in itself to the wider configuration of signifying practices within which it operates and interacts. But the contour of the argument, this new contextualist inflection having been registered, is already in place.

Nostalgia for the future

The major native precursor of the cultural materialist position, however, remains to be named. Before naming him – indeed, to prepare for
the utterance of so dreadful a name – I want to examine the frequent,
perhaps inevitable, connection between historicism and nostalgia. In
the work of Barker, Belsey, and British New Historicists generally, we
encounter not the nostalgia for presence that suffuses Greenblatt's
work, not a longing to enter into the past across the time and distance so
painstakingly established, and once there, 'to speak with the dead'
(Greenblatt 1988, p. 1). We encounter something rather more subtle,
but not less wishful: a kind of nostalgia for the future. I employ this
peculiar term to distinguish their practice from the simple back-
projection of present political belief upon the text not uncommon
among older Marxist critics, and at the same time, from a
straightforward, prospective utopianism also endemic to Marxism.
Their utopianism expresses itself not in projection, forward or back-
ward, but in nostalgia, literally understood as a communitarian longing
for home, for an England that in certain respects once was and might be
again.

This New-Historicist nostalgia should also be distinguished from
that of the old. For Renaissance scholarship, particularly that devoted
to unearthing the medieval roots of the Elizabethan drama, has often
been the medium of historicist nostalgia. 'There was once a theatre in
these islands', writes Glynne Wickham in the preface to his *Early
English stages, 1300–1600*, 'whose stage was the world instead of a
drawing-room and whose players were men and women, body and
soul, of every walk of life instead of two or three gathered together for
luncheon, high tea or even for a cocktail party' (Wickham 1966, p. ix).
Wickham's privileging of the native and medieval above the
cosmopolitan and modern (hence the snide allusion to Eliot) suggests
the nostalgic, nationalist – and not infrequently jingoistic – motives of
so much of the older historicism, so different from those of the new.
From the textualist viewpoint of the latter, Wickham's account of
English theatrical history is a myth of presence akin to that of the
'Merrie England' of which Professor Welch's lecture in *Lucky Jim* is the
comic *locus classicus*.

The consequences for cultural materialism of its open textualisation
of history and culture now become clear – by contrast with an older

empiricist and a newer structuralist version of them – and come home to roost. Wholly undeluded that the story they tell can be anything other or more than a 'text', cultural materialists – unlike their empiricist and Marxist precursors and even their structuralist counterparts – have abandoned all hope of re-entering the past or reconstructing it in its 'reality'. The abandonment of that nostalgia for 'historicity' is important, for once 'history' is framed as a textual and discursive construct never again to be confused or equated with the past 'itself' but separated from it for ever by the 'difference' of textuality, the only story that *can* be told becomes 'only a story'. There can be no more accounts of or appeals to an 'authentic' past on which a present political standpoint or future political programme with special claim to validity or necessity can be based.

For such a 'textualist historicism' there can be only 'readings'; if 'discursive knowledge' is all that it claims, then the only validity it can hope or long for will consist not in an objective or transhistorical 'truth' but in its communal acceptance: the truth of 'conventionalism', not of 'empiricism' or 'realism'. Hence the peculiar nature of cultural-materialist nostalgia, with its longing not for the historical *presence* of the past, but for the social coherence it reads out of it, and hopes to find again in the future. In Barker's reading of *Hamlet*, for example, the play stages through its action the conflict of two discourses: an older discourse of embodied, externalised presence, of 'spectacular corporeality', informing the opening court scene in the royal 'presence-chamber', and a newer discourse of modern, interiorised subjectivity foreshadowed in Hamlet's comments to his mother – 'I have that within which passes show' – and further explored in his soliloquies. It is entirely consistent with the cultural-materialist position, I am arguing, that Barker's interpretive energies and sympathies are clearly on the side of the older public discourse of embodiment and presence – itself a discourse of 'conventionalism'.

His antipathy to the newer discourse of subjective interiority struggling in and through Hamlet to emerge – and shifting uncertainly between distinct modes of expression – is registered as much in the imagery of traumatic violence – itself recalling the Jacobean drama – that characterises his prose as in its explicit statement:

That the body we see is so frequently presented in fragments, or in the process of its effective dismemberment, no doubt indicates that contradiction is already growing up within this system of presence, and that the deadly subjectivity of the modern is already beginning to emerge and to round vindictively on the most prevalent emblem of the discursive order it supersedes. (Barker 1984, pp. 24–5)

In the case of Hamlet, his ironic image of himself as a 'pipe' to be manipulated and sounded marks the metaphysical hollowing of a fully signified, because public and embodied, selfhood and the emergence of a modern and disembodied self-consciousness: 'this interiority remains in *Hamlet*, gestural . . . at the centre of Hamlet, in the interior of his mystery, there is, in short, nothing' (pp. 36–7). Yet there is still hope; for 'despite the violence unleashed against the body, it has not yet been quenched. However much it has been subsequently ignored, it remains in the texts [of Jacobean drama] themselves as a vital, full materiality' (p. 25).

If this newer discourse of interiority has been denied the status of 'transcendental' – or 'central' – signified ascribed to it by so much modern criticism, that status has been effectively re-assigned to the older discourse of presence, an inversion of privilege made possible only by reading strenuously against the grain of the text. That is, the privileging of an older cultural semiotics of extroverted fullness and presence above a more precocious semiotics of inward subsidence and subjective slippage is itself peculiarly modern, and is already represented within the play, but represented *ironically*. For Claudius's enactment of the panoply of signified monarchy, his full-dress instantiation of the king's two bodies, *is perceptibly an enactment*, a rhetorical and theatrical mimicry of a discourse and a ritual existing in the play not 'authentically' but only in the mode of recollection, that is, at a distance and in the past, if not in the 'mind's eye' or memory of Hamlet alone. And in re-enacting them, Claudius hollows them out further, whether or not they were always already hollow.

At the same time, Hamlet's descent into the new selfhood of interiority is represented as a quest for a basis for action more 'authentic' than that of the familial, social, or dramatic – i.e. public but *in*authentic – roles available to him and insouciantly (and disastrously) played out by the Polonius family. Through his indictment of the disembodied subjection of our bourgeois contemporaneity, Barker seems to express – a bit like Hamlet himself at times – a kind of nostalgia for feudalism: if not for its punitive regime of split noses and mutilated ears as such, at least for the clarity and publicity of the thoroughgoing and fully social subjection they signify. Do we really

want to return to corporal punishment, let alone to the older social
order figured, with grim irony, in the 'old commandant' and his
'infallible' judicial machinery in Kafka's *The penal colony* – even if we
could?

In Belsey's work, too, the thoroughgoing 'conventionalism' of the
older social and institutional order is also privileged, but it is the regime
of scholasticism rather than feudalism. From her opening analysis of the
discursively regulated instabilities of the hero in *The castle of per-
severance*, a later, empirical construction of the subject is implicitly
under attack, not merely for its anachronistic distortion, through its
own self-projection, of the older drama under scrutiny, but for the
selfhood that it projects: 'In the problematic of discursive knowledge
understanding is a preparation for the dissolution of the self. It is
empirical knowledge which promises dominion. In empiricism as Locke
would define it,' she concludes, 'the subject of humanism takes, in
effect, the place of God' (Belsey 1985, p. 74). Whereas in Foucault's
work all epistemes are created morally equal, even if that means equally
oppressive and objectionable, in Belsey's they are clearly not.

The 'discursive knowledge' institutionalised in medieval scholasticism and bearing the *imprimatur* of Church and State is *good*, i.e.
ideologically sound, because within it the subject is socially constructed
and defined. It is the 'empirical knowledge' newly available to the
ambiguously sovereign subject that is *bad*, i.e. ideologically unsound,
because, no longer regulated by a monologic social authority, it is
potentially unbounded and anarchic and, in its untrammelled individualism, plumes up the will to God-like power. Between the lines of
Belsey's consistent privileging of 'discursive' over and against 'emprical'
knowledge lurks a nostalgia for a universal and absolute social
authority long since unavailable, presumably for the reasons she
explicitly traces. In a study that ostensibly, even ostentatiously, celebrates 'difference' on its title-page, the undeclared object of desire is
'identity', defined no longer individualistically, to be sure, but *socially* –
as if that made all the difference. Do we really want to bring back
censorship, the Index, the Inquisition – let alone 'God'?

For such an ideological apparatus is surely what it would take to
regain for 'discursive knowledge' – however re-defined – its lost status,
and to maintain it, once regained, in place. It is thus no accident that a
pre-modern 'discursive knowledge' tends to be privileged within
cultural-materialist criticism; for once the move into textualism has

been made, that is the only kind that is available to it, even potentially: a knowledge that consists in the consensus of an 'interpretive community' rather than in correspondence to a reality outside discourse. If empirical science represents – or once represented – the paradigm-case of the latter kind of knowledge, then that of the former must be (and for some still is) religion. The thought is not quite as discouraging as it sounds, since an independently verifiable knowledge has never been necessary for political change, provided communal assent could be achieved. As Fulvia Morgana, the Marxist semiotician in *Small world*, astutely replies when asked 'What follows if everybody agrees with you?': 'What follows is the Revolution' (Lodge 1984, p. 319).

Strange as it may sound, we are not very far from the poetics and politics of – at last he can be named – F. R. Leavis. What links so apparently ill-sorted a trio as Leavis, Barker and Belsey is not only their common desire for a restored univocality of the sign, poetic and social, but their nostalgia for a time when it is supposed to have actually existed. For Leavis, that univocality, which went under such names (some of them borrowed from Eliot) as 'realisation', 'unified sensibility', and 'tradition', was grounded in the vision of the 'organic community' that was supposed to have existed before the 'dissociation of sensibility' set in during – when else? – the seventeenth century. In Belsey's nostalgia for England's future, in contrast to Leavis's, the key term is 'discourse' rather than 'sensibility', and the communitarian vision is systemic rather than organic, a matter of active cultural production rather than serene natural growth. These displacements having been registered, the similarities between her cultural materialism and Leavis's essentialist humanism are as striking as their differences.

It is surely significant in this connection that the opening essay in the founding number of *Scrutiny* was entitled 'A note on nostalgia'. Though not by Leavis but by D. W. Harding, it argued that social nostalgia – as distinct from psychological regression – could legitimately combine with 'realism' in preferring the past while resolving to act in the present. Leavis too held this view, that 'the memory of the old order [of the "organic community"] must be the chief incitement towards a new, if ever we are to have one'.[9] Formed in the depths of an economic depression that made the incitement of a 'new order' seem an urgent necessity to many others as well, Leavis's social vision was so near and yet so far from that of the Marxists with whom he could never quite come to terms. While insisting that his project was one of social

reform, the role of 'high culture' in general and 'literature' in particular
as the means to that end grew to such proportions as to become an end
in itself and an insuperable stumbling block to any possible merger
with the Marxists. For them, the key to a 'new order' was to be found
not in the cultural superstructure but in the economic base of society;
and not in the past but in the future.

That moment of high Marxism, at once 'humanist' and 'scientific',
has passed; yet for a current generation of Marxist academics, post-
imperial and post-industrial Britain is no less in crisis now than it was
in 1933, and the need for a 'new order' no less peremptory. If an older
vision of proletarian revolution arising from the imminent collapse of
capitalism – once thought an historical inevitability predictable by
'objective', 'scientific' analysis – has come to appear an all but forlorn
hope, the Marxist project has not been abandoned but re-conceived.
Having withdrawn its faith in the 'realism' of economic neces-
sitarianism, post-structuralist Marxism has re-invested it in the 'conventionalism' of ideological criticism, through which a progressive
community of the future can be educated in a certain reading of the
textuality of the past. While this metamorphosis of Marxism from an
'historical' into a 'cultural' materialism has raised problems of historical validation and political agency, it has certainly not spelled the end
of Marxism. Perhaps an older claim to scientific 'truth' could be confidently maintained only as long as science itself could make the same
epistemological claim, and that moment might also have passed.

Yet the new problems arising from a 'textualist' or 'contextualist' –
and inescapably 'conventionalist' – reading of history and literature
cannot be ignored or dismissed either. While the perpetuation of
the class structure – and struggle – virtually guarantees cultural
materialism a significant 'market share' in the teaching of literature,
this should not exempt its practitioners from concern over the
weakened philosophical basis for the historical claims they still want to
make – unless they are content to preach only to the converted, i.e. their
own 'interpretive community'.[10] To accept the relativism of their position – 'pluralism' is its cultural and institutional extension – would be
not only to abandon the 'struggle', but to invite extinction at the hands
of a dominant culture only too ready to dismiss all historical and
literary studies as a luxury society can no longer afford. How much
easier for it to do so when the 'knowledge' delivered by the latter is only
a 'reading', a matter of opinion or interpretation. Whether one is

interested primarily in the political or the philosophical dimension of historical texts – or sees them as inextricable – the problem of 'conventionalism', with its inescapable relativism, looms large at a moment when the value of studying those texts within an increasingly reactionary culture is an open question.

Notes

1 Since Jean E. Howard pointed it out (1986), the reluctance of the movement to *theorise* its own practices has often been remarked. This reluctance was understandable and excusable, given the eclecticism and pragmatism of its project. The reluctance to *historicise* itself, though also understandable and excusable, given the demystifying thrust of that project, is now beginning to be overcome: see Wayne 1987; Cohen 1987; and Montrose 1986 and 1988.

2 For a lucid exposition of 'empiricism', 'realism', and 'conventionalism' as they have emerged in the history and philosophy of science, and a useful application of these concepts to cultural studies, see Lovell 1980; see also Rorty 1982. Whereas Lovell is concerned to avoid the relativist dangers of 'conventionalism' for Marxist aesthetics, Rorty is unworried by these consequences for the 'neo-pragmatism' he advocates. The uncertainty of New Historicists themselves concerning the conventionalist status and implications of their enterprise is epitomised by Stephen Greenblatt in his introduction to *Renaissance self-fashioning*: 'The significance [of sixteenth-century texts] for us is not that we may see *through* them to underlying and prior historical principles, but rather that we may interpret the interplay of their symbolic structures with those perceivable in the careers of their authors and in the larger social world as constituting a single complex process of self-fashioning' (Greenblatt 1980, pp. 5–6). No less delicately balanced, and ultimately no less non-committal is Montrose in 'Professing the Renaissance': 'The post-structuralist orientation to history now emerging . . . may be characterised chiastically, as a reciprocal concern with the historicity of texts and the texuality of history. By *the historicity of texts*, I mean to suggest the cultural specificity, the social embedment, of all modes of writing – not only the texts that critics study but also the texts in which we study them. By *the textuality of history*, I mean to suggest . . . that we can have no access to a full and authentic past, a lived material existence, unmediated by the surviving textual traces of the society in question' (Montrose 1988, p. 20).

3 This basic difference is at last beginning to come home: 'In the British cultural context the field of literary criticism periodically takes on the appearance of a battleground on which a struggle is waged for control over the representational power of texts that are understood to be the nation's cultural patrimony – for better or worse' (Wayne 1987, p. 52).

4 For an extensive bibliography of the New Historicism, see Cohen 1987, pp. 39–47. The studies named above are cited only for their formulaic titles, which may owe as much to the *imprimatur* of the university presses under which most works of American – as distinct from British – New-Historicist studies first appeared, as to the conventions of the doctoral dissertation. Of course the two have been mutually sustaining in America for decades. The academic specialism of American New

Historicism is paradoxical, to say the least, in view of its wider political concerns. In America, where the academic system is so vast and complex as to constitute a social order unto itself, the political impulse tends to be confined and absorbed within the system, becoming 'institutional politics' or a politics of the subject, while any potential impact on the wider society is thus defused. If this proves to be the case with the New Historicism, it will be a striking example of the success of that 'strategy of containment' which Greenblatt and others identify as a ubiquitous feature of Elizabethan culture, yet on which they remain strangely silent concerning its operation in their own. The new discourse of 'power' may well signify, within such a reading of the present, a displaced expression of institutional impotence on the part of left-wing humanists, and the thoroughgoing academicisation in America of that discourse of power, a structural guarantee of their and its continuing marginalisation: 'But if new historicist reductions of Shakespeare to an agent of royal power are hard to defend in the context of the Renaissance, they acquire a certain logic and justification in the context of the present . . . New historicism should accordingly be seen as a form of leftist disillusionment. From this perspective it is possible to account for . . . the abiding concern with state power; and for the strangely quietist feel of these radical critiques' (Cohen 1987, pp. 36–7). The British situation is, as we shall see, wholly different.

5 See especially Tillyard's *The Elizabethan world-picture* (1943) which has become a recurrent target of New Historicist attack.

6 'Unlike Marxism [New Historicism] does not complement a lateral or horizontal approach with a vertical one: new historicism described historical difference, but it does not explain historical change' (Cohen 1987, p. 33). The antagonism between structuralist and historicist, synchronic and diachronic, approaches has long been recognised, particularly but not exclusively by Marxist critics. Montrose, for example, acknowledges the ahistoricity of structuralist analyses but still seems to think that more micrological historical and cultural studies modelled on Foucault can escape this structuralist limitation (1986, pp. 2–4). Yet Foucault's archaeologies of discourse have themselves been criticised – again, mainly by Marxist commentary – for the absence of any account of the transition from one discursive formation to the next: 'The emergence of such discourses is historically grounded in relatively perfunctory ways. Such discourses are concurrently in verbal, social, and material formations. But the whole question of process, of passage from one such problematic to the next, is left in abeyance' (Porter 1983, p. 180).

7 See Widdowson, ed. 1982. British New-Historicist studies, with their active, present-participial tendency, carry a similar message. Such titles might once have struck an American eye as not only unacademic but positively 'journalistic', though lately they have begun to be imitated. In Britain, as opposed to America, an intimate relation still obtains – even in the case of left-wing scholarship such as we are considering – between the academy and a wider public sphere of journalism, politics, and the media, by-product perhaps of a smaller and more strongly class-articulated society. Concomitantly, the university presses have never achieved the virtual monopoly on scholarly publication that they have in America, perhaps because the doctoral dissertation is a relatively recent innovation as a professional requirement. All but one of the British studies mentioned above were issued by commercial or 'trade' publishers, most of them highly aggressive and profitable. Their titles may also

suggest a marketing style aimed at an audience of student and 'general' readers broader than that of the libraries and scholars who purchase such books in America. Indeed, the role of Methuen (now Routledge) alone in mediating between the academy and the public sphere is a topic that deserves scholarly treatment in its own right.

8 The term 'cultural materialism', and its basic theory and practice, derive from the later work of Raymond Williams (1977). Its application to Renaissance literature is discussed in the introduction to Dollimore and Sinfield, eds. 1985.

9 Leavis and Thompson 1933, p. 97. Quoted and usefully situated by Mulhern 1979, p. 59.

10 This concern is sometimes registered by the cultural materialists themselves: 'While a genuine difficulty in theorizing "the text" does exist, this should not lead inescapably to the point where the only option becomes the voluntaristic ascription to the text of meanings and articulations derived simply from one's own ideological preferences. This is a procedure only too vulnerable to pluralistic incorporation, a recipe for peaceful co-existence with the dominant readings, not for a contestation of those readings themselves' (Barker and Hulme 1985, p. 193).

Towards a postmodern, politically committed, historical practice

JEAN E. HOWARD

The material describing the Essex Symposium brought four terms into conjunction: *postmodernism, Marxism, history* and *the Renaissance*. I think the 'power term', the one marked as threatening to throw the others into disarray, was *postmodernism*. The workshop seemed set up to ask: doesn't postmodernity throw Marxism into crisis and with it a certain view of history that has made political critics wrongly believe they produce an emancipatory and definitive knowledge of the past, in the form of an historical 'period' called 'the Renaissance', or, indeed, an emancipatory and definitive knowledge of the present? I want to add a fifth term, *feminism*, to the four on the table, my chief reason being that feminism, as a vibrant, varied and rapidly changing form of oppositional knowledge, may have the greatest potential to prevent postmodernity from entailing the delegitimisation of a politically committed historical practice; on the contrary, feminism seems poised to enlist the resources of postmodernity for the strengthening of just such a project.

I thought twice before entering this fifth term, *feminism*, into the workshop's deliberations, partly because it is all too predictable for a body sexed female to step forward to speak 'for woman', thereby essentialising woman, erasing all the material differences that keep women from an easy sisterhood, and turning feminism from a political to a biological or sociological position. Moreover, such gestures smack of the politics of 'me-tooism'; don't leave me (i.e., women) out. While it is absolutely right that feminist concerns should not be disregarded, begging for space at the pluralist table misrepresents the value of feminist thought in addressing the central concerns of the workshop. In its rapid development in the last twenty years, feminist knowledge has become something quite other than the patronisable stepchild of the academy. I write from within a feminist problematic – not so much to find the nonfeminist guilty, again, of acts of exclusion, but to argue that feminist thought offers resources one needs in thinking the question of how to address the problem of history in the postmodern moment.

Feminism is positioned to take on this issue productively in part because of its striking history of self-transformation and self-critique. Like Marxism, feminism is more than an academic movement. It's a social movement with an academic component, and, like Marxism, it is fuelled by an emancipatory telos: i.e., the end of oppression and exploitation based on gender and sexuality. But, as I hope to make clear in this chapter, both how to understand this goal and how to achieve it are issues constantly redefined and reformulated under the pressure of unpredictable historical change; and this dialectical process puts a premium on the production of new knowledges striving to be adequate to current needs. Feminism largely lacks masters to whom one must be true; the unity of its multiple manifestations comes from a shared political goal. Feminism is therefore best understood as a changing ensemble of practices and assumptions unified by the overarching goal of ending oppression by gender, but this ensemble of practices will be varied, and even contradictory in its strategies, precisely because they are developed in relation to a changing set of historical circumstances and deployed at different cultural sites. If Kristeva taught us to recognise the several 'moments' of feminism, Toril Moi has shown that these moments do not follow one another in a neat teleological progression, but overlap (Kristeva 1981, pp. 13–35; Moi 1988, esp. pp. 5–7). I am going to be arguing that feminism currently embraces several positions or moments in regard to the question of history, but that a distinctively postmodern feminist position is emerging and provides a way of thinking an address to history committed to an emancipatory politics without being committed either to Enlightenment epistemology or discourses of truth.

A final word by way of introducing the chapter and my own interests in our collective project. I see many of the same problems facing postmodern Marxism and postmodern feminism, partly because both are declared political movements owing much to the very Enlightenment traditions of thought which postmodernism critiques. Each must therefore rethink its traditional investment in absolute truth claims, in the validity of totalising master-narratives, in a politics based on the volition of rational, unified subjects capable of achieving a scientific, objective knowledge of the world. Each also must confront the limits of an agenda for social change focused solely on one axis of oppression. This much said, it is clear to me that in the United States feminism is a much more broadly based social movement than Marxism. If one hopes to effect social change in the USA, feminism arguably offers the most powerful possibilities for beginning to do so. I therefore have an interest, in several senses, in developing the radical possibilities of feminism as a mode both of making knowledge within and without the academy and of engaging in other socially trans-formative practices. In this chapter I therefore direct my attention primarily to the ways in which postmodern feminist thought provides resources for continuing – on new terms – the project of a politically committed historical practice. And while I hope what I have to say about postmodern feminism will have indirect bearing on the problems and possibilities of postmodern Marxism, the working through of the interarticulations of these two movements does not lie within the scope of this chapter. I also wish to take up feminist concerns in this paper because in the United States debates about the historical address to "the Renaissance" have in part been shaped by what has been seen as a split between New Historicist and feminist interests. From the terrain of a politically committed, postmodern feminism, I will re-examine the terms of that debate to get at what I see as the limits both of humanist feminism and also of an historicist practice tentative about its own political agenda.

I Postmodernism and the threat to humanist politics and positivist history

Perhaps no contemporary concept has been so variously defined, so contested, as *postmodernism*. Its two parts – *post* and *modernism* – seem to indicate postmodernism's temporal relationship to something – i.e., modernism – prior to it in time. Yet for Lyotard and others, postmodernity sometimes figures as a recurring condition, fixed to no historical time period, which can give rise to modernism, the relationship between the two being something like that between the sublime or the unrepresentable and that condition of representability figured as modernism. For other theorists, such as Fredric Jameson,

postmodernity marks an historical moment; it is the cultural logic of
late capitalism linking first and third worlds in new relations of
domination and dependency and producing new forms of diffused,
affectless subjectivity. For Jameson, postmodernity is not a style that
can be assumed, but a constellation of discourses and practices unique
to a particular moment in the history of capitalism and the social
relations it materially produces (Jameson 1984, esp. p. 85).

Right at the outset, then, postmodernity as a term raises questions of
history: is postmodernism a recurrent possibility within all periods and
systems of representation? or is it most meaningful as a designation for
phenomena arising within a particular set of determinate historical and
material conditions? Jennifer Wicke in 'Postmodernism: the perfume
of information' (1988) critiques certain theorists of postmodernity,
including Lyotard, for a dehistoricising inattention to the global
material conditions and divisions of labour producing aspects of contemporary Western postmodern culture and for locating a positive
alternative primarily in the aesthetic realm: in the recurrent possibility
of achieving 'the sublime' through great art. To make her case, Wicke
describes the conditions of young Asian women who, for low wages and
to the nearly universal detriment of their eyesight, assemble the tiny
components of the electronic equipment essential to the new 'age of
information'. In one factory, these young women are urged each month
to take part in a beauty contest where the prizes for winning are bottles
of Western perfume. Encouraged to see themselves not as workers, but
as sexualised women-to-be-married when their temporary stint in the
factory is over, these new subjects of Western patriarchal capitalism are
doubly and triply disabled by their overdetermined positioning within
race, gender and class hierarchies. Wicke's point, and a good one, is
that the West's contemporary culture of information rests on an international and exploitative division of labour unique to this historical
conjuncture and invisible to many Western theorists of postmodernity, rendering inadequate interventions aimed only at aesthetic
disruptions of systems of representation in the West and rendering
problematic the equation of contemporary conditions of postmodernity and the conditions of other historical moments. What
results, Wicke implies, is an erasure of historical difference, an ethno-
centricism resulting from a blindness to the 'third world' site of production in an insistent focus on the Western site of consumption, and a
severe limitation of the range and effectivity of political practices

possible within contemporary culture.

As a critique of certain dehistoricising and aestheticising tendencies in some analyses of postmodernity, Wicke's work is invaluable, but only by indirection does it imply what *would* constitute an oppositional practice adequate to the conditions of contemporary postmodernity or how to undertake the more limited project of producing oppositional histories within that moment. Moreover, if one wishes as I do to use postmodernism as a term designating a constellation of practices, discourses and social relations inhering within a particular historical moment, it must be said that as a marker of a chronological time period, postmodernism is a problematical category for all the reasons one finds it risky to homologise and essentialise any historical 'period'. Residual and emergent elements exist alongside dominant strands of a culture. Certainly modern and postmodern elements are thoroughly mixed in contemporary American culture. Postmodernity, therefore, while useful as a way to designate certain dominant and emergent elements in late capitalism, cannot be used to essentialise and totalise the current historical moment. Rather, postmodernity specifies a constellation of discourses and practices, unique to the contemporary moment but not defining it totally, which stand in a relation of difference to discourses and practices which may be chronologically deployed alongside them, but which entail different assumptions about epistemology, rationality, the self-subject, and the relationship of popular to élite culture, etc. For the moment, I want to examine the consequences of certain strands of postmodern thought for the writing of history.

In this regard, perhaps most crucial is postmodernity's challenge to the idea of the rational self, fully present to itself and able to make absolute truth claims on the basis of empirical knowledge of the real or to employ master-narratives about the real which aspire to the status of science. Recognising no outside to ideology, no discourse of science which would, for example, allow something like false consciousness to be revealed to the subject from a position of truth, postmodernity admits no means of disentangling knowledge from power or a stable and unified self from the network of contradictory discourses which constitute subjectivity in historical time. In a wonderfully simplifying phrase, Donna Haraway argues that what is ruled out of court in the postmodern moment is "the god trick" (Haraway 1988, p. 598), by which she means a mode of seeing that pretends to be outside and above the phenomena seen and capable of delivering a true and total picture of those phenomena. In 'Postmodernism and gender relations in feminist theory' (1987), Jane Flax, in part influenced by Lyotard, offers one account of what is involved in postmodernism's critique of the 'god tricks' of Enlightenment philosophy and historiography. She lists eight beliefs thrown into doubt by the conditions of postmodernity. In shorthand form these include belief in the existence of a stable, coherent self; belief in reason to provide an objective, reliable and universal foundation for knowledge; belief in the equation of reason and truth; belief in the transcendental and universal qualities of reason; belief that the right use of reason guarantees autonomy and freedom; belief that reason can arbitrate conflicts between truth, knowledge and power; the belief that science, as the exemplar of the right use of reason, is the paradigm for all true knowledge; the belief that language is transparent (Flax 1987, pp. 624–5).

It is by now a commonplace to say that the erosion of such tenets of Enlightenment thought puts both traditional politics and traditional historiography under pressure. If one has no unmediated access to the real, including past reality, what is to keep the past from being other than a fiction woven from the language games of the present? If subjects have no access to true knowledge, why should one ideologically motivated narrative have priority over others? And if subjects cannot stand outside discourse and ideology in the place of scientific reason and objectivity, what is to ground a politics, understood as any attempt to act upon the world to make it 'better'? Is there any unmediated, 'enlightened' position from which to specify that 'better'?

These are some of the questions, it seems to me, that have made many proponents of historical and political criticism, including many Marxists and feminists, eschew engagement with postmodern philosophy and cultural analysis as inimical to their work. Feminists such as Carol Neely, for example, argue that the grounds for a feminist critique of patriarchy and the necessary concept of oppositional agency are undermined if belief in a centred, rational self is given over (Neely 1988, p. 13). Even Fredric Jameson, whose attitude to postmodernity is complex and not entirely condemnatory, argues that as the cultural logic of late capitalism, postmodernity functions to produce a framentation of subjectivity and a loss of historical understanding that make collective resistance to oppression extremely difficult (Jameson 1984, esp. pp. 58–73). Postmodernity can be taken to imply, then, the end of politics, at least of a politics based on the agency of unified, rational selves who can recognise the truth of the world and persuade others of that truth. And it can seem to mean the end of historical inquiry, at least if it is understood as the quest for true, objective knowledge of the past.

In the third part of this chapter I will specify why some feminists embrace postmodernity, finding in the acknowledgement of constructed, non-unified subjectivities a release from essentialist conceptions of woman and in the critique of scientific reason and totalising master-narratives a disassembling of some of the most powerful vehicles for women's oppression and for the suppression of heterogeneity and difference.[1] I believe that while postmodern thought undermines some understandings of politics and history it opens new possibilities as well, possibilities for overcoming the dead ends of essentialist identity politics and scientism, for example, and opens space for a more mobile political practice justified less in terms of absolute truth claims and more in terms of its historically determined efficacy in attaining specific ends. In short, as Hal Foster and others have argued, part of what is happening at the present moment is a struggle over whether postmodernism will become associated with reaction or resistance, with the end of history and politics or with their fruitful reconceptualisation (Foster 1983, pp. xi–xii). In the third part of this chapter I will look at postmodern feminism's role in the latter project, but first I want briefly to glance at some of the ways feminists have in the last twenty years intervened in the production of history and to comment briefly on the local struggle between American New Historicists and feminists over 'the Renaissance'.

II Feminism and the question of history

No group has been more attentive to the negative consequences of traditional modes of historical analysis than feminists, and I wish to construct a brief genealogy of their interventions into the writing of histories in the last twenty years in order to specify some of the resources feminism can bring to bear on the question of what constitutes an adequate historicism for progressive politics at the present moment. One thing I wish to stress is the dynamism of feminist historicism during this period and, at the same time, the contradictions within feminist practice and the immense amount of effort required to keep the radical insights of feminist practice from hardening into new versions of a belief in 'true history'. From its early moments, feminist cultural analysis interrupted the dominant conventions of historical inquiry by calling attention to the fact that most accounts of culture were histories of one gender. Histories purporting to tell the truth, the whole truth and nothing but the truth were, under the pressure of feminist critique, revealed as both partial and interested. What resulted from the 1960s on was an explosion of work aimed at displacing androcentric histories which involved both writing women into history and reconceiving the very categories within which historical inquiry would proceed. When Joan Kelly asked, for example, whether there was a Renaissance for women, she questioned the very periodisations and the labels by which history had been divided into discrete 'blocks' and the changing experience of dominant groups of males taken as demarcating the essential turning points of history (Kelly 1984, esp. pp. 19–22). As feminists such as Sandra Harding and Joan Scott have made clear (Harding 1986, esp. pp. 58–110; Scott 1988, esp. pp. 28–50), feminist inquiry can mean much more than simply adding women to existing paradigms of writing history. It can refigure and has refigured those paradigms, deconstructed established oppositions (public versus private, for example), and forged new ways of understanding what constitutes the central social relations and institutions of culture.

This work has truly radical implications for beliefs about true and objective history since it reveals the interests which go into the construction of particular historical narratives, at the same time that it reveals the extent to which truth is a political as much as an epistemological category. What can be recognised as true depends, crucially, on the politically determined horizons of legitimacy prevalent at any historical conjuncture. Part of the feminist struggle, then, has been the labour of shifting, contesting and displacing oppressive understandings of what constitutes legitimate historical inquiry and knowledge. And this process has no end because it occurs in history and has to be responsive to changing conditions and political needs.

In effect, of course, the displacement of androcentric historical narratives has not always been carried on in tandem with a critique of the very idea of 'true' histories. Sometimes the attempt to write women into history has been carried on in the name of 'recovering' voices hitherto 'lost to history' but restored by the labours of feminists to their places in the historical record or the literary canon. The very idea of 'recovery' implies a stable something to be seen, grasped, or understood prior to its constitution in the investigator's discourse; and it implies, as well, that what is lost might be entirely recovered or restored, and a true and total picture of society delivered up. In short, a feminist historicism beginning with the recognition of the partial and interested nature of masculine history can, sometimes unintentionally, end up sounding as if feminist history is, by contrast, true and total, rather than, in its own way, partial and interested.

Moreover, the philosophical problems attendant upon trying to get the 'full picture' by recovering woman and her experiences and adding them to the historical record are compounded if this quest has as its goal the recovery of what is uniquely feminine – *her* voice, *her* nature, *her* mode of cognition. Critiques of essentialism are by now too well-established to need rehearsal. In their discussion of feminism and postmodernism, Nancy Fraser and Linda Nicholson point exactly to the residual essentialism lurking in the many attempts to define *the* origin or cause of patriarchal oppression (Fraser and Nicholson 1988, p. 95), and Judith Newton and Deborah Rosenfeld have cogently argued that positing the eternal and unchanging difference of woman from man not only means writing unhistorical history; it also means writing a feminist version of tragic history in which woman is endlessly written as victim, and in which gender difference becomes the unvarying ground of gender domination (Newton and Rosenfelt 1985, esp. pp. xvi–xvii). In regard to first-generation Renaissance feminist work, Jonathan Goldberg has pointed out how essentialist assumptions about binary sexual difference limit, historically and politically, the work of certain feminist critics of Shakespeare (Goldberg 1985, esp. pp. 116–18).

Consequently, a second moment of feminist historical work has turned away from ahistorical theory building (the quest, above all, for a single, transhistorical explanation for patriarchy) and away from the valorisation of essential female difference and has devoted itself to elaborating the variety of ways in which gender difference has been culturally and historically constructed. This work has been accompanied by the recognition that even within a single historical period, women are not quite all sisters in any simple sense, but bear the plural marks of difference in their various inscriptions within systems of race, class, ethnicity and sexuality. Consequently, cultural studies seem now very much in the era of the transdisciplinary microhistory. Impelled strongly by Foucauldian genealogical projects and their instantiation

in new historical practice, cultural critics are engaged in establishing
with great particularity how various social groups, including women of
particular classes and ethnicities and sexual orientations, are constituted as subjects through the overdetermined discursive networks of
a given historical conjuncture. I think it is fair to say that the extent to
which feminists have availed themselves of Foucauldian techniques of
historical investigation varies very much from field to field. In nineteenth-century studies, the work of Nancy Armstrong, Mary Poovey,
Judith Walkowitz and Catherine Gallagher, among others, has given a
strong feminist cast to the analysis of dominant and subordinated
discursive practices and cultural institutions. In fact, Judith Newton
has argued in 'History as usual?' that many of the techniques and
assumptions of new historicist practice have long been part of certain
kinds of feminist work, and she resents the construction of an
exclusively masculine genealogy for this movement (Newton 1988,
'History as usual?', esp. pp. 87–106). I am not so certain of the
accuracy of the argument that in every instance 'women were there
first', but it does seem to me that there is in theory no necessary
disjunction – at least for the present historical moment – between
feminist work and such basic tenets of new historicist practice as the
assumption that subjectivity is socially constructed, that the
reconstitution of the past is never separable from the interests and
present positioning of the inquirer, or that no texts exist 'beyond
ideology'. Ideally, such new historicist tenets should have emancipatory consequences for gender inquiry. Among other things, arguing
that gender difference and systems of domination and exploitation are
culturally produced makes it in theory possible to argue that they can
also be altered, though obviously only within the historically specific
conditions of possibility obtaining at any conjunctural moment.

What is clear, however, is that in Renaissance studies in America a
happy convergence of feminist and New Historicist concerns hasn't
quite occurred. There are exceptions to everything I am now going to
say. Karen Newman (1987 and 1989) uses new historicist methods and
assumptions in her feminist work on Shakespearean drama, and Louis
Montrose (1988) often makes the critique of Renaissance hierarchical
gender relations a major part of his New Historical practice. But as
recent essays by Carol Neely, Lynda Boose, Marguarite Waller, and
Peter Erickson make clear, many American Renaissance feminists read
new historicism as a masculinist practice striving to gain dominance in

Renaissance studies and to marginalise feminist concerns. About this reading of Renaissance New Historicism I have three things to say. First, it is no secret that many American Renaissance New Historicists are men and that the analysis of gender has often not been central to their work or has been subsumed under other concerns. To that extent 'the Renaissance' produced by New Historicism reveals itself to be a partial and interested construction demanding feminist critique and rewriting. And that rewriting is especially crucial as it bears on the question of resistance and opposition. As many have noted, many New Historical narratives of Renaissance culture focus on the ways dominant power maintains and reproduces itself (Cohen 1987, esp. pp. 35–7). They do not examine how and when it fails. It is in the interests of feminists to provide such accounts. Second, it is also no secret that much early American feminist work in Shakespeare studies, in particular, was committed to a humanist conception of the unified self and to an unhistoricised and essentialist approach to gender difference. From a New Historicist perspective, and from the perspective of a feminism like my own, both materialist and postmodernist, such a critical practice seems both theoretically and historically inadequate. British feminists such as Lisa Jardine and Kathleen McLuskie (Jardine 1983a, pp. 1–8; McLuskie 1985, pp. 88–92) have already lodged this critique of American feminist work on Shakespeare. Third, real changes have occurred in the work of both groups in the last several years, making these well-rehearsed charges and countercharges seems like out-of-date news. One wonders whose interests are served by the perpetual staging of a New Historicist/feminist 'split'? Whatever their differences, and I don't mean to minimise the importance of these and will, in fact, speak more about them in a moment, New Historicists and feminists are for the most part linked by their opposition to the 'universal, above-ideology' version of Shakespeare and other texts of Elizabethan 'golden age' culture. Both politicise literature; that is, both look at how literary texts produce, manage and sometimes destabilise the power relations of given cultures. They make it difficult to go on teaching literature as the simple expression of the best that has been said and thought with no acknowledgement of the social struggles attendant on the production of canonised 'thought' and no acknowledgement of the different ways various social groups might define 'best'. As versions of political criticism, feminism and New Historicism are more threatening when presented as contestatory allies than as enemies. The constant staging of a New Historicist/feminist 'split' may in the long run only serve the interests of those who want to reinstall 'great' literature above politics. Rather than play into a scenario in which political critics savage one another to the delight of those who wish a plague upon all the 'power people' (Marxists, feminists, New Historicists), I hope for what I would call a contestatory alliance among these groups, an alliance marked by ongoing mutual interrogation in the interest of strengthening the political analysis of past and present.

In the field of Renaissance studies, feminists have been able to learn from New Historicism, despite their critiques of it. The reverse, however, *should* be, and I hope *is*, increasingly true,[2] partly because feminism possesses what New Historicism most crucially lacks: a declared political telos which can serve as the new grounds for an historical practice which has severed itself from absolutist truth claims without succumbing to relativism or pluralist indifference about 'the matter of history'. And now my story loops round to what was promised at the beginning: an account of the usefulness of postmodern feminism for furthering the project of a politically committed, postmodern historical practice. In part this means taking seriously, and taking further, New Historicist assertions that histories of the past *can* never be disentangled from the concerns of the present, and feminist assertions that they never *should* be.

III   Beyond New Historicism: postmodern feminism and the historical project

I begin by reasserting that one of the greatest strengths of feminist work is the continuing assumption, sometimes blunted, but never entirely lost, that questions of political need and efficacy are tightly bound up with the question of how and why one writes historical criticism and historically based cultural analysis. Why do it? What is the goal or telos of such work? That question has to be asked and re-asked, with the recognition that the answers will shift and change as the horizons of (ideological) understanding and historical possibility shift. I therefore agree with Chantel Mouffe's view in 'Radical democracy, modern or postmodern?' that what endangers politics in the first instance in the postmodern moment is giving up all belief in the Enlightenment project of freedom and equality for all, which I interpret to mean a giving up of the specification of an emancipatory, if provisional, telos for one's work. What endangers an *adequate* politics, however, is believing, now, that the achievement of freedom and equality for all can be accomplished by reliance on Enlightenment epistemology and foundational discourses (Mouffe 1988, p. 34). In essence, what Mouffe wants to do is to retain the political goals of the Enlightenment while critiquing Enlightenment means of attaining those goals and, in her case, of course, this means a continuing critique of many of the teleological, deterministic, positivistic strands of classical Marxism. I hasten to add, however, that freedom and equality are not self-evident, ahistorical concepts. It is too simple merely to say we retain the Enlightenment goals of freedom and equality for all without saying how profoundly what can be signified by those terms is transformed within a postmodern problematic. For example, freedom can hardly mean freedom to find or know a 'real' self, nor can it mean the attainment of a state outside of ideology and its material instantiation in discourse. Moreover, as Wicke's essay suggests, postmodernity makes imperative a global analysis of the new conditions under which freedoms for some are premised on international division of labour requiring the enslavement of others. As middle-class American feminists rightly struggle against unequal divisions of labour within the home and unequal access to opportunities in the workplace, their relative freedom from material want in the brute form, for example, of hunger, depends on a level of prosperity shared with middle-class men that does not bear an innocent relationship to the absence of such freedom among the 'third world' societies where American electronics companies are so eager to build their factories and assembly plants. How does one specify adequate goals for feminist practice within the complex conditions of late capitalism?

I will return to this question – the most crucial of all – in a moment. But I want to emphasise that the crucial point Mouffe raises is the necessity of having a goal or telos, itself a subject of contest and debate, to organise the critique of present practices and the institution of alternatives. Whether, for example, for feminists the conditions of late capitalism privilege struggle in the domain of ideology or in economic or political spheres, and whether the alleviation of gender oppression and exploitation can be achieved without the alleviation of other kinds of exploitation as well: these are questions currently energising feminist debate and resulting in sharp divergences in feminist practice. But what unifies such disunity – and what defines a self-consciously political criticism – is the assumption that critical practice takes shape in the gap between what is and what might be, with the proviso that our understanding of what might be is constantly being reformulated in history and through historical engagements.

As a number of commentators have noted, while New Historicists repeatedly acknowledge that there are no innocent and objective histories, they are much less prone than either Marxists or feminists actually to talk about the political goals of their criticism or the contemporary determinants of their work. This can be read as a sign of intellectual sophistication, as well as modesty, since the political intentions of a writer are hardly the same thing as the political consequences of her work, and since blindness is inevitably the condition of the subject of ideology. We are all as much determined, as determining, entities. Moreover, one cannot assume that appropriation and domestication can be avoided or purity attained simply by declaring a progressive political purpose for one's work. There is a particular ugliness to self-righteous moralising. However, there are consequences of *not* declaring one's position, not foregrounding the contemporary scene of writing. One consequence is to make partial and interested histories turn back, in effect, into versions of true and complete histories. What we get are 'accounts of the past', rather than histories marked as reconstellations of the past generated for their significance to the present and its struggles over meaning and legitimacy (Arac 1987, p. 6). In the opening moments of New Historicism in Renaissance studies, the histories generated by Greenblatt, Montrose and others were so unlike 'normal' accounts of Renaissance texts that their disruptive effect was immediately felt. Literature was being politicised; the barriers between élite and popular texts broken down; humanist ideas of selfhood questioned. Now, of course, precisely because of the vigour of this initiative, it has in some quarters become a machine for producing the new kind of naturalised knowledge. There is no longer anything shocking about reading high and low texts in conjunction with one another, or talking about the contradictions in the discourses forming the emergent bourgeois subject. I want to argue that this appropriation of New Historicism for business as usual is abetted by the attenuation of New Historicist discourse about its own political agenda. The key question is: why do this work of rewriting the Renaissance? And what political imperatives in present history (other than professional avantgardism) require the rewritings to be rewritten? Unwittingly, while stressing the political nature and political consequence of all discourse but locating the object of investigation safely in the past, New Historicists can make it seem, again, as if in the present we seek disinterested truth, while in the past 'they' were endlessly implicated in power. To my mind this is one of the unintended, but potentially conservative, consequences of New Historicist practice, as it is of feminist work that simply presents itself as a 'recovery' of the past.

Before going on, let me be clear that I do not think I am placing on New Historicism a demand it does not itself invite. A critical practice so centrally committed to the political consequences of all discourse cannot, it seems to me, be reticent about the political ambitions and consequences of its own. But though it is risky and in some sense vulgar and in some sense impossible to declare the political ambitions of one's work, I think it remains important to write from an identifiable somewhere for an identifiable purpose.

Donna Haraway in her essay 'Situated knowledges: the science question in feminism and the privilege of partial perspective' brilliantly critiques 'the god trick of seeing everywhere from nowhere' (1988, p. 581) and so being accountable for nothing. To be an unmarked term, a disembodied, all-seeing, hidden eye, is one of the oldest ploys of domination, silently naturalising a partial perspective as a universal or total perspective. To write or act 'from somewhere' and 'for something' entails becoming visible and becoming accountable. It cannot ward off ideological blindness or guarantee truth, but it can begin to make some dimensions of blindness visible by opening a particular discursive site to interrogation from other sites both within and without the larger feminist project. Situated political practice therefore invites its own perpetual revision and reconstitution in historical time. It invites the supersession of its own most cherished premises in the interests of furthering a larger telos.

But what would it mean to write and work and produce histories of the past from a situated position and for some identifiable goal within the conditions of postmodernity? The dangers and problems are legion. Once one acknowledges the multiple positions from which knowledge is made and the loss of a ground of absolute truth, how does one avoid mere relativism and the loss of politics which always involves exclusions, choices and privileging of one perspective over another? Once one acknowledges the illusionary nature of a self who could know and own even its own 'experience' or 'body', how can one speak of working from a position without lapsing back into essentialism? Feminists are struggling with these issues, and I believe they take us to the very frontiers of thinking about the possibilities of a political postmodernist critical practice.

Haraway's idea of 'situated knowledges' will take us some of the way, I believe, toward a provisional answer to some of the questions outlined above. Haraway, of course, cannot 'stand for' all of postmodern feminism, but she is usefully representative of those tendencies within postmodernist feminism that continue to insist on the need for an overarching goal for feminist work, the attempt to imagine and to construct less oppressive worlds, while eschewing the Enlightenment dream of a master discourse, true for all and for everywhere, which can map the world objectively, and eschewing the Enlightenment dream of self-present individual subjects with access, through reason, intuition or science to truth. With some modifications, her idea of situated knowledges can begin to suggest what a politically committed historical practice might look like.

First of all, to work avowedly within a situated project of knowing means eschewing claims to see everything as if one were located outside of history, as if one were an omniscient, disembodied god. Feminists make feminist knowledge, not all knowledge; and they do so within the determinate ideological parameters of a specific time and place. The acknowledgement of the partial nature of all projects of making knowledge and organising praxis is, however, absolutely essential to accountability, for accepting the consequence of working from one discursive site, one situated place, and not another. For Haraway and many other postmodern feminists, acknowledgement of the many different positions from which knowledge can be made does not lead to pluralist indifference. Since different projects of knowing have such different consequences, which gains primacy and authorises action cannot be a matter of indifference. Simply put, preferred knowledges and practices are those which lead to the alleviation of oppression and exploitation. While what those knowledges and practices are will of necessity be a matter of contestation, even within feminism, and can be determined only in relation to specific and changing historical circumstances, the criterion itself remains fixed: a touchstone for keeping political work honest, flexible and situated in relationship to its motivating telos.

The second important point is that any situated production of knowledge, including feminist historiography and science, cannot arise from unmediated access to one's 'experience' or to one's 'identity'. Rather situated knowledge is a product of struggle, analysis and collective praxis.[3] It is not individual or personal knowledge, and so has nothing to do with naive forms of essentialist identity politics. A situated project of knowing and acting articulates neither the truth of a self nor the truth of everyone; it articulates a discursively generated and historically specific position which cannot be guaranteed by recourse to any transcendental or absolute grounds and which must constantly be refashioned under the pressures of historical contingencies.[4]

Where I part company with Haraway is in her lingering insistence that to work and write from the situation of the subjugated provides, in and of itself, a more objective picture of the world than to work and write from the unmarked position of the dominator (pp. 583–4). For me, all claims of greater objectivity are problematic, a way of reinstalling within postmodernist practice the discredited desire for transcendental guarantees of truth. I would frame the difference between knowledge made from the position of the dominator and that made from the position of the dominated in terms of their relative *effects*, not their relative *objectivity*. What privileges feminist historiography, for example, is its effects or consequences in disrupting and displacing historical narratives which at the crudest level erase women subjects and so further, in the present, an androcentric, oppressive understanding of the world. I hasten to add, however, that while political usefulness or efficacy are necessary, they are not sufficient criteria for a postmodern feminist political practice, including the writing of history. Like any collective project of making knowledge, feminist work has to be accountable to internal standards of coherence and adequacy to 'the facts' as they are known. Postmodernism does not mean the disappearance of the 'real', but rather of a belief in true, complete and unmediated accounts of that real. In producing accounts of the real, in contest with other accounts, feminists face a double imperative: to produce a politically necessary knowledge of the real, and what that means has to be determined historically, and to do so rigorously, all the while recognising that there are not absolute or neutral standards of evidence or agreements on what constitutes 'facts'. In producing its accounts of the real, feminist knowledge can neither escape the demand for 'accuracy' and 'coherence' nor give over the struggle to make the definition of these terms a matter of contestation and political struggle.

I hope it is beginning to be clear why I said at the beginning of this chapter that the resources of feminism could help to overcome the impasse that might be signalled by the conjunction of the terms *postmodernism, marxism, history*, and *the Renaissance* and why I said, in the middle of this chapter, that postmodern feminism could lead beyond new historicism. Neither politics nor the production of knowledges of the past are negated or cancelled by postmodern assaults on master-narratives, absolute truth claims, and the rational, self-present subject. But they have to be re-understood in a world of lost grounds, lost guarantees. Feminists, having seen women erased, 'othered', or essentialised by the old regimes of truth, are perhaps not so unsettled as some by the displacement of these regimes. Because it has always produced knowledge for political ends – to alleviate oppression and exploitation – feminism is less likely than other projects of knowing to slip into relativism when faced with the disappearance of absolute guarantees, with the death of God and the godlike capacity to see everywhere from nowhere. Instead, feminisms are situated and partial knowledges committed less to some standard of unchanging truth than to the unending struggle to remain adequate to changing historical circumstances in pursuit of their political telos. As Tony Bennett says, writing of Marxism and its encounter with post-structuralism:

> socialism can extricate itself from the mire of epistemological and ethical relativism only by means of a political desire which functions as cause and justification of itself (although it is, of course, produced by and within the complex play of social forces and relationships) and which supplies the criteria – always contested – for the determination of the ends to which political and theoretical practice are directed. If that's not felt to be enough, I would ask: what other foundation could there be which is not a demand for transcendence and which – in order to preserve things as they are – simultaneously denies the possibility that such a demand might ever be realised. (Bennett 1987, pp. 66–7)

As part of the struggle to avoid such paralysis, feminists must continue to write histories of the past, not from some belief that one can ever 'get it right', but because representations of the past (histories, readings of 'old masters', stagings of Shakespeare) continue to authorise action in the present and to constitute the categories and assumptions through which contemporary subjects live their relations to the real. How often, for example, are particular constructions of 'Shakespeare' used to legitimate some observation about 'human nature' or the near absence of women from conventional histories of art and literature used to justify the argument that women haven't the capacity for true genius?

Feminists must continue to provide counterknowledges – knowledges made from different places than those occupied by white, male, heterosexual subjects. The conditions of postmodernity, however, bring new demands to feminist practice. In the 'age of information', for example, there is a particular urgency to understanding the new modalities (advertising, cinema, Western wire services, rock videos) through which people are colonised and subjects made complicit with their own subjugation in non-coercive ways. But, and this is part of Wicke's point, it is also important to realise that old modes of oppression and domination still continue, in tandem with the new, in both the first world and the third, though the economic exploitation of a "third world" woman in a Singapore electronics factory may be invisible to Western eyes, feminist though those eyes may be. One of the dangers inherent in postmodernity's undermining of master-narratives is that all knowledges will become purely local knowledges, all politics a politics of microsituations. In the attempt to redress universalist and essentialist accounts of woman, feminists, for example, have increasingly produced carefully historicised examinations of particular categories of women and of particular productions of gender difference. The gains are obvious, the costs less so, though foremost among the costs I would cite a limitation of explanatory range and a subsequent limitation of the possibilities for significant, wide ranging political interventions based on these analyses. Paradoxically, in calling for situated projects of knowing, I may seem to be calling for work that will further the fragmentation of social analysis in the contemporary moment and so for a further blunting of the reach of political action.

My intentions are quite the contrary. A situated project of knowing is not inherently limited in scope; rather, it places limits on objectivist and foundationalist claims to see the social whole from a privileged vantage point *outside* the field of analysis or to be able to map the social whole definitively, that is, so that no remappings, no contesting mappings, are necessary or possible. Beginning 'in the midst', a situated project of knowing acknowledges the interestedness and the historicity of its constructions and categories, but does not, on that account, leave off the work of producing and refashioning them in pursuit of its telos and in historical contestation with other projects of knowing.

Materialist feminism is one such situated project of knowing, opposed to the class reductionism and economic determinism of classical Marxism but committed to the materialist position that oppression, whether by gender, race or class, involves more than 'prejudice', but is instantiated in exploitative divisions of labour, in unequal access to cultural resources (money, birth control, technical training, leisure). Consequently, interventions to alleviate oppression consist in changing not only 'minds', but also 'practices', not only systems of representation, but also systems of production and reproduction. Knowledge made from such a situated position willingly forgoes claims to provide a definitive map of the social whole or to do so from an imaginary point of disinterested objectivity. Rather, a postmodern materialist feminism offers accounts of the real which have value as emphatically 'situated' accounts that offer an alternative to common sense, the logics of domination.

At the moment, as Jennifer Wicke implies, an urgent task for feminism is to forge a new logic of interconnections in a world in which the global reach of late capitalism is accompanied by, in fact depends upon, fragmentation: of subjectivities, knowledges, polities. To the extent that an emphasis in postmodern discourse on micropolitics and local knowledges blocks analysis of macrostructures of exploitation and domination on a global scale, to that extent it becomes complicit with techniques of domination prevalent in late capitalism. An alternative logic of interconnections will provide, by contrast, a knowledge of the links between various modalities of oppression within a culture and between cultures in the global village. That means being attentive to international divisions of labour and to the different positions of masculine and feminine subjects within those divisions at different points in a world economic system.[5] It means being attentive, however, not only to how surplus labour is differentially extracted from subjects stratified by race and gender as well as by class, but also to the role of ideology in constructing exploitative and oppressive social relations in the supposedly 'private' domains of sexuality, domestic life and biological reproduction as well as in the supposedly 'public' domains of work and social reproduction. This seems to be what Nancy Fraser and Linda Nicholson are heading towards when they call for postmodern feminism to employ 'large narratives'. Writing of Lyotard they argue that his work rules out of court 'one familiar and arguably essential genre of political theory: identification and critique of macrostructures of inequality and injustice that cut across the boundaries separating relatively discrete practices and institutions. There is no place in Lyotard's universe for critique of pervasive axes of stratification, for critique of broad-based relations of dominance and subordination along lines like gender, race, and class' (Fraser and Nicholson 1988, p. 89) – and, I would add – for the analysis of interconnections among these axes. The point, according to Fraser and Nicholson, is not to confuse these provisional and historically specific narratives with foundational metatheory. These narratives, too, can be a form of situated knowledge, the forging of a new ground for knowing from the intersection of several once separated discursive sites. To locate this emergent project in relation to a genealogy of feminist interventions, one could say that if the task of feminism was once to write woman into history and so to displace androcentric narratives, then to write her into history in all of her multiplicity and historical self-difference, and so to displace essentialist narratives, a task of the future is to write her into history in a way that sets her subordination and her empowerment in relation to other axes of oppression and empowerment in a global context, and so displace narratives of atomisation. Such writing, of course, will not yield us the truth of the past or present, but it might yield a knowledge adequate to the political needs of present struggles. And that, I think, is what is required, along with a willingness to give over these histories when they, too, have become a form of naturalised knowledge no longer answerable to emergent political urgencies.

Notes

1 Flax is typical of postmodern feminism in sensing that 'the way(s) to feminist future(s) cannot lie in reviving or appropriating Enlightenment concepts of the person or knowledge' (Flax 1987, p. 625) and that 'transcendental claims reflect and reify the experience of a few persons – mostly white, Western males' (p. 626).

2 Consider, for example, Louis Montrose's recent statement that 'it is Feminism and the Women's Movement which in recent years have provided the most powerful infusion of intellectual and social energy into the practices of cultural critique, both written and lived' and his acknowledgement of a 'tendency in much New Historicist work produced by American male academics to displace and contain its own cultural politics by at once foregrounding relations of power and confining them to the English past that is presently under study' (Montrose 1988, p. 26).

3 For a nuanced discussion of the role of theory in constructing a position from which cultural analysis can proceed, see Resnick and Wolf 1982.

4 As Tony Bennett writes, in regard to Marxist theory: 'It is only by being ongoingly revised that a body of theory retains any validity or purchase as a historical force. To

construe the relations between the formulations of classical Marxism and those which have been developed in the wake of structuralism as if the latter could be assessed in terms of the degree of their fidelity to or compatibility with the former would be unduly restricting. That way, a body of theory could never be allowed to develop other than via the germination of the seeds of development sown during the crystallising phase of its inception – a profoundly unhistorical conception of the ways in which theoretical ideologies are adapted to changing theoretical and political circumstances. Rather than testing the value of theoretical innovations via such backward-looking glances, the acid test should always be: What do they enable one to do? What possibilities do they open up that were not there beforehand? What new fields and types of action do they generate? (Bennett 1987, pp. 63–4).

5 For an ambitious attempt at such a narrative of interconnections see Maria Mies, *Patriarchy and accumulation on a world scale: women in the international division of labour* (Mies 1986).

'No offence i' th' world':
Hamlet and unlawful marriage

LISA JARDINE

Ham.	Madam, how like you this play?
Queen.	The lady doth protest too much, methinks.
Ham.	O, but she'll keep her word.
King.	Have you heard the argument? Is there no offence in't?
Ham.	No, no, they do but jest – poison in jest. No offence i' th' world.[1]

This piece is part of the groundwork for a larger project on the relationship between cultural history and textual studies.[2] It is therefore both exploratory and incomplete – characteristics which will, I hope, make the work available for use by others besides myself who are trying to make explicit some of the assumptions behind recent historically-based text-critical practice. The aim is to set up a dialogue with others writing similarly reflectively – an aim which was the starting-point for the Essex Symposium for which an earlier draft of this chapter was written.[3]

As a start, the remarks which follow are prompted by my reading of a helpful article by David Simpson, entitled 'Literary criticism and the return to "history" ' (in double inverted commas).[4] It is that 'return to', and then "history" in double inverted commas, in his title, which immediately takes my attention. And indeed, Simpson sets out to show that

> the status of historical inquiry has become so eroded that its reactive renaissance, in whatever form, threatens to remain merely gestural and generic. 'History' promises thus to function as legitimating any reference to a context beyond literature exclusively conceived, whether it be one of discourse, biography, political or material circumstances.[5]

In other words, he believes that many so-called historicist critics are using the catchword 'history' to mask a quite conventional (and conservative) commitment to a set of unscrutinised, idealised premises about a past already modelled to the ideological requirements of the present.[6] The implication of that idea of 'return', then, is that there is something retrograde, and above all something *positivistic*, about the undertaking – that is, that in invoking history we are privileging something called 'facts' or 'real-life events', whereas in truth we are all now supposed to know that there are only texts, that our access to facts and to history is only and inevitably textual.[7]

I start my own argument by making it clear that I do not regard the present endeavour as either a turn or a *return*. I do not think that we should let the marketing tag, 'new' (targeted at eager academic consumers, after the latest product), suggest fashionable change, any more than we should allow 'historicist' to suggest retroactive, backward-looking positivism (once historicism always historicism). What we should be looking at, I suggest, is the converging practices of social historians, intellectual and cultural historians, text critics and social anthropologists, as they move together towards a more sensitive integration of past and present cultural products. It is to this generally progressive trend or development that I consider my own work belongs.[8]

Both historians and text critics have learnt a lot from recent literary theory. We do, indeed, now begin from that position of understanding that our access to the past is through those 'textual remains' in which the traces of the past are to be found – traces which it will require our ingenuity to make sense of. Nevertheless, it is by no means the case that this inevitably leaves us in a position of radical indeterminacy. In fact, I begin to believe that it only appears to lead us in such a direction if we are committed (wittingly or unwittingly) to the view that what textual remains yield, in the way of an account of the past, is evidence of *individual subjectivity*. In this case, indeterminacy is apparently doubly inevitable. For what we recognise as individual subjectivity is the fragmented, partial, uncertain, vacillating trace of first-person self-expression. And if we take on board Stephen Greenblatt's suggestive idea of *self-fashioning* – an aspiration on the part of the individual, embedded in past time, towards a coherence of self, which is inevitably endlessly deferred, and historically incomplete – it can be argued that what the cultural historian can retrieve and reconstruct of the past will of necessity be correspondingly incomplete and indeterminate. Here, Greenblatt's primary model is an anthropological one, his methodology that of the social anthropologist (and with it some of his assumptions about the strangeness of other selves).[9]

But those of us who are committed to social and political change may consider that we have another agenda altogether, the focus of which is *group* consciousness (and intersubjectivity).[10] In my recent work, I have emphasised that the specified ground for my own textual and cultural interpretations is a strongly felt need to provide a historical account which *restores agency to groups hitherto marginalised or left out of what counts as historical explanation* – non-élite men and all women. And since that means the focus of my critical attention is social relations within a community, the shaping of events in telling the tale is part of the given of the kind of excavation of the past I am engaged in.[11] In other words, I find that I am able to accommodate competing accounts of a set of textually transmitted events (competing versions of what makes collections of incidents in past time culturally meaningful), without discarding as illusory the lost incidents in past time which gave rise to them. That is a methodological matter to be negotiated, the very fabric out of which perceived social relations are constructed, not a break-down or paradox within the community as such. Texts may be *generated* by individual, gendered selves, but we may nevertheless choose to give our attention to the way in which in any period, membership of a community is determined by a shared ability to give meaning to the shifting unpredictability of everyday life. This is the group consciousness on which social practice depends, and which provides the boundary conditions for individual self-affirmation and action.

'Restoring agency' is, for me, a matter of countering the apparent passivity of non-élite groups within the historical account. But this needs a little further glossing. The counter-position to passivity (by implication, powerlessness), is *active participation*, but not (without falsifying the account) *power*. In my recent exploration of the defamation of Desdemona in *Othello*, I was not able to give back to Desdemona *power* to accompany her activity – but I was able to reposition our attention in relation to the events which take place on the stage, so that representation no longer overwhelmed the interpersonal dynamics of an early modern community to which the text gives expression.[12] In so far as I was successful, this retrieval of agency for Desdemona was achieved by my treating the individual subject in the drama as a 'cultural artefact':[13] the play gives us a tale of Desdemona's actions in the (then) recognisably shared terms of the early modern community. We can retrieve that recognition, I argued, by juxtaposing the tales told in contemporary court depositions (where the recognition of the *infringing* of shared codes of behaviour is the essence of the story) with the dramatic text – both being 'performances' before 'audiences' in that same community. Our access to something like 'who Desdemona is' is given by learning to 'read' in the social relations dramatised, those situations which were meaningful – which established or expressed Desdemona's relationship to her community in ways acknowledged as socially significant. Those 'events' (as I choose to call such socially meaningful sets of relationships) are the expressed form of Desdemona's 'lived experience', and I mean that, since in my view it will not make a significant difference whether the 'person' who is presented via this shaped version of experience is real or fictional.[14]

What distinguishes this kind of retrospective critical activity from that of the social historian, I think, is that we want to position ourselves so as to *give meaning* to early modern agency, not simply to record it, to show that it was there. As Geertz says:

> We are seeking, in the widened sense of the term in which it encompasses much more than talk, to converse with [our 'native' informants], a matter a great deal more difficult, and not only with strangers, than is commonly recognized. 'If speaking *for* someone else seems to be a mysterious process,' Stanley Cavell has remarked, 'that may be because speaking *to* someone does not seem mysterious enough.'[15]

Or as Greenblatt puts it – consciously alluding to the Geertz, as he specifies his own methodological starting-point:

> I began with the desire to speak with the dead.
> This desire is a familiar, if unvoiced, motive in literary studies, a motive organized, professionalized, buried beneath thick layers of bureaucratic decorum: literature professors are salaried, middle-class shamans. If I never believed that the dead could hear me, and if I knew that the dead could not speak, I was nonetheless certain that I could re-create a conversation with them.[16]

What distinguishes the kind of analysis I am after, in the new 'inter-discipline' I see my work as moving towards, from much literary criticism, and from much recent text criticism, is that it seeks to engage with the *external manifestations* of selfhood. It does not treat the 'lived experience' of the individual, as something with which the modern critical self can engage, and which it can make meaningful in its own terms. Nor does it posit an unchanging human nature immune to local circumstances, which it is the critic's task to retrieve.[17]

This brings me to a crucial distinction which in the consideration I shall be giving to *Hamlet* I shall particularly need to sustain, between the version of the term 'subject' which my own approach addresses, and the one which I introduced earlier – individual internalised selfhood (of which the related term 'subjectivity' is symptomatic).

The form that the pursuit of the 'lived experience' or untramelled universal selfhood in textual criticism currently takes is grounded in psychoanalytical theory. It is the pursuit of a gendered first-person, authentic utterance – a discourse which inscribes the individual's unique experience of reality. The *subject*, in this sort of textual study, *is* that first-person discourse – which is the only access we have to individual selfhood.[18] And this discourse, which inscribes the individual's experience and determines her selfhood, is a discourse of desire and sexuality. And since this symbolic construction of the subject depends on a sign system which the receiver of the discourse shares with the discourser, subjectivity, in so far as it is grasped and understood is transhistorical.

In Greenblatt's pioneering work, this pursuit of the psychoanalytical subject via psychoanalytic theory coexists with the methodology of social anthropology.[19] The individual critic acknowledges the distance which separates him from the discoursing subject in past time; he (*sic*) attempts to 'speak with the dead'. It follows that the *terms* of the dialogue he establishes are those which he can 'hear' as the textual trace of selfhood, within his own discursive formation: desire and sexuality. By reaching back into texts which preserve desirous discourse in the early modern period, the new historicist critic retrieves those sign systems which he (from his own position in time and culture) can recognise; it is those shared discursive strategies which are, for him, all we can know of selfhood in past time.

The drawback in such an approach for the feminist critic is that sexuality is explicitly assumed to code 'power' in ways which lead to the *subjection* of women (no longer *qua* women, but ostensibly as *standing for something else*) – even (ironically, and anachronistically) the subjection of Elizabeth I to her desirous male subjects.[20] But the main point to note is that, on this account of subjectivity, the 'actual' is coextensive with what two discourses *share* – a matter of intertextual identity. This is, in my view, a fundamental difficulty for such a theory, and its methodology of power relations and subjectivity construction, when we are trying to deal with an inaccessible historical past, and particularly when we are trying to recover female agency from the cultural traces of the past.[21]

Which brings me finally to the problem of 'feeling', and our access to it, in *Hamlet*. Hamlet's feelings towards his mother Gertrude were already described in recognisable terms of incestuous desire in the classic 1919 article on the play by T. S. Eliot:[22]

> The essential emotion of the play is the feeling of a son towards a guilty mother ... Hamlet (the man) is dominated by an emotion which is inexpressible, because it is in *excess* of the facts as they appear.... Hamlet is up against the difficulty that his disgust is occasioned by his mother, but that his mother is not an adequate equivalent for it; his disgust envelopes and exceeds her.[23]

This is an appropriate starting point, both because this idea of excess has been a feature of all *Hamlet* criticism since Eliot, and because it already makes clear that an account of Hamlet's 'excessive' feelings in terms of *desire* (inexpressible emotion), immediately makes concrete and specific his *mother* as focus of attention for her *guilt* – she is pronounced guilty not as a judgement on her actions, but as a condition of her presence in the play in relation to Hamlet (thus textual rather than historical in my sense). If Hamlet's feeling is excessive it is because his sense of his mother's guilt exceeds what could possibly fit the facts of the plot: the guilt of a mother who has stimulated sexual desire in her son. Here 'desire' is taken in the psychoanalytic and deconstructive sense, and is not an event but (according to Lacanian theory (and then Derrida)) a permanent condition of language, with regard to which Hamlet adopts a particular (problematic) orientation, one which produces mothers as guilty of arousing excessive desire in their sons.[24]

If desire is taken to be 'a permanent condition of language', then the analysis of the subject, and the interpretation of the text (in our case, the text of *Hamlet*) tend increasingly towards one another. In a recent article entitled 'Sexuality in the reading of Shakespeare', Jacqueline Rose writes:

> The psychoanalytic concept of resistance ... assumes that meaning is never simply present in the subject, but is something which disguises itself, is overwhelming or escapes. Freud came to recognize that its very intractability was not a simple fault to be corrected or a history to be filled. It did not conceal a simple truth which psychoanalysis should aim to restore. Instead

this deviation or vicissitude of meaning was the 'truth' of a subject caught in the division between conscious and unconscious which will always function at one level as a split. Paradoxically, interpretation can only advance when resistance is seen not as obstacle but as process. This simultaneously deprives interpretation of its own control and mastery over its object since, as an act of language, it will necessarily be implicated in the same dynamic.

In both *Hamlet* and *Measure for Measure*, the play itself presents this deviant and overpowering quality of meaning which appears in turn as something which escapes or overwhelms the spectator.[25]

And if we add the increasing interest of some critics in social anthropology, and in kinship systems as reflected in social forms, including language, the collapse of (specifically) 'incest' from a specified, forbidden sexual union into a universal tendency towards non-conforming, problematic forms of desirous social relationships (manifested above all *in language*) is complete. In his recent book, *The end of kinship: 'Measure for measure', incest and the idea of universal siblinghood*, Marc Shell writes:

I have tried to bring to light a literary tradition associating physical and spiritual kinship and to suggest the manifestation of this tradition in the politics of the modern world. . . . [This] project involves reconsidering the polarity or the opposition between ascent into kinship and descent from kinship (or between incest and chastity) just as though 'the way of descent and the way of ascent were one and the same.'

Some literary works display an inescapable vacillation between such descents and ascents, a vacillation from which society as we know it begins in an archaeological sense. Such vacillation takes place in *Hamlet*, where the hero thinks both about descent into incest or parricide, which he both desires and fears . . . and also about ascent into universal kinship. . . . The movements to and from absolute chastity and unchastity (incest), taken together, lend credence to a discomforting thesis: that there is no ultimately tenable distinction between chastity and incest, so that our ordinary understanding of marriage – as a middle way or as an adequate solution to the difficulties posed by society's exogamous need for an intersection of intertribal unity and intertribal diversity – is mistaken.[26]

I am not pretending, here, to cover this issue adequately. But I use this abbreviated discussion as a way of distinguishing 'subjectivity' approaches from my own approach, focused as it is on *agency* and *event*, in terms I outlined at the beginning of this chapter. In my terms, what is striking in the play *Hamlet* is that Hamlet does not sleep with Gertrude; there is no incestuous 'event' in the play, between mother and son, to match the excessive emotion on his side, and the excessive guilt on hers.[27] *Claudius* sleeps with (marries) Gertrude, and it is in fact on her sexual relations with *him* that Hamlet's excessive emotion concerning Gertrude is focused. And the point about Claudius's marriage to Gertrude historically (as event) is (a) that it is 'unlawful' and (b) that it deprives Hamlet of his lawful succession. So I first turn my attention to what constituted unlawful marriage in the early modern period, and then show how the social relations of the play are altered if we put back the Gertrude/Claudius marriage in history – reinstate it as event – and look at the *offence* that it causes to Hamlet.

'Unlawful marriage', in early modern England, was a matter for the Ecclesiastical Courts. It is a key feature of the church canons (the legislation in canon law) that someone is *offended* by incest/unlawful marriage. As the 1603 canons put it:

> If any offend their Brethren, either by Adultery, Whoredome, Incest, or Drunkennesse, or by Swearing, Ribaldry, Usury, or any other uncleannesse and wickednesse of life, the Church-wardens . . . shall faithfully present all, and every of the said offenders, to the intent that they may be punished by the severity of the Lawes, according to their deserts, and such notorious offenders shall not be admitted to the holy Communion till they be reformed.[28]

And the crucial passage on incest itself in these canons runs:

> No person shall marry within the degrees prohibited by the lawe of god, and expressed in a table set forth by authority in the year of our lord 1563; and all marriages so made and contracted shall be adjudged incestuous and unlawful, and consequently shall be dissolved as void from the beginning, and the parties so married shall by course of law be separated. And the aforesaid table shall be in every church publickly set up, at the charge of the parish.[29]

Two depositions from the Durham Ecclesiastical Court Records, concerning an 'unlawful marriage' (around 1560) show clearly how this idea of 'offence caused' has a bearing on individual cases brought to the notice of the church courts:

> EDWARD WARD of Langton near Gainford husbandman, aged 40 years.
> He saith that ther is dyvers writing hanginge upon the pillers of ther church of Gainford, but what they ar, or to what effect, he cannott deposse; saing that he and other parishioners doith gyve ther dewties to be taught such matters as he is examined upon, and is nott instruct of any such.
> He saith, that he was married with the said Agnes in Gainford church by the curat Sr Nicholas, about 14 daies next after Christenmas last past, but not contrary to the lawes of God, as he and she thought. And for the resydew of the article he thinks nowe to be trewe, but not then. Examined whither

that he, this deponent dyd knowe at and before the tyme of their mariadg, that she the said Agnes was, and had bein, his uncle Christofore Ward's wyfe, ye or no, he saith that he knew that to be trew, for she had, and haith yet, fyve children of his the said Christofer's. Examoned upon the danger of their soules, and evyll example, he saith that both he and mayny honest men in that parish thinks that it were a good deid that thei two meght still lyve to gyther as they doo, and be no further trobled. + AGNES WARD, ALIAS SAMPTON, aged 40 years.

– all the Lordship and paroch of Gainford knew howe nighe hir first husband and last husband was of kyn, and yet never found fault with their mariadg, neither when thei were asked in the church 3 sondry sonday nor sence – they haith bein likned [linked?] to gither more and 2 yere, and yett never man nor woman found fault – but rather thinks good ther of, bicause she was his own uncle wyf.+[30]

The purposive narrative of these depositions is not difficult to unravel: Edward Ward's marriage to his uncle Christopher Ward's widow, Agnes, is incest under ecclesiastical law, but 'mayny honest men in that Parish thinks that it were a good deid that thei two meight still lyve to gyther as they doo, and be no further trobled', and, as Agnes testified, everyone in the parish knew 'howe nighe hir first husband and last husband was of kyn', 'and yett never man nor woman found fault'. Not only did no one find fault; they 'rather thinks good ther of, bicause she was his own uncle wyf'.

Church law holds the marriage unlawful; Christian charity suggests that no one is harmed by the marriage, and widow and children are appropriately cared for. The 'dyvers writing hanginge upon the pillers of ther church' that Edward Ward refers to are the 'table [to] to be in every church publickly set up, at the charge of the parish', specified in the 1603 canons quoted above: the tables of consanguinity and affinity which specified who might legally marry whom (as Edward Ward clearly deposes, he himself is illiterate, and unable to read the tables). And we may, I think, extend the idea of 'offence caused' one stage further. *Someone* had to draw the marriage to the attention of the courts; that person had to be someone to whom the 'unlawfulness' of the marriage gave some (material) offence.[31] This charge laid by another is what is referred to (but permanently uninterpretable without information now lost to us) in the sentence in Edward Ward's deposition: 'And for the resydew of the article he thinks nowe to be trewe, but not then'.[32]

If we look at the Levitical degrees, the tables of consanguinity and affinity, we see how these already incorporate the idea of 'offence caused'. 'Consanguinity' conforms broadly with what we might expect: a man may not marry his mother, his father's sister, or his mother's sister, his sister, his daughter, or the daughter of his own son or daughter.[33] The table of consanguinity prohibits marriages with close blood ties, in the generations in which it might plausibly occur (parent, sibling, offspring, grandchild). The table of affinity, by contrast, reflects unions which might produce conflicting inheritance claims.[34] A man might not marry his father's wife, his uncle's wife, his father's wife's daughter, his brother's wife, or his wife's sister, his son's wife, or his wife's daughter, nor the daughter of his wife's son or daughter. None of these are blood ties, but each creates complications over the *line*. In particular, the marriage of a widow to her dead husband's brother threatens the son's inheritance claim. The son is first in line, his father's brother second; the marriage of the dowager widow to the second in line threatens to overwhelm the claim of the legitimate heir.

Notoriously, Henry VIII's marriage to his dead brother Arthur's widow, Catherine of Aragon, was incestuous under the Levitican tables of affinity.[35] Since Claudius's marriage to Gertrude is, like Henry VIII's, a marriage to a dead brother's widow, there is no doubt in the play of the incest, and Hamlet states the case directly:

> Let me not think on't – Frailty thy name is woman –
> A little month, or ere those shoes were old
> With which she follow'd my poor father's body,
> Like Niobe, all tears – why, she –
> O God, a beast that wants discourse of reason
> Would have mourn'd longer – married with my uncle,
> My father's brother – but no more like my father
> Than I to Hercules. Within a month.
> Ere yet the salt of most unrighteous tears
> Had left the flushing in her galled eyes,
> She married – O most wicked speed! To post
> With such dexterity to incestuous sheets![36]

The ghost of Hamlet senior puts the case more forcefully still, but unlike Hamlet, gives the active part in the incest entirely to Claudius:

> Ay, that incestuous, that adulterate beast,
> With witchcraft of his wit, with traitorous gifts –
> O wicked wit, and gifts that have the power
> So to seduce! – won to his shameful lust
> The will of my most seeming-virtuous queen. . . .

> O horrible! O horrible! most horrible!
> If thou has nature in thee, bear it not,
> Let not the royal bed of Denmark be
> A couch for luxury and damned incest.[37]

An offence – incest – but (as in the case from the court records), some anxiety as to *who* has been materially offended. In kinship terms there is an offence. It goes unrecognised until someone claims it as such.

Kinship and inheritance are remarkably strong themes in the play from its opening moments.[38] Young Hamlet is heir to Old Hamlet, just as young Fortinbras is heir to Old Fortinbras: *he* comes at the head of an army to reclaim his inheritance.[39] Claudius's first entrance as King, with Hamlet as not-King (dressed in mourning black), immediately emphasises the alienation of the Hamlet line. Indeed, what is striking about this first entrance is that it is entirely *unexpected* in revealing to the audience *Claudius* as King (referred to throughout the play simply *as* 'King' – here only as 'Claudius King of Denmark'), sumptuously, with Hamlet in mourning black. Everything in the earlier scenes has prepared the audience for *Hamlet's* appearance as King. The prolonged mourning (an interesting topic itself in early modern history) insistently keeps the direct line, Old Hamlet/Young Hamlet present. And Claudius's opening words fix for the audience the *usurpation*:

> Though yet of Hamlet our dear brother's death
> The memory be green, and that it us befitted
> To bear our hearts in grief, and our whole kingdom
> To be contracted in one brow of woe,
> Yet so far hath discretion fought with nature
> That we with wisest sorrow think on him
> Together with remembrance of ourselves.
> Therefore our sometime sister, now our queen,
> Th'imperial jointress to this warlike state,
> Have we . . .
> Taken to wife.[40]

The first exchange of words between Claudius and Hamlet (somewhat late in the scene – it follows the 'fatherly' exchange with Laertes) underlines the fact that the 'unlawful' marriage has strengthened the line in Claudius's favour, and to Hamlet's detriment:

> *King.* But now, my cousin Hamlet, and my son –
> *Ham.* A little more than kin, and less than kind.
> *King.* How is it that the clouds still hang on you?
> *Ham.* Not so, my lord, I am too much in the sun.[41]

If Hamlet is Claudius's cousin, Hamlet should be king; if Hamlet is Claudius's son, then he is confirmed as line-dependent on Claudius, who sits legitimately on the throne. I suggest that Act I in its entirety dwells deliberately on *incest* as a material offence committed against Hamlet.[42]

Claudius's unlawful marriage to Hamlet's mother, Gertrude, cuts Hamlet out of the line.[43] The offence is against Hamlet. But for a mother to connive in wronging her own blood-son (even if passively) makes her an *emotional* focus for the blame – not simply the unlawful marriage, but the unnatural treatment of a son.[44] She has indeed committed a sinful and unlawful act, on which Hamlet obsessively dwells. He does so as one to whom that act has caused harm, disturbing the conventional relationship between blood-bond and line-bond, so that his filial duty towards his mother is now at odds with his obligations towards his father and himself (the legitimate line). The act is sexual (as Hamlet insistently reminds us). Its consequences are *material* for the line, and Hamlet is equally insistent about that:

> Ham.   Now mother, what's the matter?
> Queen.   Hamlet, thou hast thy father much offended.[45]
> Ham.   Mother, you have my father much offended. . . .[46]
> Queen.   Have you forgot me?
> Ham.   No, by the rood, not so.
> You are the Queen, your husband's brother's wife,
> And, would it were not so, you are my mother. . . .[47]
> Queen.   What have I done, that thou dar'st wag thy tongue
> In noise so rude against me?
> Ham.   Such an act
> That blurs the grace and blush of modesty.[48]

Offence against Old Hamlet ('my father'); offensive behaviour towards Claudius ('thy father', because Gertrude is '[her] husband's brother's wife', and thus he her son's father). Hamlet is caught between the knowledge of an unlawful marriage, a crime committed (and perhaps two), to which the community turns a blind eye,[49] and a sense of personal outrage at a wrong perpetrated against himself, by his close kin, when to rectify that outrage would be to commit petty treason.[50]

Here, I suggest, we have an alternative account of '(the man) . . . dominated by an emotion which is inexpressible, because it is in *excess* of the facts as they appear' – one in which we can see quite clearly that in so far as Gertrude is supposed to have behaved monstrously and unnaturally towards her first husband *and* her son, her guilt – in direct contrast to Claudius's – is culturally constructed so as to represent her as responsible without allowing her agency.[51] In my version, the intensity of feeling, the sense of outrage on Hamlet's behalf is still there, but it is produced as a consequence of offences recognised within the early modern community (in which Gertrude is much more straightforwardly and specifically implicated). In *this* account, Gertrude has participated in the remarriage – has (literally) *alienated* her son, and Old Hamlet's name (and does not apparently accept Hamlet's urging to leave Claudius's bed, because that argument (his) does not effect *her*).

We have not, then, exonerated Gertrude, but we have recovered the guilt surrounding her as a condition of her oppression: she is required by the kinship rules of her community to remain faithful to her deceased husband; that same community deprives her of any but the proxy influence her *re*marriage gives her, over her son's future. Yet she is the emotional focus in the play's cultural construction of the guilt which taints the State of Denmark.

Let me end by reminding you of something I said at the start: that there are grave reasons why I have found myself pushed to look for evidence of such agency in history – this is by no means simply an urge to identify my own critical position as an end in itself. It is above all the consequences for women of thus shifting the focus from text and discourse to history and agency, which, for me, currently, 'motivates the turn to history'.[52] As a Shakespeare critic, I have become tired of having to listen to offensive critical discourses, for which the author need apparently take no responsibility, which excavate desire in discourse so as to 'objectivate' the female subject – object of desire, object of blame, permanently victim.[53] After my initial reaction, which was one of anger (as some people will remember all too well),[54] it occurred to me that there must be something *wrong* with such accounts in relation to women, whether or not such critical enterprises were valuable in relation to men and patriarchy. For in history, women are *not* permanently in the object position, they are subjects. To be always object and victim is not the material reality of woman's existence, nor is it her lived experience. If we look at event, at agency in history, the inevitability of these accounts disappears. And we find that we are once again entitled to ask (as I have done in the case of Gertrude): Who, after all, has been wronged, and by whom?

Notes

1 *Hamlet*, III.ii.224–30. All references are to the Arden edition, ed. Harold Jenkins (London, 1982).
2 *Reading Shakespeare historically* (forthcoming).
3 I am particularly grateful to Annabel Patterson and Jean Howard, with whom I discussed that earlier draft at length, on that occasion, and to Bill Sherman, who couldn't be there, but who criticised the paper at length and in detail afterwards.
4 Simpson 1987–8.
5 *Ibid.*, 724–5. For another powerful argument which meshes with Simpson's doubts about the authenticity of discourse theorists' commitment to 'history' see Montrose 1986.
6 'In particular, given the current popularity of discourse analysis, it seems likely that for many practitioners the historical method will remain founded in covertly idealist reconstructions' (*ibid.*).
7 Catherine Belsey, in her chapter in this volume, 'Making histories then and now: Shakespeare from *Richard II* to *Henry V*', gives an elegant account of the ideological motivation for the privileging of a master-narrative version of history in criticism of Shakespeare's 'history' plays (for a similarly astute account of the ideology of Hamlet criticism, see Terence Hawkes, 'Telmah', in Hawkes 1986). Unlike Simpson, however, she sees the possibility of a post-modernist deconstruction which 'uncovers the differences *within* rationality, and thus writes of it *otherwise*', and which will thereby 'activate the differences and promote political intervention'. She proposes this as an alternative to both 'the master-narrative of inexorable and teleological development' and 'a (dis)continuous and fragmentary present, a world of infinite differences which are ultimately undifferentiated because they are all confined to the signifying surface of things'.
8 For a challenging account of these developments in cultural history see Chartier 1988.
9 See, for instance, Geertz 1984; M. Rosaldo 1984; Shweder and Bourne 1984; Bruner 1986.
10 For a clear account of the way in which political commitment sharpens the focus of feminist historical work, see Jean Howard's chapter in this volume, 'Towards a postmodern, politically committed, historical practice.'
11 See most eloquently Davis 1987.
12 See Jardine 1990.
13 See first of all Geertz 1973, p. 51; then Greenblatt 1980, p. 3.
14 See Geertz 1973, pp. 15–16.
15 Geertz 1973, p. 13.
16 Greenblatt 1988, p. 1. I am grateful to Bill Sherman for making this helpful connection for me, and for his continued support for my efforts to get to grips with recent writings in social anthropology.
17 See Geertz 1973, p. 35: 'The image of a constant human nature independent of time, place, and circumstance, of studies and professions, transient fashions and temporary opinions, may be an illusion, that what man is may be so entangled with where he is, who he is, and what he believes that it is inseparable from them. It is precisely the consideration of such a possibility that led to the rise of the concept of culture and the decline of the uniformitarian view of man. Whatever else modern anthropology

asserts – and it seems to have asserted almost everything at one time or another – it is firm in the conviction that men unmodified by the customs of particular places do not in fact exist, have never existed, and most important, could not in the very nature of the case exist. There is, there can be, no backstage where we can catch a glimpse of Mascou's actors as 'real persons' lounging about in street clothes, disengaged from their profession, displaying with artless candor their spontaneous desires and unprompted passions.'

18 I leave aside here the issue of the disadvantaging of women *per se* in Lacanian theory, see Jardine 1989.

19 This coexistence is made easier by the fact that social anthropologists like Geertz have thoroughly absorbed psychoanalytical theory, and tend to assume the Freudian subject as the starting point for their discussions of the cultural construction of selfhood. See Geertz 1973; Rosaldo 1984.

20 See Neely 1988, pp. 5–18.

21 In our Symposium discussions it became clear, I think, that in this respect (and this respect *only*) feminist critics are currently at an advantage in the critical debate being conducted around historicist and deconstructive critical approaches to text. Since they have a declared political objective, they are entitled to discard methodologies which fail to contribute constructively to it.

22 I concede, after many discussions on the subject, that taking Eliot as starting-point is in some sense a rhetorical device. But I find it striking that Eliot is fully aware of Freud, and thus that psychoanalytical reading of the play is established before psychoanalytical theory is explicitly introduced into literary studies.

23 Eliot 1932, pp. 144–5.

24 For a clear account of the consistent allocation of blame to the woman in psychoanalytical readings of *Hamlet* and *Measure for measure* see Rose 1985.

25 *ibid.*, pp. 116–7. See also her very clear rehearsal of a series of psychoanalytical readings of *Hamlet* prompted by Eliot's essay.

26 Shell 1988, p. 24.

27 The same kind of account can be given of Ferdinand's 'incestuous desire' for his sister, in *The Duchess of Malfi*. See Jardine 1983b.

28 Gibson 1730; Burn 1763.

29 Gibson 1730; Burn 1763.

30 Surtees Society 1845, p. 59. The 'marks' made by both dependents indicates that they were illiterate (a fact which is confirmed within Edward Ward's deposition).

31 See Davis 1983 for a clear case in which an unlawful relationship goes unreported in the community until a charge is brought by an individual who regards the 'marriage' as depriving him of something (land) due to him: 'The new Martin was not only a husband, but also an heir, a nephew, and an important peasant proprietor in Artigat. It was in these roles that the trouble finally began' (p. 51).

32 In fact, the canons of 1603 were drawn up hastily upon Elizabeth's death, since at her death it was suddenly realised that there now was no body of valid ecclesiastical law (her own legislation having been specified as for the duration of her reign). Owing to an oversight, the 1603 canons did not go through Parliament until some three years later, when it was realised that the clergy was probably operating outside statute law, and the situation was rectified. Patrick Collinson has recently suggested to me that these canons in fact *never* went on to the statute book – that in fact the Tudor and

Stuart governments left church law in a kind of deliberate limbo. All of this is really to suggest that (a) it was extraordinarily difficult to operate the various competing demands of common law, statute, and canon law, and (b) 'moral' and 'legal' demands might readily be perceived to be in opposition, the legal contrary to custom, or the moral dubious within the technical law.

33 There are exactly comparable tables of consanguinity and affinity for the woman.

34 Indeed, this is how theological dictionaries traditional describe the rules of affinity – as concerning *property*.

35 So was Henry's marriage to Ann Boleyn, since he had already had a relationship with her sister (Catholic propaganda, interestingly, claimed more obvious incest: that Ann was in fact Henry's daughter).

36 *Hamlet* I.ii.146–57. And see the Book of Common Prayer, cit. Jenkins, *Hamlet*, 319, n. 14. For another example of explicit affinity incest in the drama see Spurio's relationship with his stepmother in Tourneur's *The revenger's tragedy*. There, as here, the unlawfulness of the relationship is emphasised by the repeated formula from the tables of affinity: '*Spurio*. I would 'twere love, but 't 'as a fouler name / Than lust; you are my father's wife, your Grace may guess now / What I call it' (I.ii.129–31). In *Cymbeline* Cymbeline tries both to force Imogen to divorce her true husband, Posthumous, and to enter into an incestuous marriage with her stepbrother, Cloten.

37 I.v.42–6; 80–3.

38 For extended discussion of the 'elective' monarchy in Denmark, see Harold Jenkins's discussion in the recent Arden edition. I point out for brevity that Scotland was an elective monarchy: the eldest son of the reigning monarch was removed at birth to the care of the Earl of Marr. In due course the clans were assembled, and he was 'elected' her to his father.

39 'Now sir, young Fortinbras, . . . [comes] to recover from us by strong hand . . . those foresaid lands / So by his father lost.' I.i.98–107.

40 I.ii.1–14.

41 I.ii.64–7, and then see 107–12: 'You are the most immediate to our throne, / And with no less nobility of love / Than that which dearest father bears his son / Do I impart toward you.'

42 The offence is committed against Hamlet senior *and* Hamlet junior. See Greenblatt 1986, p. 219: 'The ghost of Old Hamlet – 'of life, of crown, of queen at once dispatched' – returns to his land to demand that his son take the life of the imposter who has seized his identity.' There seems to be a useful notion here of 'Hamlet' as an identity, a nexus of relations that Hamlet junior *ought* to occupy. See Girard 1986, 285–6: 'This significance of twins and brothers . . . must be present . . . if we are to interpret correctly the scene in which Hamlet, holding in his hands the two portraits of his father and his uncle . . . tries to convince his mother that an enormous difference exists between the two. There would be no Hamlet 'problem' if the hero really believed what he says. It is also himself, therefore, that he is trying to convince.'

43 Had Hamlet an heir himself his position would be strengthened (the play stresses Gertrude's maturity). I have come to think that *this* is the emphasis which so insistently produces Ophelia as fallen woman – were she pregnant she would threaten the (new) line in Denmark.

44 The intensity of the blame this occasions stands comparison with the blame which drives Ophelia insane – the murder of a father by the daughter's 'husband' (an act of

petty treason, carried out by a king's son). Early modern inheritance law consistently reflects anxiety as to whether mothers can be expected to act reliably on their male offspring's behalf, in the absence of a male head of household. See Jardine 1987, p. 9.

45 That is, 'been offensive to'.

46 That is, 'committed an offence against'.

47 See Bullinger: 'A woman maye not mary husbandes brother' (fol. xvir.

48 III.iv.7–41.

49 On this account the possible *murder* of the king is a secondary issue.

50 On murder by wife or child as petty treason see Sharpe.

51 It is because this particular cultural construction of female guilt is still current that it remains plausibly 'real' to critics.

52 The phrase comes from Howard 1986, p. 13, and is a question addressed to all those whose work has been called 'New Historicist' – 'What motivates the turn to history?' (p. 14).

53 'Objectivate' is Chartier's term. See, for instance, Chartier 1988: 'To combat [the] reduction of thoughts to objects or to "objectivations" . . . a definition of history primarily sensitive to inequalities in the appropriation of common materials or practices has come into being' (p. 102). 'Foucault has a lot to say about the way 'public' discussion of sex constitutes the chief way in which public institutions manipulate the consciousness and intimate experiences of great masses of people' (Sintow, Stansell and Thompson 1983, p. 9).

54 San Diego, 1984.

Whose crisis? AIDS/plague and the subject of history[1]

JOHN J. JOUGHIN

If post-Marx the future of historical materialism is in question, if the subject of history is in crisis again, if after Lyotard an extreme exception is taken to the rule of a metanarrative; for some of us on the left, the suspicion remains that the problem was always more multiplex than that, or, to be more exact, that these latest revisions are merely old problems making final *re*-solutions possible, that in truth apocalyptic moments have always come and gone, and that this latest post-history would not be the first to claim to be the last.

By way of an open rejoinder I want to recollect some critical moments from moments of crisis, arresting some fragments from an early modern affliction loosely allocated The Plague alongside today's epidemic, all too often figured by the same trope, actually an Acquired Immune Deficiency Syndrome. In part, and pieced together, these fragments constitute a continuum. Post-histories from the past, in the present, and for the future. They outline the configuration of a history of histories in crisis.

I

The lack of resolution

Physick himself must fade
All things to end are made
(Nashe, *Summer's last will and testament* (1978, p. 195))

London 1563, 1578, 1593, 1603, 1625, 1636, 1665 – the chronicle is sited and sequential, yet, in situ, the early modern plague city must always more properly come together as a place apart. It is secure only in its dislocation. And unsurprisingly, perhaps, just as the Corporation's regular form collapses, the establishment of continuity and containment feature as civic priorities.[2] For here, just where time is out of joint the order of the day is to make space mark time. And so it is that within London's walls Certain Directions are customarily laid down for the duration, and that the micropolities of its wards and parishes deploy an auxiliary apparatus of surveillance, hoping that, in accordance with Foucault's formulation, discipline can correct disorder (cf. Foucault 1977a, esp pp. 195ff.). Coterminously, between quarantine, and around and within the stratified codification which partitions this polis, a place is cleared for counting. The civic calculus is Aristotelian and its function is to measure mortality as an integral motion. The weekly bills which log their account with the itemised rigour of a balance sheet are a detailed part of this whole, whilst church bells register as a scaled down counterpoint conveying a continual metre with which to mark out the dead. And as bills tell and bells toll a premium is placed on repetition and fixity, for compassing adversity rests on constant correlation and computation, soothsayers chart the aspect and influence of planetary conjuncture and eclipse, preachers divine providence.

And, in the archives, if we grubbed around in the right ruins, we'd find a monument to these moments. For the official civic history and its sequential framing narrative comprise an aggregate of all these fractions. The statistical accumulation of the bills, the steady monotony of the bells, the assured trajectories religous and astrological, each combines and crosses co-ordinates, to provide an amalgam of field data with which to plot the authentic unilinear logic of disease, and to protest its full and true relation, from first symptoms to full recovery.

Yet that these finite parabolas of redemption, remembrance and resolve should customarily commence by protesting their historical accuracy is, of course, only the most evident index of a marked deficiency. For despite open-ended declarations and a durative appearance the official plague scripts are principally an imposition of hindsight, and their bona fide claims to currency (mostly counterfeit) are coined in the cast of an older contingency. Tending towards a realised end before it can begin, such historiography is predictably ahistorical, its thanksgiving for deliverence already forestalling any interrogative account of its recent arrival. It is what Walter Benjamin would term an historicism. For regardless of its dedication to posterity, it writes history posthumously. Telling their sequence of events like the

beads of a rosary, what these civic remembrancers forget to remember
or (more probably) remember to forget, is that in the event there's little
or no time for reverence or commemoration. For civic historicism,
common interment is an unremarkable episode, merely an instalment
on the outskirts of the polis.[3]

Exhumation (w)rites

In every era the attempt must be made anew to wrest tradition away from a
conformism that is about to overpower it. The Messiah comes not only as
the redeemer, he comes as the subduer of Antichrist. Only that historian will
have the gift of fanning the spark of hope in the past who is firmly convinced
that even the dead will not be safe from the enemy if he wins. And this enemy
has not ceased to be victorious. (Walter Benjamin, 'Theses on the philosophy
of history' (1968, p. 257))
For Walter Benjamin Tradition is the practice of ceaselessly excavating.
(Terry Eagleton, *Walter Benjamin or towards a revolutionary criticism*
(1988, p. 59))

But during the crisis, that the plague pits should amass an
indiscriminate *bricolage* of the high and the low is a remarkable and
untimely matter to be sure. It breaks the monolithic decorum of civic
monumentalism which cannot yet re(s)crypt this non-alignment, or
carry out its overpowering undertaking to 'preserve' the past in homo-
geneity. Lest we should forget that in this last respect the official tome
(however weighty) details an empty uniformity, latter-day excavation
inadvertently locates the fuller content at the site of its original
displacement. Assaying its spade at a deeper level and dislodging as
many leather shoes as disordered bones, it stumbles upon the plague
dead, where they fell, dead in their tracks, with no proper plaque or
stone to remark their unhallowed congregation. Remaining only without some trace that is whole it transpires that these dead are not
altogether without trace, for memory tallies as an uneven multiple
which only begins to be reckoned at such distant and disjunctive points
of departure 'ever new places' and old places too, from whence, to
which, fragments of history are unpredictably destined to return. This is
the pit without the pendulum. And it marks a site where we can finally
wrest tradition away from conformity. Where the forgotten can finally
be re-membered and reinstalled as a recollection of the dispossessed (cf.
Benjamin 1968, pp. 255–66).

Remembering resistance

'Cancer' would seem to symbolize (and 'realize') the refusal to respond: here is a cell that doesn't hear the command, that develops lawlessly, in a way that could be called anarchic. It does still more: it destroys the very idea of a programme, blurring the exchange and the message: it wrecks the possibility of reducing every thing to the equivalent of signs. Cancer, from this perspective, is a political phenomenon, one of the rare ways to dislocate the system, to disarticulate, through proliferation and disorder, the universal order and signifying power. This task was accomplished in other times by leprosy, then by the Plague. Something we cannot understand maliciously neutralizes the authority of a master knowledge. (Maurice Blanchot, *The Writing of the Disaster* (1986, pp. 86–7))

Then and now, and now as then, the recollections of the dispossessed and the tradition of their oppression teach us, that the 'state of emergency' in which we live is not the exception but the rule. And during the crisis, just as this loose arrangement holds, then all is not lost. For while the Corporation is thus caught off kilter and in the throes of restraint, then at least this is a turning point and a dislocation which the oppressed (for whom misplacement is always binding) can and will gauge for themselves. As official routes of social and economic exchange break down, their unlikely tactic for survival is to stand firm on a transmutational threshold. Long accustomed to the shifting solidarities of contingency, moving with the contraflow of liquidation, they break open new channels of circulation. The statistical accompt of bills and bells can't begin to figure these infractions, corpses removed under cover of darkness, clothes and possessions illicitly redistributed, so many transactions realised in the twilight zone. This community of the suffering traffics in tales of the living dead, for its act of remembering is always aligned to a freshly reactivated expectation.[4] Their collective account is unscripted, courageous and cunning, an unauthorized response, a cell which doesn't hear the command, it proves too streetwise for the normative master syntax of the State's emergency. Confronted with the firm forecasts of civic determinism the oppressed fix their mark by the current constellation, projecting a past against their present they make *ends* meet outside the narrative frame. They develop lawlessly. For them the exception is the rule.

II

Into the crypt

Meanwhile still inside the narrative frame, and during those two weeks which cut a section through the meridian peak of the official narrative curve of London's Great Plague, at that conjuncture we'd have to term critical, for some, the imperative to write the disaster remains. I want to blast one such text out of the homogeneous civic historicism where it currently resides.[5] And I single out this account, John Allin's account, because it claims to be an authority on its own founding moment of danger. For Allin is if nothing else in part a purveyor of master knowledges – an astrologer, a medic, a mystic, a man of the cloth – and just as his correspondence is steeped in anxious incredulity it is never lacking in resolve. As a series of moments in crisis his letters remain as yet unknowing, but not yet wholly unwary, of their own critical moment:

> London August 24th 1665
> – I am, through mercy, yet well in middest of death, and that, too, approaching neerer and neerer: not many doores off now, and the pitt open dayly within view of my chamber window. The Lord fitt mee and all of us for our last end! Surely if my friends be afrayd of my letters, I would be afrayd of theirs. The sickness yet increseth: this bill is 249 more than the last, viz. – of all diseases, 5,568: of the plague, 4,237; but rather in verity 5,000, though not so many in the bill of the Plague. Here are many who wear amulets made of the poison of the toad, which, if there be no infection, workes nothing, but, upon any infection invadeing from time to time, raise a blister, which a plaister heales, and so they are well: perhaps I may by the next get the true preparation and send you. (Cooper 1856, p. 8)

Almost inevitably there's a circumscription here, a will to closure that's missing from a collective account of the same epidemic. But just as Allin polices the borders of his own confinement, marking termination and taking time out to tally the dead, note that that open text which is outside intrudes. Through his chamber window (outside the frame yet still within view) he reads a tale which can't fully be told, a writerly text which reminds him of poison pen letters that are best left unwritten and unsent. For even as the minister insists upon an orthodox and confined sense of an ending here 'The Lord fitt mee and all of us for our last end!' the mystic construes the double logic of the amulet. And, in truth, before the true preparation or preservative could ever be fowarded the blister would burst, for the space of Allin's scripting is also the space of a dangerously unstable crypting. Two weeks later the crisis is upon him:

> September 7th 1665
> – The increasing sicknesse hath now drawn very nigh mee, and God
> knoweth whether I may write any more or no: it is at the next doore on both
> hands of mee, and under the same roofe . . . but I have no place of retireing,
> neither in the city or country; none in heaven nor earth to go unto but God
> only; the Lord lodge me in the bosom of his love, and then I shall be safe
> whatever betides . . . There is in my deske a little book new written, I
> intituled it 'Liber Veritatis': it is the true use of the elixir magnu for physi-
> cke, phitt, or delight, given by a true master of the arte to a friend whence I
> transcribed it. I would have Mr. Jeake to have that, and you to transcribe it;
> but be sure to keep it both of you a secrett. (Cooper 1856, p. 9)

As the sickness draws on, not even a plaister can cover the cracks, for
there's no room for hiding here. Though the amulet, of course, returns,
no longer a keepsake, but a cure in safekeeping none the less, his *Liber
Veritatis* which is in verity an obnoxious mixture, the word of a 'true
master' already sullied by the vagaries of transcription. Even the Lord's
bosom which by the same token is also a keepsake will not afford protection. For nothing's certain here. Only the inside could secure against
the outside by an act of exscription but Allin must keep his writing
deske closed, for inside, his last zone of exclusion is enveloped by that
which it seeks to contain. Only in time, as the point of turning is past
will the painful threshold relent, and only then can the writerly sickness
be written out. The crypt emptied. The secret secreted in another place:

> September 14th 1665
> – This sickness, though more dye, because more are infected, yet, thanks be
> to God, is not so mortall as at the first, for more recover of it now than
> formerly . . . If we knew how to trust the bills, it is decreased in the general
> . . . Our friend Dr. Starkey is dead of this visitation, with about 6 or more of
> them chymicall practitioners, who in an insulting way over other Galenists,
> and in a sorte over this visitation sicknes (which is more a judgement than a
> disease) . . . were too confident that their chymicall medicines would doe,
> they would give money for the most infected body they could heare of to
> dissect, which they had, and opened to search the seat of this disease, &c;
> upon the opening whereof a stinch ascended from the body, and infected
> them every one, and it is said they are all dead since, the most of them are
> distractedly madd, whereof G.Starkey is one . . . God is resolved to stain the
> pride of all glory; there is no boasting before Him, and much less against
> Him. (Cooper 1856, p. 10)

Just as the visitation departs, here at the site of its unseating the seat of
Allin's dis-ease is finally reinstated. As the body politic recovers, a

corpse can now safely transfigure for a Corporation or substitute for a
corpus. And that which was privately unutterable can now be publicly
spoken 'upon the opening . . . a stinch ascended from the body.' An
open text to be sure, full of tokens, too full for those in hand with the
body. They desired a consultation and now, it is said, they are dead, or
distractedly madd, infected every one. Among those undone one
Star-key, who despite himself breaks the civic code, though this
abberancy can't eclipse the sure projection of Allin's salvation, his
confidence in the end (God's re-solve) is now restored. And restorative
too. A week later. He writes. Protesting a cure:

> September 20th 1665
> It is refreshing to mee to thinke you are yet willing to receive a line from mee.
> It was an affliction to mee that I knew not to whom I might send a letter with
> acceptance. I am afrayd that some of my friends there are this day too much
> afrayd where no feare need to bee, for were my pen infectious my hand
> would soon let it drop. (Cooper 1856, p. 15)

Ramifications here then, for the relations between writing and history.
Ramifications then and now. For Allin's case history is very much to the
case in point, rehearsing and remarking the terms and situations of a
medico- historiographic problematic which, for some, still endures: a
Galenic history, 'natural', developmental, and above all teleological,
co-constituted and rewritten against the grain of an-other (that Allin
would term Paracelsian) which is chymicall, contingent, indeterminate.

III

The dis-ease of writing histories of disease. I want to move forward
now to discuss the theoretical problems posed by such a project in our
own conjuncture. Forward to a retrovirus which works its wiles in
reverse transcriptions, breaks codes, and en(s)crypts itself within a
body/text which can no longer distinguish inside from outside. Foward
to another poison chain of correspondence which can't yet be properly
deciphered or addressed, because even now, we're told, the *envelope* of
the virus seems to be changing (quoted by Treichler 1988, p. 60).

And if such a recitation of the figurality of HIV's bio-logic is
necessarily playful, it is not trivial, for those metaphors which in-form
(and some would claim infect) the prevailing medico-scientific
discourse on AIDS, also determine the epidemic's broader transmis-
sions and receptions, its real- world intelligibility within the social and
cultural domain. And that to this *end* for those living and articulating

the crisis, it is imperative to listen, to speak carefully, and to be heard:

> In January, 1986, I lost a friend to AIDS. I weigh these words carefully, as I
> weigh my sense of loss, and my motives for writing this book . . . [Bruno's]
> funeral took place in an ancient Norman church on the outskirts of London.
> No mention was made of AIDS. Bruno had died, bravely, of an unspecified
> disease. In the congregation of some forty people there were two other gay
> men besides myself, both of whom had been his lover. They had been far
> closer to Bruno than anyone else present except his parents. Yet their grief
> had to be contained within the confines of manly acceptability. The irony of
> the difference between the suffocating life of the suburbs where we found
> ourselves and the knowledge of the world in which Bruno had actually lived,
> as a magnificently affirmative and life enhancing gay man, was all but
> unbearable. (Watney 1987, p. 8)

On the outskirts of the polis another crypt. Containing their grief AIDS
activist Simon Watney and his friends stand closest to the bereaved yet it
is required that they stand furthest apart. Inside the outside of the inside
they experience the unbearable irony that difference can make. Alone in
mutual exclusion, they are surrounded by the solitarising silence of the
communal.

We need to remark Watney's founding moment, and to listen to the
resonance of its suffocated silence. To remember that just as AIDS is a
writerly sickness writ large, an epidemic of, and in, signification, the
skewed parameters and loaded positionalities of its reinscription function within a complex discursive field in which many reactionary and
entrenched narratives already intersect. In short, we need to remember
that the signifier 'AIDS' is wielded as much in silent domination as in
signification (cf. Treichler 1988). Meanwhile, that radical counter-
discourse which would resist such uniformly coercive formations continues to find itself in some disarray, at odds even in opposition.[6] And
towards formulating and formalising a strategy in respect of all of this, I
want (very briefly) to rehearse one such ongoing oppositional
divergency – where, in an apparent dialogue of the deaf, comrades find
themselves adversaries, divided, albeit in a common cause.

Of recent interventions in the current crisis, Susan Sontag's highly
visible (and frequently cited) *AIDS and its metaphors* (Sontag 1988)
commands continued attention. She speaks and many listen. Sontag's
(ostensibly radical) 'point of resistance', here, and in previous polemics
(cf. esp. Sontag 1983) is to refuse that punitive metaphoricity which
contaminates illness and its representations. Her pledge is for
abstention, a programme of figural detoxification: '[though] one

cannot think without metaphors . . . that does not mean there aren't some metaphors we might well abstain from or try to retire. As, of course, all thinking is interpretation. But that doesn't mean it isn't sometimes correct to be 'against' interpretation' (Sontag 1988, p. 5) Whilst Sontag's ensuing exposition of the stigmatization of those who suffer is substantial and necessary, and her refutation of the linguistic excess and execration of a Jerry Falwell (p. 61) or a Jean-Marie Le Pen (p. 62) is taken as read, her opening agenda also surrenders a considerable hostage to fortune. 'Against interpretation' she must opt instead for the 'demysified' narratives of modern science (cf. esp. Sontag 1983, p. 65), arguing for a reading of illness that is mono-causational, developmental, naturalistic and (by imputation at least) Galenic. Needless to say such a move is counterproductive in every sense. For all their notional 'neutrality' these master discourses of preservation, rationality and enlightenment have a darker flip-side, and are, in any case, always already politically active and socially overdetermined. Unwittingly (and inevitably), it follows that Sontag eventually finds herself writing inside the outside of her own exclusion zone, re-articulating those futilities and fatalities she had hoped to oppose, disseminating the very same 'loaded meanings and misleading metaphors' she had once refused:

> AIDS may be extending the propensity for becoming inured to vistas of global annhilation . . . the look into the future . . . has . . . turned into a vision of disaster . . . Like the effects of industrial pollution and the new system of global financial markets, the AIDS crisis is evidence of a world in which nothing important is regional, local, limited; in which everything that can circulate does, and every problem is, or is destined to become worldwide . . . AIDS is one of the dystopian harbingers of the global village, that future which is already here and always before us which no one knows how to refuse. (Sontag 1988, pp. 87, 89, 92, 93)

Plagued even within the confines of her own figural cordon sanitaire, unable, finally, to offer 'refusal' or contemplate resistance, Sontag's high profile volubility amounts to a kind of silencing.[7]

Meanwhile, back in the figural frontline, within those same 'regional, local (and) limited' sites of confrontation which her unitary notion of 'global circulation' would elide or override, the struggle to be heard continues. And the resounding response to silence is – 'SILENCE = DEATH' – the slogan (first coined by the AIDS Coalition to Unleash Power of New York City (ACT-UP) and now customarily stencilled white on black beneath a pink triangle – a 'point-up' version of that

proscriptive symbology deployed by the Nazis) is a call for sustained
vocal and discursive intervention which sites its ongoing cultural and
political praxis within a deconstructionist framework that aims to
'deessentialize power metaphorized as epistemological centre . . .
opening up space for marginalised voices and subversive practices of
resistance' (cf. Patton, 1989 pp. 30, 31, 36, 37). Yet as an alternative
oppositional strategy this stance on the margins will also prove
untenable, a victim, finally, of its own tropological pitfalls – even
ACT-UP's rallying cry is by its own (omissive) admission always
already assailable, for as AIDS activist Lee Edelman explains: '. . . the
defensive appeal to literality in a slogan like Silence = Death must
produce the literal as a figure of the need and desire for the shelter of
certain knowledge, such a discourse is always necessarily a dangerously
contaminated defense.' (Edelman 1989, p. 313). The poignant paradox
of these and other alternative readings is that for all their apparent
marginality it is precisely the shelter of a certain knowledge by which
they too must eventually set their mark. So it is that just as Edelman
assures us that there is no 'natural or literal discourse beyond rhetoricity' (p. 313) he 'find[s] himself' seeking the centre of his own remove,
gravitating back (at a point of departure) to the urgency of the literal,
anxiously re-marking a painful displacement where it is written, outside
the inside of his own discursive 'zone of infection':

> If my conclusion presents the somber circularity of Discourse = Defense =
> Disease = Discourse, I cannot conclude without trying to locate the zone of
> infection within these remarks . . . As much as I would insist on the value and
> urgency of examining the figural inscriptions of AIDS, I am sufficiently
> susceptible to the gravity of the literal to feel uneasy, as a gay man, about
> producing a discourse in which the horrors experienced by my own com-
> munity, along with other communities in America and abroad, become the
> material for intellectual arabesques that inscribe those horrors within the
> neutralizing conventions of literary criticism. Yet as painfully as my own
> investment in the figure of literality evokes for me the profound inhumanity
> implicit in this figural discourse on AIDS, I am also aware that any discourse
> on AIDS must inevitably reproduce that tendentious figurality . . . for
> discourse, alas, is the only defense with which we can counteract discourse,
> and there is no available discourse on AIDS that is not itself diseased.
> (Edelman 1989, pp. 315–6)

Futility if not fatality. Silence, still, even around and within so much
rhetoricity.

IV

Whose crisis?[8]

What, then, is to be done, if Sontag's cure is Edelman's poison, if each writes on the left only for each to write the other in an otherness to his or her self? Clearly we cannot merely choose sides, or opt for options here, where there are only unstable boundaries. Nor, can we, should we, I think, want to plunge into the playful irreducibilities of such a structural abyss. We need, rather, to remark or query the extent to which such a variance in formalistic oscillation is already itself a located event. And to recall that beyond the divide of so much indeterminancy there lies the situated experience of the contradiction which that divide itself implies. In the crypt, as we saw, that experience can never merely be resolved. So it is that John Allin marks time on the threshold between exscription and envelopment, while Simon Watney must mourn in mutual exclusion. Each of these founding moments serves as a painful reminder of the difference that differences can and do make, that in life if not in logic difference is the producer as well as the product of coercion. Yet, if the fate of the subject in history is to remain silenced and unresolved, we cannot consider it sealed. For it is politically imperative that we also reflect on the possibility of resistance. That there is a way out of the crypt. That mutual exclusivity is not an inevitability. To this end we need to acknowledge and recognize the extent to which a true identity would also be permeable to the possibilities of its own non-identical moment. That even in its critical moment, a particular moment of non-identity stands in a pattern of relations to other particulars which define its identity.[9] So it is that, as we saw, misplacement can be binding, that for those with a consciousness of the constellation in which they stand, contingency can and does bring its own shifting solidarities.

In our wider work as we struggle in and for representation, we too might reactivate such a standpoint. That (to echo Walter Benjamin one last time) we might be able to fan a spark of hope in the past and to grasp the constellation which our own era has formed with a definite earlier one, but that to do so we must remain critical of our own founding moment of difference by invoking the locational question of historical identity and asking – Whose crisis? – A crisis for whom? And within the limited confines of the present chapter, and elsewhere as we continue to attempt an evaluation of the contemporary health crisis of AIDS, such a critical interrogative, if it were truly critical, would necessarily want to begin by verifying the premise of its own critical content. For it would surely reflect that historically it is the ruling class that has had a substantial investment in raising the question of crisis and its control, only and especially when it (the ruling class) is in control. That critical moments, apocalyptic moments, occupy a necessary space in the oppressor's imaginary where there is never a lack without an attendant resolution. And that in our own conjuncture, despite incredulity master tropes remain empowered and in place, secured and legitimated in, and by, crisis. So that currently in the 'AIDS crisis' the 'healthy' and efficient narration of a master discourse of preservation, sustains a tale of corruption (and homophobia), with which to nurture 'The Nation'. Policing desire as disease in order to safeguard the micro-moral polity of the family (cf. Watney 1987 and 1988). And, of course, this is a 'threat' to which a latter-day moral etiology with a more orthodox sense of an ending is all too ready to respond. Listen to the postmodern medic, and remember his resolve, for he too divines the signs '. . . we face . . . an impending Armageddon of AIDS, and the salvation of the world through molecular genetics' (quoted by Treichler 1988, p. 62).

In order to carry on wresting tradition free from the resolve of conformism, and in order to formulate strategies for different futures, we must continue to locate the displacements of the historical process as they constellate around the reflex of the relation of the past to the present. And as we do so we must remember that it is not enough to simply mark the difference between then and now, but that we must also continue to reflect upon the difference that that difference is able to make, and for whom. That for the subject of and in history to finally break out of the crypt, it is necessary to recognize the need to accommodate the oppositional formation of an identity within the contingencies of situational change.

Notes

1 This paper owes much to the forum provided by Essex's Early Modern Research Group, viz: Francis Barker, Maurizio Calbi, Al Constantine, Tracey Hill, Paula Hutchings and Steve Speed. I would like to thank them for their collective encouragement and comradeship and to record a particular indebtedness to Francis for his sustained support. Needless to say none of those mentioned above can be held responsible for those errors and eccentricities which remain in the present version of the paper, they are mine alone.

2 A few of the following formulations presume a familiarity with the various conventions and practices which surrounded early modern epidemics, and some readers might feel

in need of further contextualisation. By far the most recent and comprehensive resource is Paul Slack's *The impact of plague in tudor and stuart England* (Slack 1985) to which I'm indebted. Those requiring a thumbnail sketch of the plague polis are strongly recommended to consult F. P. Wilson's virtuoso piece on *The plague in Shakespeare's London* (Wilson 1927).

3 For more on the customary distinction assumed between common and commemorative interment cf. Philippe Ariès's extensive account of *The hour of our death* (Aries 1981).

4 I'm indebted here to Giulia Calvi's work on the Florentine plague of 1630. Her analysis of the dynamic motive in social networks under duress is given in 'A metaphor for social exchange: the Florentine plague of 1630' (Calvi 1986) and should be considered alongside Victor Turner's definition of 'the community of the suffering' which can be consulted in *The ritual process* (Turner 1969) – (also invoked by Calvi 1986, cf. esp. pp. 147ff). For more on collective or 'popular' resistance during epidemics cf. Paul Slack's 'Responses to plague in early modern Europe: the implications of public health' (Slack 1988, esp. pp. 443–6).

5 It can be located in part in W. G. Bell's antiquarian history of *The great plague in London in 1665* (Bell 1924, esp. pp. 255–66).

6 A useful introductory guide to the multiplex discursive field of 'AIDS commentery' pro and contra is provided by Simon Watney in his *Policing desire: pornography, AIDS and the media* (Watney 1987). Amidst the plethora of additional material available, some of the best individual accounts of AIDS as a broad social and cultural crisis are to be found in a collection of essays which originally appeared in a special issue of *October* (43, 1987) now available as *AIDS: cultural analysis/cultural activism* (Crimp, 1988) wherein I am especially indebted to Paula Treichler's 'AIDS, homophobia, and biomedical discourse: an epidemic of signification' (Treichler 1988) and Simon Watney's 'The spectacle of AIDS' (Watney 1988). The need to set a political agenda for debate and action on AIDS is also advanced in (and by) *Taking Liberties*, (Carter and Watney (eds) 1989). The 'historical dimensions' of the epidemic have recently been surveyed (somewhat unsatisfactorily) in *AIDS: the burdens of history* (Fee and Fox 1988). Currently (and not before time) attention is focused on HIV/AIDS in the third world, again Treichler and Watney are recommended: 'AIDS and HIV infection in the Third World: a first world chronicle' (Treichler 1989); and 'Missionary positions: AIDS, "Africa", and race' (Watney 1989).

7 I'm partially indebted here to D. A. Miller's recent overview of Sontag's text. Though I should note that in the main Miller's attention is focused (quite rightly, I think) on those more localised and detailed silences, exclusions and preteritions which surround Sontag's 'treatment' of gay men – 'a homophobia "of omission" [which] . . . comes to betray its collusion with more active forms of abuse' (Miller 1989, esp. pp. 92–6 and 101).

8 An answer returning as a question, my interrogative responds to the resonance of Francis Barker's 'Which dead?'.

9 I owe these insights on reflection and 'true' identity to Peter Dews cf. his rigorous exploration of 'Adorno, post-structuralism, and the critique of identity' in Dews 1989, esp. pp. 12ff). also see his *Logics of disintegration; post-structuralist thought and the claims of critical theory* (Dews 1988).

Production, reproduction, performance: Marxism, history, theatre

GRAHAM HOLDERNESS

A metatheatrical approach to the dramatic and theatrical dimensions of the 'story' of the *Henriad* presupposes a standpoint outside the normal limits of what has been called 'stage-centred' reading. It calls for a project that is doggedly textual in orientation, and is thus *anti*theatrical: it will generate readings that do not readily lend themselves to performance and that will necessarily draw fire from stage-centred critics. But that, in a perverse way, is my point: that the antitheatricality of the readings I shall give reflects an antitheatricality in the Shakespeare text. (Harry Berger, Jr)[1]

An alternative must lie in a response to the full implications of the Shakespearian texts that confront us and in an attempt to give their textuality full rein.
    The play-text as play . . . sees the play-text referring to a 'reality' lying beyond it. However, in this case that 'reality' consists of an actual play, realized on the stage. The action on the stage has priority, and the text serves a secondary role as a kind of 'score' for the performance . . . each of these approaches seeks to recuperate the play-text on behalf of a tried and trusted genre, and to limit its potential, accordingly . . .
    The Shakespearian texts . . . are not plays. (Terence Hawkes)[2]

I feel here especially at a disadvantage in never having been at a performance of *Coriolanus*. But I find on reading this passage, or rather in imagining it said (sometimes as by specific actors; Olivier, of course, among them, and the young Brando), that it takes a long time to get through. (Stanley Cavell)[3]

Leftist cultural work has frequently been marked by exhortations to theorise and historicise the activity of the 'critic' (an ideologically-loaded term which might more appropriately be replaced by other figurative personae – the writer, the reader, the teacher): to reflect self-consciously on the practices of politically radical cultural analysis. This motivation towards self-exposure – which derives from a theoretical rejection of the pseudo-objectivity characteristic of traditional forms of criticism, from a methodological acknowledgement that a criticism committed to disclosing the ideological infrastructure of cultural works cannot operate by concealing its own ideological problematic, and from a 'post-modernist' preoccupation with metadiscourse – has featured strongly in specifically-focused feminist writing, but in other areas has remained relatively undeveloped. Walter Cohen's pioneering essay 'Political criticism of Shakespeare' (1987) is therefore an important contribution to a necessary operation: the observations I wish to make about it should be received in the context of an applauding recognition of its decisive significance for politically-conscious work in the cultural field.

Cohen's detailed and extensive discussion of the growth and development of 'political criticism' in Renaissance studies provides a model example for the cultural analysis of academic and educational institutions, and shows a critic beginning to take seriously the poststructuralist imperative to investigate and identify all ideological positions, including our own. In the course of his analysis Cohen suggests some points of distinction between 'political criticisms' as they are practised on opposite sides of the Atlantic, in Britain and in North America. Through the contrasting influences of New Criticism, with its cultivation of 'emotional distance' between reader and text, and Leavisite criticism, with its insistence on moral commitment, British criticism emerges from such a comparison inflected by 'a far greater orientation towards the present and toward explicitly political concerns than one finds in the United States' (Cohen 1988, p. 21). 'British Marxist discussions of Shakespeare' are thus characterised by a combination of traditional and innovative practices: 'a revisionist historical analysis of the plays in their own time and a radical account of their ideological function in the present' (p. 27). Surveying the 'far smaller field of American Marxist writing on Shakespeare', Cohen asserts that 'none of these critics even addresses the issue that British Marxists have successfully begun to explore: the contemporary institutional force and social function of Shakespeare'.

This seems to me a key distinction between forms of critical enterprise which, although cognate, convergent and closely interlinked, are moving increasingly into positions of mutual antagonism and contestation. But what divides them is not entirely or necessarily geographical location. If we were looking for examples of this kind of politically-engaged contemporary focus on Renaissance reproductions, it would certainly be to British cultural work that we would look – to

Simon Barker's 'Images of the sixteenth and seventeenth centuries as a history of the present' (1986), to the second half of *Political Shakespeare* (Dollimore and Sinfield 1985), to *The Shakespeare myth* (Holderness 1988), to the work of Hawkes (1986) and Evans (1986) and Drakakis (1986). By contrast the work that is currently dominating the American Renaissance journals, either directly or in the form of recuperative opposition, has its gaze firmly located on the past, if only by virtue of an attention to contemporary intellectual work that is itself a processing of history.

The critical anthology in which Cohen's essay appears seems to mediate between these competing tendencies. An international though predominantly American product, emanating from the International Shakespeare Congress held in West Berlin in 1986, *Shakespeare reproduced* is co-edited by two women, one American and one British (Howard and O'Connor 1988). It contains eleven contributions from America, two from the former GDR and one from Britain. Most of the contributions adopt what is by now a familiar form, the discussion of one play in relation to the literary and philosophical problems and methods of deconstruction, feminist and psychoanalytic criticism, race, politics, history. While these are in their way impressive pieces of work, they leave a sense of unfulfilment: not simply because they operate within a well-tried professional format, but because the editors and contributors are continually promising or demanding something more:

> Other work beckons, as well. We need examinations of Shakespeare's use at *all* levels of the educational system, and not just in colleges and universities; and we need to investigate the ideological use of Shakespeare in other wide-reaching cultural practices such as television and film. But even then, we would argue, the work of a political and historical criticism of Shakespeare will not be done. Shakespeare is constantly reproduced in the general discourses of culture and is used to authorize practices as diverse as buying perfume, watching Masterpiece Theatre, or dispatching troops to far-flung corners of the globe. We need studies which consider particular uses of the name or image of Shakespeare or of Shakespearean play-titles, speeches or snippets of verse in advertising, in popular culture magazines, in political rhetoric. Ignoring these uses of Shakespeare as trivial or beyond our expertise means acquiescing in the separation of the academy from general culture and means ignoring, as well, much of what in our own time may be of significance to a political and historical criticism. (Howard and O'Connor 1988, pp. 15–16)

Few of the writers actually address these issues: and the one contribution that really takes the volume into new territory is Marion F. O'Connor's examination of the 'Shakespeare's England' exhibition at Earl's Court, 1912: 'Theatre of the Empire'. This fascinating essay moves quite beyond the well-trodden paths of textual re-reading to the elaborate decoding of another kind of text, one of those significant 'reproductions' of Shakespeare with which the volume as a whole so clearly fails to engage. Moving from society costume-balls, through the productions of William Poel's Elizabethan Stage Society, Queen Victoria's Jubilee, *Country life illustrated*, and the architectural style of Edward Lutyens, O'Connor takes us to view the simulated reconstructions of Drake's *Revenge* and Shakespeare's Globe Theatre at an exhibition which expresses vividly and eloquently the spirit of imperial Britain shortly before the First World War. In place of the 'arbitrary connectedness' which Walter Cohen identifies as the key method and the structural weakness of 'New Historicism' (Cohen 1988, p. 34), O'Connor links her diversified and disparate elements into a powerful analysis of ideological and institutional reproduction. This is 'history', of course: but formulated in terms of a cultural historiography that looks far beyond a distanced, periodised 'Renaissance', to the institutional origins and concrete forms of cultural reproduction in a particular, relatively accessible, 'present'.

The strategies and methods of such a cultural historiography can easily be applied to a contemporary process of Renaissance reproduction in which other Globe theatres, other royal jubilees, other wars, continue to be implicated; and the political repercussions of such study are correspondingly direct and unmistakable. The contrast with 'New Historicism', which can describe its motivation as 'a desire to speak with the dead', is extreme. Although 'New Historicism' has frequently in the past been regarded as indistinguishable from Marxist 'cultural materialism', the true distance between them is disclosed with particular clarity by the publication of Stephen Greenblatt's *Shakespearean negotiations* (1988). The basic theoretical approach of Greenblatt's 'New Historicism' takes its starting-point from an interdisciplinary convergence of literary and historical methodologies. The traditionally constitutive structures of literary understanding – the author, the canon, the organic text – are deconstructed, and the dramatic texts returned to the historical culture from which they emanated. The traditionally indispensable techniques of literary investigation – verbal analysis, qualitative identification, evaluation – are largely abandoned in favour of an intertextual juxtapositioning of authorised literary works with the products of 'non-literary' discourses. Other plays and other texts, together with contemporary beliefs and cultural customs, social practices and institutional structures, are continually thrown into an exciting and liberating interplay of discourses, as Greenblatt traces the continuous flow and circulation of ideological forms and political interventions throughout the complex body of Renaissance society. The isolation of Shakespeare as deified author, and the strict perimeters of demarcation between Shakespearean texts and other forms of writing, are convincingly broken down, and Renaissance culture opened up to new methods of literary and historical analysis. The ultimate objective of that analysis is certainly the sphere of the political: through verbal and structural investigation of a range of rhetorical strategies, the critic discloses the conditions of cultural, ideological and political power, and the dramatic texts become sites for the negotiation and authorisation, interrogation and subversion, containment and recuperation of the forms of Renaissance power. But the political situation into which those demystified forms are then decanted, the present context of the critical utterance itself, is not specifically an object of address, or is constituted only rhetorically by means of a mannered postmodernist self-consciousness.

Some of the important differences between American 'New Historicism' and British 'cultural materialism' are now through such contrasting examples becoming more clearly visible than they were a mere few years ago. Cultural materialism is much more concerned to engage with contemporary cultural practice, where New Historicism confines its focus of attention to the past; cultural materialism can be overtly, even stridently, polemical about its political implications, where New Historicism tends to efface them. Cultural materialism partly derives its theory and method from the kind of cultural criticism exemplified by Raymond Williams, and through that inheritance stretches its roots into the British tradition of Marxist cultural analysis, and thence into the wider movement for socialist education and emancipation; New Historicism has no sense of a corresponding political legacy, and takes its intellectual bearings directly from 'post-structuralist' theoretical and philosophical models. American 'political' critics seem to think of their ideology as having been formed in the environment of 1960s campus radicalism – in 'the political crucible of the 1960s' (Howard and O'Connor 1988) – where their British counterparts are at least as likely to have imbibed their ideological formation from the free milk and orange juice of the post-war socialist reconstruction. Cultural materialism accepts as appropriate objects of enquiry a very wide range of 'textual' materials – social rituals, historical objects, material from popular culture, buildings, theatres, actors and actresses, performances of plays. New Historicism concerns itself principally with a narrower definition of the 'textual': with what has been *written*, rather than with what has been enacted, performed, uttered, built, organised, collected or exhibited.

Political criticism, like sex, is something you can't do effectively on your own: and on this side of the Atlantic the natural form for radical criticism to take seems to have been the critical anthology, the forum for a collaborative but abrasive conjuncture of different voices – the Essex conference on *1642*, *Political Shakespeare*, *Alternative Shakespeares*, *The Shakespeare myth*.[4] Precisely because Greenblatt's work has been developed within such a system of collaboration, and has appeared so often already in the context of these collective forms, its manifestation in the form of the elegant, urbane and learned monograph seems strikingly to characterise an individual voice, unmistakably distinctive even as it denies its own autonomy:

> I began with the desire to speak with the dead . . . It was true that I could hear only my own voice, but my own voice was the voice of the dead, for the dead had contrived to leave textual traces of themselves, and those traces make themselves heard in the voices of the living. (Greenblatt 1988, p. 1)

On the strength of this style, if Roland Barthes had met T. S. Eliot somewhere on the road to Little Gidding, Stephen Greenblatt would have been the third who walked always beside them. This is not only an individual voice, and the voice of an accomplished rhetorician: it is also a highly mannered voice bespeaking a form of cultural authority. Evidently when New Historicism seeks to give utterance to the voices of those witnesses normally eliminated from the history of a culture – the subversive and the oppressed, the marginalised and the dispossessed – it encounters a need simultaneously to adopt a voice capable of contesting power and authority within the apparatus of that very academic institution established to suppress those lost voices. Greenblatt's work has already, significantly, been widely acknowledged as the acceptable face of political criticism; and many a voice crying compellingly in the wilderness has ended up as a voice droning unopposed through the

Senior Common Room.

Walter Cohen effectively accounts for this abstracted quality of New Historicism; and in pointing to the moral fervour and nonconformist evangelical zeal of Leavis, he correctly diagnoses one possible route through which a socialist cultural politics found it possible to develop (via that cultural and educational configuration summed up in the useful term 'left-Leavisism'). But Cohen's analysis fails to account for the most obvious reason for the relatively contemporary focus of attention to be found in British Marxist criticism: a reason which lies in the existence of a British tradition of Marxist literary criticism and Marxist cultural analysis, preceding even the *annus mirabilis* of 1968, certainly pre-dating the incorporation of French theoretical work in the 1970s. Cohen's bibliographical compilation of political studies of Shakespeare (appended to Cohen 1987) takes as its starting-point the year 1980: and although he admits that the list is 'arbitrary in its boundaries', that particular *terminus a quo* effectively occludes the historical roots of British Marxist criticism and its specific forms of political engagement. Cohen is aware that in Britain 'leftist cultural criticism developed earlier', but still wishes to nominate 1980 as a 'significant point of demarcation, with an intensified radical response to the recent victory of Thatcher, the extension of this work to Renaissance literature, and the publication of an important marxist study of Middleton' (p. 19). That the work of a veteran communist critic and activist such as Margot Heinemann should be regarded as the inception of a new age of theory, rather than as the development and consolidation of a long tradition of Marxist cultural practice, is sufficient indication of the deformation introduced into cultural analysis of the British experience by this particular attempt at periodisation.

I have no wish to isolate this historical continuum, the 'tradition' of British Marxism; or to reflect nostalgically on the achievements of that tradition in the 1930s and 1950s – though they are there, and they were mediated into our modern cultural practice by the work and example of Raymond Williams. Still less would I wish to minimise the importance of post-Althusserian Marxist philosophy, its wholesale revision of earlier variants of Marxism, its transformation of terms such as ideology, base and superstructure, humanism, its capacity to enter into dialectical relations with linguistic, psychoanalytic and feminist theories. There are however certain other characteristics of that earlier cultural work which might instructively be re-examined. Like Marxist philosophy itself, it took as a model for any kind of political, economic or cultural analysis the unity of theory and practice. Also in keeping with Marxist philosophy, it maintained a constant focus on the political present: there was never any possibility of regarding Marxism, as New Historicism tends to regard it, simply as a means of explaining the past. And it was always inseparable from clearly-defined political commitment, and from direct or indirect political or quasi-political involvement: you would expect a left academic in the late 1960s or early 1970s to be a member of a specific political party – Communist Party, International Socialists (later Socialist Workers' Party), International Marxist Group, Marxist wing of the Labour Party – or at least to be active in those branches of adult and 'political' education which ramified, often through the unions, into the labour movement itself.

I know I will be accused of retrospective political nostalgia: though to have been present and politically active in a period, the early 1970s, when the mobilisation of the labour movement could free workers imprisoned for trades union activity, or bring down a Tory government, is to have acquired a concrete awareness of political possibilities that I would not, in this dark and bitter time of defeat and retrenchment, willingly relinquish. I know we cannot revive old policies, or follow an antique drum: but it was certainly in those conditions of direct struggle that I acquired my sense of the inescapably political nature of all culture. Political conditions today are so different as to throw those direct struggles of the early 1970s into sharp historical relief, as the victory of 1974 was eclipsed by the terrible defeat of 1984: where now are the crystal-clear imperatives of political struggle?

Linked to this general crisis and failure of the political will are the philosophical anxieties associated with 'postmodernism'. Setting aside the question of whether a *cultural* theory like postmodernism could really ever be held to compromise and undermine a *political* philosophy like Marxism, it seems to me that the revisionist Marxism we are likely to be holding on to today is not so very different from the Marxism we inherited at the end of the 1960s. It was never, in my experience of Marxist political practice in that period, an item of belief that the proletarian revolution was inevitable; the 'scientific' element in 'scientific socialism' was always subjected to deeply critical question; and I can recall very few instances of Marxist analysis or political action that were entirely free from scepticism, relativism, the awareness of manifold possibilities. Certainly we used to construct a 'grand

narrative' in which 'history' was imputed to be always and ultimately
'on the side of the people': but 'history' was understood with absolute
clarity to be 'nothing more or less than the activity of man pursuing his
aims'. And although the subject of that operation would now
(correctly) require instantaneous redefinition, the concrete presence in
the labour movement of the early 1970s of militant and articulate
women made it abundantly clear that Marx's generic term for humanity
was not in practical application to be understood as in any way
patriarchally-inflected. In the Marxist texts themselves (which I used
to teach to workers in Communist Party education classes, and in
classes for trades unionists organised by the Workers' Educational
Association), the 'master-narrative' describing successive phases of
economic development, and adumbrating the final overthrow of capitalism by socialism, was never read as metaphysical prophecy, but
rather as political exhortation. The Marxist philosophy of history, and
the Marxist methods of economic and political analysis, were means of
understanding the developments of the past: which could then be
applied to specific tasks of political action which would, if successful,
realise the political development of the future.

The Marxism that I first absorbed in that crucial period was a
Stalinist deformation already de-stabilised by the assault of
Althusserian philosophy, and its interaction with a Hegelian humanist
variation of Marxism developed in resistance to Althusser. Marxism
was very much, in the late 1960s and early 1970s, a philosophy in crisis
and change. Politically it contained and retained a version of the
'Popular Front' strategy of a broad-based alliance of anti-capitalist
groups (one example is the Communist Party programme known as
'The British Road to Socialism') which in turn bears a striking resem-
blance to the loose co-ordination of separate interest groups that Jean
Howard talks about in her chapter in this volume. Althusserian
Marxism, with its emphasis on the relative autonomy of separable
cultural, political and economic spheres, of activity seemed to me to
endorse this political strategy (though it was then, and has subsequently
been, interpreted quite differently, as the vindication of a theoretically-
empowered vanguard élite). The key problem was, and still is, whether
Marxist philosophy could ever hope to offer a macro-narrative
complex enough to incorporate this pluralism, without either excluding
or oppressing particular groups which would wish to be part of the
progressive movement, but not on terms which would marginalise their

own interests; or becoming so attenuated as to disappear altogether as a totalising force. My own view is that this project is still perfectly feasible: but then I have always regarded the *analytical* content of Marxist politics – specific analysis of concrete historical situations, and applied political strategies designed to realise ultimate objectives – to be far more important than the *theoretical* content of Marxist philosophy. I agree with Jean Howard that very broad, 'Enlightenment' categories such as 'universal emancipation' can be used as ultimate goals, because the crucial imperative in any historical situation is to co-ordinate, in some broad-based programme, forces capable of working towards both particular and general forms of human emancipation.

What we can carry forward from that earlier tradition of *praxis*, contemporary engagement and direct commitment, into a greatly strengthened and theoretically-developed historical materialism, are certain methods of political analysis and cultural intervention. We can draw on the 'empiricist' leanings of an earlier form of Marxism, to re-introduce methods of concrete historical and cultural analysis; our earlier fears of empiricism seem naive in the context of the New Right's formidable rejection of the empiricist method in favour of a radical and stridently ideological critique. We can focus our attention much more firmly on contemporary cultural conditions, consolidating and developing a continuous analysis of immediately contemporary forms of cultural construction; building on work that has been extensively proposed but only fitfully achieved. And we can seek more overt and declarative forms of political consciousness: taking a lead from feminism, and stepping out from behind the defensive shield of postmodernist self-consciousness, it may be possible to open up more direct, more confessional, more communicative modes of political dialogue.

Despite the evident theoretical and institutional divergences between 'New Historicism' and cultural materialism, they should still be considered as cognate enterprises, often converging into a strategic synthesis, frequently intermeshing across the ground of a single critical initiative. The task of analysing subsequent, and particularly contemporary, Renaissance reproductions, could scarcely be attempted without the kind of work already performed on the original historical moment of production. What I am advocating here is not a theoretical witch-hunt against New Historicism, but rather a different kind of application or strategic mobilisation of finely-crafted methodologies already effectively exercised on Renaissance historical materials. I am also advocating however that as we broaden the focus of our attention to assimilate hitherto neglected materials, so we might also incorporate new and alternative methodologies; perhaps in the meantime reflecting critically on the ideological implications of some of the methods that have already been established, and that seem to be growing into a strange and unforseen currency.

I have already emphasised, after Walter Cohen, the desirability of a more open political consciousness, and of a more consistent focus on the present: these seem to me inseparable from any kind of Marxist perspective. In addition I think we should be more willing, as Jean Howard proposes, to approach popular culture: not the popular culture of the past, the historical institutions of Renaissance carnival, but our own contemporary popular culture of print and image and audio-visual medium. If our sphere of cultural attention, even the educational work by means of which we all earn our living, is to be considered in any kind of democratic perspective, we have to recognise that in so far as the majority of people encounter 'the Renaissance' at all, they do so through the media of contemporary popular culture. The material available for comment and analysis in this context is much more extensive than we normally think. To approach it we need of course the tools of media study, sociological inquiry and semiotic analysis: many of the comments we have all made, *en passant*, about such phenomena suffer from theoretical naivety and oversimplification. Our attention should be focused more broadly on the educational systems as a whole: our work in higher education is not in any except an illusory sense separable from educational practice at all 'levels'.

Lastly, it seems to me that we should consider overhauling quite radically some of our assumptions about the nature of Renaissance *drama*, and of the appropriate methods radical critics may employ in analysing its processes of production and reproduction. Drama has in too much radical criticism and cultural analysis been treated in much the same way as it always has in traditional literary criticism – as written text. If you extracted from the critical anthology *Shakespeare and the question of theory* (Parker and Hartman 1986) Elaine Showalter's wonderful essay on the image of Ophelia, you could read through 238 closely-printed pages on Shakespeare which manage not to mention the name of a single actor or actress, a single director, a single theatrical production. Remove Robert Weimann's contribution on

'Mimesis in *Hamlet*' and the term 'theatre' itself disappears entirely as a material institution, suffering abstraction to a theoretical category. For a number of reasons connected with the institutional relationship between 'Literature' and 'Drama' as academic subjects, which I will discuss more extensively below, there is a history here of rival appropriations, with disciplines vying with one another to constitute this prestige cultural material into different forms. As we can see from *Shakespeare and the question of theory* (and as the writers quoted in the epigraph to this chapter amply demonstrate), American deconstructionism merely confirms that divergence, taking the printed play-text itself (invariably a modern scholarly edition) to be quite iterable and pluralistic enough for the purposes of radical analysis. Some of the authors openly proclaim the 'anti-theatrical' character of their criticism: a stage-production can only represent an attenuation and fixing of the play-text's fertile semiotic instability. This remarkable claim (not by any means restricted to American colleagues) can be arrived at from a number of different routes: from a deconstructionist preoccupation with verbal language, which simply ignores the dimension of the stage, or from a hostile and detached sociological perspective which regards the theatre as a subsidised imposition on an unwilling population. It is rarely if ever reached through a serious study of *theatre*: stage and production history, the theories and practices of acting, directing, stage design, the complex semiotics of performance art itself. I want to argue that we should place at the centre of our critical enterprise a different conception of Renaissance drama as *theatre*: as dramatic materials that were devised specifically for performance, and that display in their Renaissance forms a diversity and plurality firmly banished from the modern scholarly edition; as 'texts' that have a performance history often separable from their history as written texts – a history that cannot be reduced to a simple series of ideological appropriations; as cultural products that are designed for mobilisation in theatrical rather than literary-critical ways, and therefore require correspondingly more flexible methods of semiotic analysis; as play-scripts that are available for kinds of educational work in which dominant structures of authority and power can be convincingly called into question.

One of the determinants of my particular emphasis here is a professional involvement with the teaching of Drama. Many of us have been engaged, over the past twenty years, in an intellectual struggle to

develop and establish a body of cultural theory that would not only
have the power to pose an effective challenge to dominant ideological
'explanations' of culture in history, but would also have the capacity,
given sufficient purchase on the institutional apparatus of the
'academy', to supplant that hegemonic world-view with an alternative
understanding of culture, rooted in a socialist philosophy of history and
politics. One key feature of this long ideological battle has been a
restless, chafing dissatisfaction with the imposed educational conditions structured into British academic culture; an insistence on
rupturing the traditional boundaries of established 'disciplines', a
sustained determination to draw together conventionally 'separate'
fields of inquiry – literary studies, history, philosophy, sociology – into
the kind of active, interventionist, interdisciplinary forms of knowledge
represented pre-eminently, for most of us, by Marxism. It is in the
context of a continuing commitment to that enterprise that I venture to
offer some observations which could easily be misinterpeted as an
attempt to forestall the dismantling of disciplines, or to privilege one
particular form of academic discourse: defending, in a sectarian and
partisan manner, the potentialities of 'Drama' over those of other
systems of knowledge. I have no desire to emulate earlier forms of
academic imperialism by seeking to establish the discipline of Drama at
the centre of progressive intellectual culture. On the contrary, as my
arguments will indicate, there seem to me to be very good reasons why
radical forms of cultural criticism and theory have shunned some of the
mysticism and metaphysics with which Drama is frequently associated.
My argument for the incorporation into progressive Renaissance
studies of specifically *theatrical* methodologies is based initially on the
premise that drama is in any case a highly pluralistic, heterogeneous
discipline, more a site of conflicting ideologies than a securely
hegemonic cultural apparatus. And although I have argued, in other
contexts, that Drama should be seeking a cohesive theoretical centre,
that proposal is founded on the assumption that historical and
sociological and anthropological and political contexts and perspectives should become as natural a part of Drama's methodologies as
they are of Marxist literary criticism, historical analysis and cultural
history.
   The tension between 'Drama', and 'humanities' disciplines like
English and History, can be located in certain peculiar cultural conditions, rooted in turn in certain historical divisions of labour that have

accompanied the development of British academic culture. The new critical approaches, from structuralism onwards, which began to penetrate British academic discourse from the early 1970s, tended to find a 'natural' home within institutions and departments of 'Literature', while simultaneously influencing fields of inquiry which had already to one degree or another broken away from the would-be hegemonic apparatus of traditional literary studies – linguistics, cultural studies, film, media and communications studies. Prior to the post-structuralist 'revolution', British literary studies had been dominated jointly by Cambridge English and by American New Criticism, both schools obsessed with evaluation and with textuality: with the process of privileging the morally beneficial and aesthetically 'great', and with textualised language as the concrete embodiment of experiential meaning. Neither method had anything useful to say about 'Drama' except as literature: the fact that a great deal of what is conventionally designated 'Literature' (including the work of the 'greatest' English author) actually originated as non-literary performance art was conveniently ignored, and the category of the 'dramatic' theoretically collapsed into the subject-centred process of textual reading – the critic (who was always assumed to be male) was simply exhorted, after D. H. Lawrence, to read with his testicles as well as with his brains.

It was partly as a consequence of this combination of indifference and hostility on the part of literary-critical establishments and institutions that 'Drama' began to emerge as an independent discipline: in the form of autonomous sections within English departments, or as separate departments with their own distinct philosophy and method. The key distinction of method was of course Drama's commitment to performance as a necessary, or even as the true or only medium by means of which dramatic literature could be experienced and understood. The traces of that original schism can still be observed by comparing the teaching of Drama between different insitutions and across different sectors: you can find Drama students reading and analysing texts (though the object of the analysis may be an absent performance rather than a present meaning), or you can find them performing those texts in workshops, rehearsals or productions. In some locations Drama has moved much further away from the original *rapprochement* of literary, historical and practical studies, towards an educational model in which performance, and the skills of performance, are the substance of the learning process. Frequently in this context Drama can be found linked with Dance and Music, in a 'Performance Arts' scheme which can often look very close to professional training. It is at this point, of course, that Drama touches the professional theatre, and is to be found supporting strictly 'vocational' programmes in technical theatre, theatre design, stage management, theatre administration. If on the other hand a student is approaching Drama as an educational medium, in for example a course of teacher-training, then the substance of the discipline is likely to be at the furthest remove from the professional theatre and from vocational training. In educational Drama the discipline is conceived as an exploratory medium that can be used for discovery of the self and for exploration of the world. This model can be observed both in schools and in such initiatives as 'Theatre in Education' and some forms of 'community' theatre. By linking Drama with television and film, or by emphasising its character and potentiality as a specifically audio-visual communicative discourse, it is possible without violence to nudge the subject into the environment of 'media' or 'communications' studies.

Since the primary target of post-structuralist criticism has been the text-centred approaches of *Scrutiny* and New Criticism, Drama could be seen as an already partially-liberated area: there is nothing new or surprising in many of the propositions of post-structuralist theory for Drama specialists, who become understandably irritated at the laborious expositions of post-structuralist critics striving to demonstrate that the works of Shakespeare or Ben Jonson are iterable and pluralistic. Drama teachers have in a sense always known from the very nature of their subject, though they may have used a very different language to formulate their knowledge, that 'reading' is an active process of constructing meaning, not a passive assimilation of encoded truths; that historical institutions and practices are important not as a shadowy 'background' to the corporality of texts, but as constitutive determinants of those texts and their reproduction; that the meanings of dramatic texts are never stable and authoritative, but always (and perhaps infinitely) deconstructable. At the same time an awareness that the 'language' of drama is only partially verbal, that the expressive art of drama involves a much wider range of signifying practices, has made Drama a natural home for developments in semiotics.

These observations should not, however, lead us to conclude that Drama is, or is generally organised and communicated as, a 'naturally' radical art or cultural study: although some of its most eminent practitioners have argued as much. The very eclecticism of the discipline renders it capable of both radical intervention and conservative reproduction: its scholarship and 'theatre history' can be dominated by nostalgia and escapism; its 'practical' element can often be reduced either to therapeutic play or to mere training for professional success; its interpretative strategies can be as formalistic as those of Literature, and its Educational theories are frequently escape-hatches to all kinds of metaphysical notions about the self and human nature. In the model National Curriculum that forms a central plank of Kenneth Baker's Great Education Reform Act, Drama does not appear as a core subject. The ideologues of Drama claim that this proposed act of suppression by educational policy indicates the truly radical character of Drama as an activity. It is far more probable that this marginalisation is not a consequence of Drama's being perceived as a potent and dangerous revolutionary force, but rather because the disicpline has come to be associated with precisely the kind of woolly thinking and vague, semi-mystical psychologising that the hard-nosed Mr Gradgrinds of the New Right are determined to eliminate from the curriculum.

Much contemporary work on Renaissance drama, particularly on Shakespeare, is dominated by methods derived from traditional Literary studies: the hegemonic discourse of this particular cultural practice derives from a *rapprochement* of activities such as textual scholarship, interpretative criticism, subject-centred 'reading' and journalistic reviewing. 'Literature' specialists of the more traditionalist kind dominate the columns of the academic reviews and the various publication projects which address the analysis of Renaissance drama in performance. That fact in itself does not of course obviate the possibility of progressive individual interventions: but in terms of a large-scale cultural analysis, it is clear that the initiative in this area has been taken by the hegemonic institution of Literature, so that neither the radical potentialities of new approaches to literary criticism nor those of Drama itself have been incorporated into this area of work.

The investigation of drama as a performance art should be supported by a serious engagement with post-structuralist criticism, for the interpretation of dramatic literature; with cultural sociology, for analysis of the institutional and ideological contexts of theatrical production; with history, both for a broader cultural perspective and for an understanding of the nature of theatrical spaces, audiences, ideologies;

with theatre semiotics, for methods of decoding the signifying practices of drama; with practical experimentation, for concrete explorations of the pluralistic character of all performance art; with politics, both in a general sense and in relation to specific issues of race, sexuality and gender; and with progressive currents in film and media studies, where examples of theoretical rigour can take the analysis of drama on the screen far beyond the flabby platitudes of much current criticism and reviewing. Despite the fact that my general argument is one in favour of adjustments in radical criticism and theory to incorporate the methodologies and perspectives of Drama, it will be evident from the above that I see the reverse of that process as an equal priority: Drama should also be seeking to incorporate into itself the dialectical methodologies of radical criticism.

To present some demonstrative illustrative material, I have chosen to look at, or rather to look round, a text that has already been established as one of central concern to progressive cultural criticism: *The taming of the shrew*. It is noteworthy that the important Marxist, deconstructionist, and feminist discussions of this play are all located firmly within a particular play-text, that to be found in the First Folio of 1623, which represents the one version of the dramatised 'shrew' narrative that has authority beyond all others: 'Shakespeare's' *The taming of the shrew*. As interesting and important as that play-text is, there are certain contextual and intertextual features of Shakespeare's Shrew-play that relativise its existence within a broader and more complex cultural configuration. The performance history of this play, as distinct from its textual history, presents us with a clear example of a deeply unstable, volatile entity, chameleon in its adaptability, vertiginously pluralistic in its continual metamorphoses.

To begin with, in its Renaissance form it exists, like *King Lear*, in two quite distinct textual forms, the text in the First Folio, and the anonymous play *The taming of a shrew*, printed in 1594. While the Quarto and Folio texts of *King Lear* have been confidently designated, by the contemporary *gurus* of textual authenticity, as respectively Shakespeare's 'original' and 'revised' versions of the play (Wells and Taylor 1988, p. 909), *The taming of a shrew* (together with many another variant version of a canonised Shakespeare text) has been brusquely marginalised into the category of 'Bad Quarto'. If we take no interest in these evidences of the concrete plurality of the Renaissance play-text, then we are implicitly acknowledging the authority of these

very dubious bibliographical and scholarly procedures, accepting that
the true significance of these texts lies in the character of their relationship to the controlling authority of the Bard.

That formal instability of the *Shrew*-text can be traced per-
formatively through the stage-history of Shakespeare's play, or textually through a long series of free adaptations – John Lacey's *Sauny
the Scot*, James Worsdale's *A cure for a scold*, Garrick's *Catherine and
Petruchio*, the musical *Kiss me, Kate*, Charles Marowitz's collage *The
shrew* – a history that is regarded by conventional scholarship as
peripheral to the evolution of the 'real thing', Shakespeare's play; but
which should in my view become the real focus of our critical, historical
and political attention. One of the methods I will be proposing is a form
of 'peripheral analysis', which strategically avoids the authenticated
authoritative 'Shakespeare' text, and addresses instead a theatrical
narrative in a diverse and continual process of reproduction. There is, it
is true, no compelling reason why this history of textual improvisation
should not be recognised as a literary history, and acknowledged as
necessarily contingent upon the contemporary textuality of *The taming
of the shrew*. But in practice these variant versions belong, if only for
reasons of institutional territorialism and disciplinary apartheid, not to
a literary but to a performance history: to a history not of the text but of
the theatre.

In most scholarly editions of *The taming of the shrew*, the principal
editorial concern is of course with establishing the authoritative
('Shakespearean') text, and fending off the distracting untidiness of this
confusing peripheral history. Ann Thompson's 'New Cambridge
Shakespeare' edition (1984) displays rather more theoretical
sophistication in its discussion of the other texts, but its overriding
institutional function remains that of formulating and establishing the
'Shakespeare text':

> throughout its stage history *The Taming of the Shrew* has probably received
> fewer completely straight performances than any other Shakespearan play
> of comparable popularity on the stage. The apparently unrelieved ethic of
> male supremacy has proved unpalatable, and generation after generation of
> producers and directors have altered and adapted the text in more or less
> flagrant ways in order to soften the ending. Of course, responses to the play
> are bound to be affected by the status of women in society at any given time
> and by the way that status is perceived by both men and women. Reading
> through the reviews, one sees the play acting as a kind of litmus paper,
> picking up worried and embarrassed reactions from men who were probably

just as committed to male supremacy as they take the play's hero to be but whose methods of oppressing their women were less obvious and more socially acceptable. Productions of the play have frequently attracted whatever thoughts were in the air on the perennially topical subjects of violence and sexual politics, and this tendency can hardly fail to increase in our own time. (Thompson 1984, p. 24)

Now whether there can ever be such a thing as a 'straight' performance of any play of course remains open to debate. Ann Thompson is talking here specifically though about alterations made to 'the text' in the course of preparing a performance-script for a production. This argument presupposes that the verbal component of a performance-text has a far more determinant influence over a production than it ever actually has: we need go no further than some of the productions cited by Ann Thompson herself to see that the *same* verbal text can be used to signify utterly divergent meanings on stage. The iterability of the play is not seen in this argument as an inherent characteristic of the dramatic medium, but as the combined result of a certain fixed and ideologically-closed character in the play itself, and of the anxiety of masculine observers afraid that the play might let the cat of male supremacy out of its theatrical bag. Shakespeare's play is thus in this problematic a fixed entity, that can be altered from its original and immanent form by textual tampering (as an editor of course Ann Thompson is directly responsible for constructing such an effect of fixity) but which remains in place as an inviolable essence, of sufficiently constant and stable a shape to be compared with 'litmus paper'. The play is capable of registering the contemporary attitudes and anxieties that permeate the cultural and political world in which it is produced; yet it is not, essentially, changed by them − it does not absorb their colour and substance.

The metaphor of the litmus-test works in exactly the same contradictory way as the mimetic image of the mirror. To call a play a mirror is to distinguish between the reflection and the reflective medium: the latter remains constant while varying images play across its surface. Similarly litmus paper identifies the divergent substances, the acidity or alkalinity, into which it may be dipped, without its own physical properties undergoing any real change. In each case the argument presupposes in the play a stability of signification, a constancy of immanent structure. The deconstructionist method would dispose of these distinctions by insisting that the 'play' is at any given point no more than the *reflection* in the mirror; no more than the pink or blue trace that stains with significance the blank neutrality of a litmus paper. The mirror and the experiment are symbols for the cultural and institutional context within which such images may be observed. But while the deconstructionist method is in a sense correct as an account of the original nature of this type of drama, it is continually falsified by the existence of an authoritative text. And since deconstruction seems happy to work with authoritative texts, finding in their authority an exciting challenge, and in their textuality no impervious obstacle to deconstructive operations, this methodology perversely and para-doxically continues to authenticate and endorse the centralised, canonised 'Shakespearean' text.

Anyone present at a performance of Shakespeare's *The taming of the shrew* in Britain at any time since 1913 is quite likely to have witnessed a hybrid amalgamation of the two discrete Renaissance play-texts: the text contained in the First Folio, and that of the anonymous *The taming of a shrew*. Shakespeare's play in the 'authorised' form of the Folio text contains of Christopher Sly only the two opening scenes known as the 'Induction', and a moment of foregrounding at the end of Act I, Scene i: from the second scene of the *Shrew* action, nothing more is seen or heard of the dreaming drunken tinker. In *The taming of a shrew*, by contrast, the Sly-narrative is not a prologue but an extended dramatic framework: Sly and his attendants are kept on stage more or less throughout, and are given several further comments on and inter-ventions in the action of the play.

Even the two-scene 'Induction' disappeared from the play (Haring-Smith 1985) for centuries while Garrick's *Catherine and Petruchio* and other adaptations held the stage: in 1900 Frank Benson was still pro-ducing the play with no trace of Christopher Sly.[7] Subsequent directors such as Oscar Asche (1904), W. Bridges Adams (1933) and F. Owen Chambers (1936) restored the 'Induction', but often in a cut form. It was Martin Harvey, acting under the advice and influence of William Poel, who in a 1913 production at the Prince of Wales's Theatre decided to supplement Shakespeare's text by interpolating the Christopher Sly scenes from *A shrew*: and to develop the Sly-framework into a constitutive element of the drama. In this and many subsequent produc-tions, Sly and his attendants were kept on stage, where they functioned as a surrogate audience: in accordance with the Lord's directions, the actors involved in the *Shrew* narrative constantly referred and deferred to them as the privileged audience of their presentation. Directors would give Sly lines which belong in the Shakespearean text to other characters: e.g. Tranio's observation (I.i.169) 'That wench is stark mad, or wonderful froward' became, in Theodore Komisarjevsky's 1939 Stratford production, a spectator's observation from outside the dramatic event. In the same production Sly made several abortive attempts to intervene in the action in the manner of Beaumont's intrusive grocer in *The knight of the burning pestle*: at several points he tried to join the actors in the *Shrew* narrative, and had to be forcibly restrained by the Page.

Since Martin Harvey's pioneering production, the Christopher Sly framework has been embraced by the modern theatre with particular enthusiasm: to such an extent that it became commonplace to augment the play with the Sly interventions and epilogue preserved in the 1594 Quarto text. By contrast, within the dominant discourses of literary criticism and textual scholarship, the relation between, on the one hand, a 'good' text like that of the Folio, or that of a 'good' Quarto, and on the other, that of a so-called 'bad' Quarto, is clear: the latter is an inferior, garbled version of the authorial intention faithfully preserved in the former. An editor may believe (as does Ann Thompson) that *A shrew's* complete Sly-framework probably indicates the existence of a similar theatrical structure in Shakespeare's play; but no editor has yet thought it appropriate to amalgamate the two texts to the extent of incorporating as a whole the theatrical device preserved in an unauthorised, non-Shakespearean text.

The approach of theatrical practitioners has been quite different. In the case of *The taming of the shrew*, theatrical practice began many years ago to prefer the dramatic opportunities offered by the text of *A shrew* to considerations of textual purity and authorial ascription. Initially this strategy of theatrical appropriation was quite at odds with the views of the literary-critical and scholarly establishment, which was in search of textual and authorial authenticity: for not only was the incompleteness, the insufficiency of Shakespeare's play acknowledged; in addition elements of a text generally regarded as inadequate and self-evidently un-Shakespearean were incorporated to satisfy the requirements of theatrical practice. Those requirements, for whatever complex cultural reasons, operate in this instance to produce a different kind of dramatic text: a *Shrew*-play in which the choric observer remains present throughout, rather than enduring summary banishment after one scene, constitutes a much more sustained and consistent exercise in theatrical alienation than the version in which those devices of alienation are ignored or suppressed.

The science of textual scholarship as applied to Shakespeare has seen considerable change in recent years: contemporary scholarly editions now aim to acknowledge these plays as dramatic scripts as well as written texts, and to take into account a play's theatrical history when attempting to produce an authoritative text. Most scholarship remains none the less committed to discovering or inferring the author's original intentions, and to producing a text which a reincarnated Shakespeare would be able to recognise and approve. In the theatre, the presence of that forbidding and ghostly mythological creature, the absent author, does not always bear with quite the same gravity on the activities of those who work on and reproduce the plays in performance. Hence in the theatre history of *The taming of the shrew* we can witness a bold opportunism that can be regarded either as iconoclastic or as pioneering: the amalgamation of 'good' and 'bad' texts is taken to an extreme that more conservative scholars may disapprove, while their more progressive colleagues may look for ways of pursuing the theatre's natural dramatic instincts.

Whether we think of the Quarto as a script for performance or a transcript *of* performance, it is clear that it brings us closer to contemporary Elizabethan theatrical practice than does the Folio text. I am not arguing that we can distinguish in any evaluative way between a more strictly 'literary' mode of production traceable to the cloistered creativity of the 'author', and a 'theatrical' mode deriving from the rough practicalities of the playhouse. Since the author in question was no poet hidden in the light of thought, but a species of theatrical entrepreneur – actor, writer and speculative businessman – his role in the process of production is likely to have been a more consistent and sustained involvement than the transmission of a completed text to a distinct group of actors. It is now widely recognised by scholars that the discrete texts of a Renaissance play represent a cultural activity in process, glimpsed at different stages of a productive working in which the 'text' was primarily regarded not as a finished commodity but as a script for performance, remarkably alterable and subject to the conditions governing theatrical presentation at any given time. The comparitively rudimentary stage directions of the folio thus represent not naive gesturings towards an absent performance but specific proposals to be attempted, improvised, modified or rejected by a collaborative team of theatrical practitioners at work. As the example of the two *Shrews* indicates, the modern descendants of those Elizabethan actors have focused not with the critics and scholars on the internal organisation, formal coherence and imaginative unity of individual texts; but on the lost but recoverable theatrical practice still visible in the interstices of a text, eloquent in the lacunae between one text and another, and implicit in the material conditions of a theatre eternally restless to interrogate and re-open the closures of written fiction, perpetually resistant to the notion of a sealed and finished form.

When describing the obstacles that customarily prevent us from engaging in this kind of fully intertextual study of Renaissance drama, we usually nominate a range of 'external', institutional constraints: the curriculum, the syllabus, the machinery of assessment, the 'external' examiner, the expectations of the student, even the simple availability of published texts. A deconstructionist conviction that the 'text' is in any case – however authoritatively canonised and edited into fossil form – merely the focus of rival appropriations and completely at the service of competing ideologies, can paradoxically work to endorse the adherence to a mainstream text, at the same time as it can validate any text as equally available for analysis. If 'Shakespeare's' *The taming of the shrew* can be shown, simply through analysis of the verbal text in a modern scholarly edition, to be demonstrably mobilised in the service of ideological structures which lay/lie outside the text and bear upon it as constitutive determinants; or fissured and dis-integrated by ideological contractions; or unsealed and porous, absorbing at every point the dynamics of history, class- and gender- struggle; or internally mobile, continually denying, as it is read, the fulfilment of any stable relationship between sign and signified – then the kind of margin-scraping peripheral pursuit I am advocating will begin to seem by contrast an esoteric branch of cultural archaeology.

It is entirely possible, given the kinds of change currently happening in our educational system, that these constraints may in any case be relaxed, making a genuinely intertextual cultural studies seem an appropriate completion at tertiary level of the centrifugal, project-based methodology available at the Secondary Level in the General Certification of Secondary Education qualifications and even more so in the increasingly important form of British Technical Education Certificate. It is equally likely however that such forms of learning will be consolidated rather as strategic points of access to an educational system which must ultimately impose and test the student's absorption of the mainstream literary heritage. If the broad-based and student-centred methods of GCSE are not permitted to filter up, then we could well see our sixteen-year-olds watching *West Side Story*, improvising 'Romeo and Juliet' situations from their own experience, and gathering links between the play and contemporary issues of family, race, class, gender; while our students in higher education continue to be measured by their ability to analyse what is ironically called 'the text' of Shakespeare's *Romeo and Juliet*.

One pedagogic form in which I have found it possible to mobilise some of these concerns in a direct though academically structured way is that of the integrated theoretical-and-practical Drama course. I currently teach in an institute of higher education on such a course, one unit of which is devoted to Renaissance drama. Since the course addresses 'Renaissance drama in modern performance', and makes extensive use of film and video productions for comparative analysis, it 'naturally' concentrates on Shakespeare. Since the course employs a fully-integrated methodology in which practical experimentation is conceived as a means of intellectual enquiry rather than as preparation for a separable 'performance', the practical workshop process can readily incorporate elements from the theoretical, historical and textual studies that are proceeding alongside it. The physical engagement of practical drama forces contextual issues that bear immediately on the students' own lives – for example those of gender politics, patriarchal violence and feminine resistance – into immediate and visible illumination. At the same time the open-ended 'workshop' situation, which does not demand intensive work on practical skills, or exhaustive preparation for a stageable 'production', allows for a constant interpenetration of theoretical, historical and textual material.

A one-term workshop project on *The taming of the shrew* developed from comparative textual work on the Shakespeare-text, *The taming of a shrew*, the Restoration and eighteenth-century 'free adaptations' including Garrick's *Catherine and Petruchio*, Charles Marowitz's 'collage' version, and *Kiss me, Kate*; concentrating on the induction/Sly-frame, and on the various problems of gender-relations provoked by different episodes in the 'taming' action – the courtship, the marriage, the character of Petruchio's domestic polity and Katherina's final speech of obedience. Improvisation sessions played with alternative versions of the Induction, circulating gender roles (female Hostess, male Sly – male Host, female Sly) as do the Elizabethan texts; and produced radically divergent tones and meanings from different scenes. Eventually it became apparent that a constant presence of Sly as surrogate audience, and clearly-differentiated contrasts of style, would be needed in order to force from the action an acceptable range of meanings. The Induction scene was drawn from *A shrew*, and emphasised a medium of broad popular comedy. The next scene was a courtship scene, with a script derived from Garrick's version, played to Sly as a kind of pantomime on a shallow, one-dimensional 'Restoration' stage. The scene in Petruchio's house, staged in torch-lit darkness as a 'madhouse' scene, represented the 'medieval dungeon' of Marowitz's Gothic fable. The shifts of style and genre produced a clearly-visible series of 'framing' effects, but also constructed a narrative of deepening anxiety as Katherina's plight became more intense and disturbing. For the final scene the students wanted to break this empathetic development, so as to deflect any possibility of complicity with Katherina's anti-feminist apology. The homily on obedience was delivered to the studio audience, in a challenging, interrogative tone. At one point the actress asked the Lord if it was absolutely necessary to go through with it. This interruptive technique was then developed to a further level as the actress resentfully pleaded with the male 'director' (myself, seated in the audience) to be excused from the humiliation of her textually-imposed discipline.

This example is not offered as in any way a historic or memorable 'production', but only as exemplifying an educational situation in which a combination of deconstructionist work on authorised texts can be combined with 'peripheral analysis' and practical experimentation, to produce a learning model in which the 'plays' are still very much there (not dissolved into 'themes' or immediate contemporary issues), yet capable of delivering from their own transformational potentialities an urgent address to immediate and inescapable political realities.

Notes

1 Berger in Parker and Hartman 1986, p. 213.
2 Hawkes 1986, pp. 76–7.
3 Cavell in Parker and Hartman 1986, p. 258.
4 Barker, *et al.* 1981; Dollimore and Sinfield 1985; Drakakis 1986; Holderness 1988.
5 e.g. McKluskie n.d.; Fineman in Howard and O'Connor, 1987.

6 Wells and Taylor 1988, p. 25; Morris 1982; Oliver 1984.
7 Productions by Atkins, 1946; Benthall, 1948; Divine, 1953; Barton, 1960; Nunn, 1967; Kyle, 1982.

Bibliography

Arac, Jonathan (1987) *Critical genealogies: historical situations for postmodern literary study*, New York.

Ariès, Philippe (1981) *The hour of our death*, Harmondsworth.

Barker, Francis (1984) *The tremulous private body: essays on subjection*, London.

—— (forthcoming) *Signs of invasion.*

—— and Peter Hulme (1985) ' "Nymphs and reapers heavily vanish": the discursive con-texts of *The tempest*', in Drakakis (1986), pp. 191–205.

—— *et al.* (eds.) (1981) *1642: literature and power in the seventeenth century*, Colchester.

Barker, Simon (1986) 'Images of the sixteenth and seventeenth centuries as a history of the present' in Francis Barker *et al.* (eds.) *Literature politics and theory*, London, pp. 173–89.

Bell, Daniel (1960) *The end of ideology: on the exhaustion of political ideas in the fifties*, Glencoe, Ill.

—— (1973) *The coming of post-industrial society: a venture in social forecasting*, New York.

—— (1976) *The cultural contradictions of capitalism*, New York.

Bell, Walter George (1924) *The Great Plague in London in 1665*, London.

Belsey, Catherine (1985) *The subject of tragedy: identity and difference in renaissance drama*, London.

Benjamin, Walter (1968) 'Theses on the philosophy of history' [1940], in *Illuminations* trans. Harry Zohn, ed. and introd. Hannah Arendt, London, pp. 255–66.

Bennett, Tony (1987) 'Texts in history: the determinations of readings and their texts', in D. Attridge, *et al.* (eds.) *Post-structualism and the question of history*, Cambridge, pp. 63–81.

Berger Jr., Harry (1985) 'Psychoanalysing the Shakespeare text: the Henriad', in Parker and Hartman (1986), London, pp. 210–29.

Berman, Marshall (1983) *All that is solid melts into air: the experience of modernity*, London.

Blanchot, Maurice (1986) *The writing of the disaster*, trans. Ann Smock, London.

Boose, Lynda (1987) 'The family in Shakespeare studies; or – studies in the family of Shakespeareans; or – the politics of politics', *Renaissance Quarterly*, 40, pp. 707–41.

Brennan, T. (ed) (1989) *Between feminism and psychoanalysis*, London.
Bruner, E. M. (1986) 'Experience and its expressions', in Turner and Bruner (1986).
Burn, R. (1763) *Ecclesiastical law*.
Calvi, Giulia (1986) 'A metaphor for social exchange: the Florentine plague of 1630', *Representations*, 13, pp. 139–63.
Carter, Erica and Simon Watney (eds.) (1989) *Taking liberties*, London.
Cavell, Stanley (1985) ' "Who does the wolf love?": *Coriolanus* and the interpretations of politics' in Parker and Hartman (1986).
Chartier, R. (1988) *Cultural history: between practices and representations*, trans. L. G. Cochrane, Cambridge.
Cohen, Walter (1987) 'Political criticism of Shakespeare', in Howard and O'Connor (1987), pp. 18–46.
Cooper, William Durrant (1856) 'Notices of the last Great Plague, 1665–6; from the letters of John Allin to Philip Fryth and Samuel Jeake. In a letter to SIR HENRY ELLIS, K.H., Director, by WILLIAM DURRANT COOPER, F.S.A.', *Archaeologia*, 37, pp. 1–22.
Crimp, Douglas (ed.) (1988) *AIDS: cultural analysis/cultural activism*, Cambridge, Mass.
Davis, N. Z. (1983) *The return of Martin Guerre*, Cambridge, Mass.
—— (1987) *Fiction in the archives: pardon tales and their tellers in sixteenth-century France*, Stanford, Cal. and Cambridge.
Derrida, Jacques (1978) 'Cogito and the history of madness', in *Writing and Difference*, trans. Alan Bass, London, pp. 31–63.
—— (1982) 'Différance', in *Margins of Philosophy*, trans. Alan Bass, Brighton, pp. 1–27.
—— (1987) *Positions*, trans. Alan Bass, London.
Dews, Peter (1988) *Logics of disintegration: Post-structuralist thought and the claims of critical theory*, London.
—— (1989) 'Adorno, post-structuralism, and the critique of identity', in Andrew E. Benjamin (ed.) *The problems of modernity: Adorno and Benjamin*, London, pp. 1–22.
Doane, Janice and Devon Hodges (1987) *Nostalgia and sexual difference: the resistance to contemporary feminism*, New York.
Dollimore, Jonathan (1985) 'Introduction: Shakespeare, cultural materialism and the new historicism', in Dollimore and Sinfield (1985), pp. 2–17.
—— and Alan Sinfield (eds.) (1985) *Political Shakespeare: new essays in cultural materialism*, Manchester.
Drakakis, John (ed.) (1986) *Alternative Shakespeares*, London.
Eagleton, Terry (1985) 'Capitalism, modernism and postmodernism', *New left review*, 152, pp. 60–73.
—— (1988) *Walter Benjamin or towards a revolutionary criticism*, London.
Edelman, Lee (1989) 'The plague of discourse: politics, literary theory, and AIDS', *The South Atlantic quarterly*, 88 (1), pp. 301–17.
Eliot, T. S. (1932) *Selected essays*, London.
Erickson, Peter (1987) 'Rewriting the Renaissance, rewriting ourselves', *Shakespeare quarterly*, 38 (3), pp. 327–37.
Evans, Malcolm (1986) *Signifying nothing*, London.
Fee, Elizabeth and Daniel Fox (eds.) (1988) *AIDS: the burdens of history*, California.
Fineman, Joel (1985) 'The turn of the screw' in Parker and Hartman (1986), pp. 138–60.

Flax, Jane (1987) 'Postmodernism and gender relations in feminist theory', *Signs*, 12, pp. 621–43.

Foster, Hal (1983) 'Postmodernism: a preface' in H. Foster (ed.) *The anti-aesthetic: essays on post-modern culture*, Port Townesend, Washington, pp. ix–xvi.

Foucault, Michel (1972) *The archaeology of knowledge* [1969], trans. A. M. Sheridan Smith, London.

——— (1977a) *Discipline and punish: the birth of the prison*, trans. Alan Sheridan, London.

——— (1977b) 'Nietzsche, genealogy, history', in Donald F. Bouchard (ed.) *Language, counter-memory, practice: selected essays and interviews*, Oxford, pp. 139–64.

——— (1978) 'Politics and the study of discourse' [1968], *Ideology and consciousness*, 3, pp. 7–26.

——— (1979) 'Truth and power', in Meaghan Morris and Paul Patton (eds.) *Michel Foucault: power, truth, strategy*, Sydney, pp. 29–48.

Fraser, Nancy and Linda Nicholson (1988) 'Social criticism without philosophy: an encounter between feminism and postmodernism', in A. Ross (ed.) *Universal abandon?: the politics of postmodernism*, Minnesota and Edinburgh, pp. 83–104.

Fukuyama, Francis (1989) 'The end of history', *The independent*, London, 20 and 21 September.

Garber, Marjorie (1987) *Shakespeare's ghost writers: literature as uncanny causality*, New York.

Geertz, Clifford (1973) *The interpretation of cultures*, New York

——— (1984) ' "From the native's point of view": on the nature of anthropological understanding', in Shweder and LeVine (1984), 123–36.

Gibson, Edmund (1730) *Codex Iuris Ecclesiasticae Anglicanae*.

Girard, René (1986) 'Hamlet's dull revenge', in Parker and Quint (1986), pp. 280–302.

Goldberg, Jonathan (1985) 'Shakespearean inscriptions: the voicing of power', in Parker and Hartman (1986), 116–37.

Greenblatt, Stephen (1980) *Renaissance self-fashioning: from More to Shakespeare*, Chicago.

——— (1985) 'Invisible bullets: Renaissance authority and its subversion, *Henry IV* and *Henry V*', in Dollinore and Sinfield (1985), pp. 18–47

——— (1986) 'Psychoanalysis and renaissance culture', in Parker and Quint (1986), pp. 210–24.

——— (1987) 'Capitalist culture and the circulatory system', in Murray Krieger (ed.) *The aims of representation: subject/text/history*, New York.

——— (1988) *Shakespearean negotiations: the circulation of social energy in Renaissance England*, Oxford.

——— (1990) 'Resonance and wonder', in Peter Collier and Helga Geyer–Ryan (eds) *Literary theory today*, Cambridge, pp. 74–90.

Habermas, Jürgen (1985) 'Modernity – an incomplete project', in Hal Foster (ed.) *Postmodern culture*, London, pp. 3–15.

Haraway, Donna (1988) 'Situated knowledges: the science question in feminism and the privilege of partial perspective', *Feminist studies*, 14 (fall), pp. 575–99.

Harding, Sandra (1986) *The science question in feminism*, Ithaca.

Haring-Smith, Tori (1985) *From farce to melodrama: a stage history of 'The taming of the shrew'*, London.

Hawkes, Terence (1986) *That Shakespeherian rag; essays on a critical process*, London and New York.

Herr, Michael (1978) *Dispatches* [1968–77], London.

Holderness, Graham (ed.) (1988) *The Shakespeare myth*, Manchester.

—— (1989) *The taming of the shrew*, Manchester.

Howard, Jean (1986) 'The new historicism in Renaissance studies', *English literary renaissance*, 16 (1), pp. 13–43.

—— and Marion O'Conner (eds.) (1987) *Shakespeare reproduced: the text in history and ideology*, London.

Jameson, Fredric (1972) *The prison-house of language*, Princeton.

—— (1984) 'Postmodernism, or the cultural logic of late capitalism', *New left review*, 146, pp. 53–92.

—— (1988) 'Cognitive mapping', in Cary Nelson and Lawrence Grossberg (eds.) *Marxism and the interpretation of culture*, Basingstoke, pp. 347–60.

Jardine, Alice (1985) *Gynesis: configurations of woman and modernity*, Ithaca.

Jardine, Lisa (1983a) *Still harping on daughters: women and drama in the age of Shakespeare*, Brighton.

—— (1983b) '*The Duchess of Malfi*: a case study in the literary representation of women', in S. Kappeler and N. Bryson (1983), pp. 203–17.

—— (1987) 'Cultural confusion and Shakespeare's learned heroines: "These are old paradoxes" ', *Shakespeare quarterly*, 38, pp. 1–18.

—— (1989) 'The politics of impenetrability', in T. Brennan (ed.) *New directions in psychoanalysis and feminism*, London.

—— (1990) ' "Why should he call her whore?": defamation and Desdemona's case', in M. Warner and M. Tudeau–Clayton (eds.) *Strategies of Interpretation: essays in honour of Frank Kermode*, London.

Kappeler, S. and N. Bryson (eds) (1983) *Teaching the text*, London.

Kelly, Joan (1984) 'Did women have a renaissance?' in *Women history and theory*, Chicago, pp. 19–50.

Kristeva, Julia (1981) 'Women's time', *Signs*, 7 (autumn), pp. 13–35.

Leavis, F. R. and D. Thompson (1933) *Culture and environment*, London.

Lodge, David (1984) *Small world*, London and New York.

Lovell, Terry (1980) *Pictures of reality: aesthetics, politics and pleasure*, London.

Lyotard, Jean-François (1984) *The postmodern condition: a report on knowledge* [1979], trans. Geoff Bennington and Brian Massumi, Manchester.

—— (1987) 'The sign of history', in D. Attridge *et al.* (eds) *Post-structuralism and the question of history*, Cambridge, 162–80.

McLuskie, Kate (n.d.) 'Feminist deconstruction: the example of *The taming of the shrew*', *Red Letters*, 12, pp. 15–22.

—— (1985) 'The patriarchal bard: feminist criticism and Shakespeare: *King Lear* and *Measure for measure*', in Dollimore and Sinfield (1985), pp. 88–108.

Marx, Karl (1970) *The Eighteenth Brumaire of Louis Bonaparte* [1851–2], in K. Marx and F. Engels *Selected works*, Moscow.

—— (1973) *Grundrisse* [1857–8], trans. Martin Nicolaus, London.

Mies, Maria (1986) *Patriarchy and accumulation on a world scale: women in the international division of labour*, London.

Miller, D. A. (1989) 'Sontag's urbanity', *October*, 49, pp. 91–101.

Moi, Toril (1988) 'Feminism, postmodernism and style: recent feminist criticism in the United States', *Cultural studies*, 9 (spring), pp. 3–22.

Montrose, Louis A. (1980) ' "Eliza, Queene of Shepheards" and the pastoral of power', *English literary renaissance*, 10, pp. 153–82.

—— (1986) 'Renaissance literary studies and the subject of history', *English literary renaissance*, 16 (1), pp. 5–12.

—— (1988) 'Professing the Renaissance: the poetics and politics of culture', in H. Aram Veeser (ed.) *The New Historicism*, London, pp. 15–36.

Moretti, Franco (1988) 'The great eclipse: tragic form as the deconsecration of sovereignty' in F. Moretti (1988) *Signs taken for wonders: essays in the sociology of literature*, trans. Susan Fischer, David Forgacs and David Miller, London, pp. 42–82.

Morris, Brian (ed.) (1982) *The new Arden Shakespeare: The taming of the shrew*, London.

Mouffe, Chantal (1988) 'Radical democracy: modern or postmodern?' in A. Ross (ed.) *Universal abandon?: the politics of postmodernism*, Minneapolis and Edinburgh, pp. 31–45.

Mulhern, Francis (1979) *The moment of Scrutiny*, London.

Nashe, Thomas (1978) *The unfortunate traveller and other works*, London.

Neely, Carol Thomas (1988) 'Constructing the subject: feminist practice and the new Renaissance discourses', *English literary renaissance*, 18, pp. 5–18.

Newman, Karen (1987) ' "And wash the Ethiop white": femininity and the monstrous in *Othello*' in Howard and O'Connor (1987), pp. 141–62.

—— (1989) 'City talk: women and commodification in Jonson's *Epicoene*', *English literary history*, 56, pp. 503–18.

Newton, Judith (1988) 'History as usual?: feminism and the "new historicism" ', *Cultural critique*, 9, pp. 87–122.

—— and Deborah Rosenfelt (1985) 'Introduction: towards a materialist feminist criticism', in J. Newton and D. Rosenfelt (eds.) *Feminist criticism and socical change*, New York and London, pp. xv–xxxix.

Nietzsche, Friedrich (1983) 'On the uses and disadvantages of history for life' [1874], in Nietzsche, F. *Untimely meditations*, trans. R. J. Hollingdale, Cambridge.

Oliver, H. G. (ed.) (1984) *The taming of the shrew*, Oxford.

Orgel, Stephen (1975) *The illusion of power: political theater in the English Renaissance*, Berkeley.

Parker, Patricia and Geoffrey Hartman (eds.) (1986) *Shakespeare and the question of theory*, London.

Parker, Patricia and David Quint (eds.) (1986) *Literary theory/Renaissance texts*, Baltimore and London.

Patterson, Annabel (1989) *Shakespeare and the popular voice*, Oxford.

Patton, Cindy (1989) 'Power and the conditions of silence', *Critical quarterly*, 31 (3), pp. 26–39.

Pechter, Edward (1987) 'The New Historicism and its discontents: politicising Renaissance drama', *Proceedings of the Modern Language Association*, 102, pp. 292–303.

Porter, Dennis (1983) '*Orientalism* and its problems', in F. Barker *et al.* (eds) *The politics of theory*, Colchester, pp. 179–93.

Rabkin, Norman (1981) *Shakespeare and the problem of meaning*, Chicago.

Resnick, Stephen A. and Richard D. Wolf (1982) 'Marxist epistemology: the critique of economic determinism', *Social text*, 2 (3), pp. 31–72.

Righter, Anne (1961) *Shakespeare and the idea of the play*, Harmondsworth.

Rorty, Richard (1982) *Consequences of pragmatism*, Minneapolis.

Rosaldo, M. Z. (1984) 'Towards an anthropology of self and feeling', in Shweder and LeVine (1984), pp. 137–57.

Rose, Jacqueline (1985) 'Sexuality in the reading of Shakespeare', in John Drakakis (1986), pp. 95–118.

Scott, Joan Wallach (1988) *Gender and the politics of history*, New York.

Shakespeare, William (1951) *The complete works*, (ed.) Peter Alexander, London.

Shell, M. (1988) *The end of kinship*, Stanford, Cal.

Shweder, R. A. and E. J. Bourne (1984) 'Does the concept of the person vary cross-culturally?', in Shweder and LeVine (1984), pp. 158–99.

Shweder, R. A. and R. A. LeVine (eds.) (1984) *Culture theory: essays on mind, self and emotion*, Cambridge.

Simpson, David (1987–8) 'Literary criticism and the return to "history" ', *Critical inquiry*, 14, pp. 721–47.

Sintow, A., C. Stansell and S. Thompson (1983) *Powers of desire: the politics of sexuality*, New York.

Slack, Paul (1985) *The impact of plague in Tudor and Stuart England*, London.

—— (1988) 'Responses to plague in early modern Europe: the implications of public health', *Social Research*, 55 (3), pp. 433–53.

Sontag, Susan (1983) *Illness as metaphor*, Harmondsworth.

—— (1988) *AIDS and its metaphors*, Harmondsworth.

Spivack, Bernard (1958) *Shakespeare and the allegory of evil*, New York.

Surtees Society (1845) *Depositions and other ecclesiastical proceedings from the courts of Durham, extending from 1311 to the reign of Elizabeth*, London.

Thompson, Ann (ed.) (1984) *The new Cambridge Shakespeare: The taming of the shrew*, Cambridge.

Tillyard, E. M. W. (1943) *The Elizabethan world-picture*, London.

—— (1969) *Shakespeare's history plays*, London.

Treichler, Paula (1988) 'AIDS, homophobia, and biomedical discourse: an epidemic of signification', in Crimp (1988), pp. 31–70.

—— (1989) 'AIDS and HIV infection in the Third World: a first world chronicle', in Barbara Kruger and Phil Mariani (eds.) *Remaking History*, New York, pp. 31–86.

Turner, Victor (1969) *The ritual process*, London.

—— and E. M. Bruner (eds.) (1986) *The anthropology of experience*, Urbana, Ill. and Chicago.

Waller, Marguerite (1987) 'Academic Tootsie: the denial of difference and the difference it makes', *Diacritics*, 17 (spring), pp. 2–20.

Watney, Simon (1987) *Policing desire: pornography, AIDS and the media*, London.

—— (1988) 'The spectacle of AIDS', in Crimp (1988), pp. 71–86.

—— (1989) 'Missionary positions: AIDS, "Africa", and race' in *Critical quarterly*, 31 (3), pp. 45–62.

Wayne, Don E. (1987) 'Power, politics, and the Shakespearean text: recent criticism in England and the United States', in Howard and O'Connor (1987), pp. 48–68.

Wells, Stanley and Gary Taylor (eds.) (1988) *William Shakespeare: the complete works*, Oxford.

Wicke, Jennifer (1988) 'Postmodernism: the perfume of information', in *The Yale journal of criticism*, I (2) (spring), pp. 145–60.

Wickham, Glynne (1966) *Early English stages, 1300–1600*, vol. I, London.

Widdowson, Peter (ed.) (1982) *Re-reading English*, London.

Williams, Raymond (1977) *Marxism and literature*, Oxford.

Wilson, F. P. (1927) *The plague in Shakespeare's London*, Oxford.

Wordsworth, Ann (1987) 'Derrida and Foucault: writing the history of historicity', in Attridge *et al.* (eds.) *Post-structuralism and the question of history*, Cambridge, pp. 116–25.

Notes on contributors and editors

Francis Barker teaches critical theory and the culture of the English Renaissance at the University of Essex where he is a senior lecturer in the Department of Literature. His books include *The tremulous private body: essays on subjection* (1984). A book on tragedy and history, *Signs of invasion*, is forthcoming, and a further volume on culture and violence is in preparation. He is a founding member of the Essex Early Modern Research group.

Catherine Belsey is the chair of the Centre for Critical and Cultural Theory at the University of Wales College of Cardiff. Her principal publications include *Critical practice* (1980), *The subject of tragedy* (1985), *John Milton: language, gender, power* (1988).

Howard Felperin is a professor of English at Macquarie University, Sydney, Australia. His books to date are *Shakespearean romance* (1972), *Shakespearean representation* (1977), *Beyond deconstruction* (1985), *The uses of the canon: Elizabethan literature and contemporary theory* (1990). *A new history of Shakespeare criticism* is forthcoming. He has lectured on Shakespeare and Critical theory on four continents and is a fellow of the Australian Academy of the Humanities.

Graham Holderness is head of Drama at the Roehampton Institute where he teaches Renaissance and Modern literature and drama. He is the author of *Shakespeare's history* (1985) and *Shakespeare: out of court* (1990) co-authored by John Turner and Nicholas Potter. He is also the editor of *The politics of theatre and drama* (1991). In addition, he is working on a book to be called *The cultural production of narrative form*.

Jean E. Howard is a professor of English at Columbia University, New York. She teaches Renaissance drama and literary theory and is the author of *Shakespeare's art of orchestration* (1984) and the editor (with Marion O'Connor) of *Shakespeare reproduced: the text in history and ideology.* (1987) She is also completing a book entitled *Discourses of the theatre: the stage and social struggle in early modern England.*

Peter Hulme is a senior lecturer in Literature at the University of Essex where he teaches literary and cultural theory. He is the author of *Colonial encounters* (1986).

Margaret Iversen is a lecturer in the Department of Art History and Theory at the

University of Essex. She teaches the historiography of art history and contemporary theory including psychoanalysis and feminism. She has just completed a book on the art historian Alois Riegl and is working on another called *Theories of the visual sign from structuralism to poststructuralism.*

Lisa Jardine is professor of English at Queen Mary and Westfield College, University of London, where she teaches Shakespeare and feminist theory. Her principal publications are *Still harping on daughters* (1984) and, with Julia Swindells, *What's left: woman and culture in the labour movement* (1989). Another book, *Reading Shakespeare historically,* is in preparation.

John Joughin is a research student and graduate teacher at the University of Essex where he is currently completing his thesis entitled *The constellations of capital: situating London in the early modern.* He is a member of the Essex Early Modern Research Group.

Index

Index